THE CALLED TO PEACE
WORKBOOK

Includes
*Called to Peace: A Survivor's Guide to Finding Peace
and Healing After Domestic Abuse*
with Foreword by Chris Moles

Updated and Revised Editions

JOY FORREST

BLUE INK
PRESS

I have tried to recreate events, locales and conversations from my memories. In order to maintain anonymity in some instances I have changed the names of individuals and places, I may have changed some identifying characteristics and details such as physical properties, occupations and places of residence.

THE CALLED TO PEACE WORKBOOK
Published by Blue Ink Press, LLC
Copyright © 2025 Joy Forrest
All rights reserved, including the right of
reproduction in whole or in part in any form.

All scripture quotations, unless otherwise indicated, are taken from The Holy Bible, New International Version ®, NIV ®. Copyright © 1973, 1978, 1984 by Biblica Inc.TM Used by permission of Zondervan. Scripture quotations marked (NKJV) are taken from the New King James Version ®. Copyright © 1982 by Thomas Nelson Inc. Used by permission. All rights reserved. Scripture quotations marked NASB are taken from the New American Standard Version ®. Copyright © 1960, 1962, 1963, 1968, 1971, 1972, 1973, 1975, 1977, 1995 by The Lockman Foundation Printed in the United States of America

www.blueinkpress.com

ISBN-13: 978-1-948449-24-3

Library of Congress Control Number: 2024947751

Defend the weak and the fatherless; uphold the cause of the poor and the oppressed. Rescue the weak and the needy; deliver them from the hand of the wicked.

~ Psalm 82:3-4

Table of Contents

NOTE ON REVISED EDITION — VII

FOREWORD BY CHRIS MOLES — XV

PREFACE — XVII

INTRODUCTION — XIX

PART ONE: A STORY OF ABUSE

CHAPTER 1	A Fragile Foundation	5
CHAPTER 2	Becoming a Victim	7
CHAPTER 3	Perishing	9
CHAPTER 4	Hope Deferred	12
CHAPTER 5	Losing Ground	15
CHAPTER 6	The Tempest	17
CHAPTER 7	Light in the Darkness	20
CHAPTER 8	Facing the Truth	25
CHAPTER 9	New Beginning	29
CHAPTER 10	Reaching Back	32

PART TWO: KEYS TO FINDING PEACE & HEALING

CHAPTER 11	Education & Truth	41
CHAPTER 12	Managing Your Emotions	50
CHAPTER 13	Knowing God	61
CHAPTER 14	Finding Your Worth in Him	64
CHAPTER 15	No Longer a Victim	68

CALLED TO PEACE WORKBOOK

WORKBOOK INTRODUCTION   76

    LESSON 1   Knowing God   78
    LESSON 2   Finding Your Worth in God   87
    LESSON 3   The Most Powerful Instruments of Healing   95
    LESSON 4   The Path to Healing, Facing the Truth   108
    LESSON 5   Healing From Trauma   119
    LESSON 6   Managing Your Emotions   131
    LESSON 7   Overcoming Fear   140
    LESSON 8   Dealing With Anger   149
    LESSON 9   Managing Sadness and Grief   155
    LESSON 10   Overcoming Shame, Guilt, and Regret   164
    LESSON 11   The Power of Disengagement   175
    LESSON 12   Learning to Set Healthy Boundaries   183
    LESSON 13   Understanding Forgiveness   191
    LESSON 14   Worship Him   199
    LESSON 15   Finding Beauty in Suffering   207

AFTERWORD   214

SUPPLEMENTAL LESSONS

    Is it Sexual Abuse?   221
    Loving Your Enemy   224
    The Importance of Community in the Healing Process   226
    Characteristics & Tactics of Coercively Controlling People   228

APPENDICES

    APPENDIX A: Finding Peace After Abuse Recovery Groups   231
    APPENDIX B: Power & Control Wheel   233
    APPENDIX C: Healthy Relationships Begin With Healthy People   234
    APPENDIX D: Developing a Safety Plan   235
    APPENDIX E: Checklist of Abusive Behaviors   236
    APPENDIX F: Scripture Database   237
    APPENDIX G: Additional Resources   241

ACKNOWLEDGMENTS   245

ABOUT THE AUTHOR   246

Note on Revised Edition

In the years since *Called to Peace: A Guide to Finding Peace* and *Healing After Domestic Abuse* (2018) and the *Called to Peace Companion Workbook* (2019) were released, the world has changed significantly, especially when it comes to matters related to abuse. Social media, beginning with the "MeToo Movement," has kept abuse of all kinds in the spotlight. We have moved from a dearth of information on the subject to an overabundance in a relatively short timeframe. Remarkably, this barrage of information has not eluded the church, which has historically been hesitant to address such issues. Most notably, evangelical Christian women coming out of domestic abuse began to create online forums for other survivors, resulting in a tidal wave of resources—some good and others not so good. In the wake of this new abundance of information, I have found many misconceptions need to be cleared up. In addition, CTPM support leaders and participants have provided a great deal of feedback since the inception of the groups in 2017, and I want to incorporate many of their suggestions as well.

The primary goals in revising the books are:

- To better define the scope of the books
- To address currently widespread, and sometimes harmful, teaching
- To update terminology
- To share updates about Called to Peace Ministries (CTPM)
- To make the workbook more user-friendly, including a new lesson order, spelling out the names of the Bible, and writing out more Scriptures, as requested by support group participants and leaders.
- To address domestic abuse and coercive control issues in the church
- To add clarifying footnotes to issues that have been misconstrued

Scope of the Books

The *CTP* book and workbook are not intended to be comprehensive works on domestic abuse. Neither are they intended to tackle a multitude of theological issues related to domestic abuse. Instead, they are primarily devised to help survivors find God's heart for them along with His path to healing. The secondary goal is to help people helpers get a better picture of how abuse impacts and entraps victims, along with a general understanding of the healing process. There are numerous other resources for people helpers (counselors, ministry leaders, etc.) that will better equip you to effectively respond to the devastation that is called domestic abuse.[1]

---

[1] For a more in-depth look at the dynamics of domestic abuse and coercive control, see Appendix G.

AUDIENCE

I originally wrote most of the workbook curriculum for a women's bible study class at my church. The lessons were based on Scriptural truths I had learned coming out of abuse and from interactions with women I worked with through our church counseling ministry. They were not originally written specifically for abuse survivors. After launching Called to Peace Ministries we began to get requests for a support group, so I tweaked the curriculum to make it more specific to domestic abuse (DA). However, I believe the truths here will apply to anyone experiencing the common issues addressed in the book (anger, fear, unforgiveness, grief, etc.). I also believe these lessons will benefit those who have experienced other types of abuse, including childhood sexual abuse and spiritual abuse. If you're reading the books from a perspective other than domestic abuse and coercive control, I believe you will still find these biblical principles helpful. If you are a counselor, you might consider using these Scripture-based lessons as counseling homework; I did for years prior to writing the books. This is not my wisdom. It took decades for me to finally yield to our Divine Counselor and find the freedom He offers. Once I did, I wanted to tell everyone I met! I pray you will find the truths contained here as exciting and life changing as I have found them.

As I've been working with DA/CC victims at CTPM, we've seen a considerable overlap with victims of other kinds of abuse, such as childhood sexual abuse (CSA), ritual abuse, and even trafficking. While these books are not specifically written for these survivors, I believe that the material contained within them will be helpful for them. However, I have come to recognize that, generally, the earlier in life abuse occurs, the longer the healing process takes. Shame, for CSA survivors, is exceptionally stubborn because it is cultivated while the personality is still forming. However, God's Word is powerful, and I believe that, in addition to trauma-informed counseling, the most traumatized of us can find a path to healing as we meditate on and internalize Scriptural truths.

UPDATED LANGUAGE

The current plethora of information on abuse caused me to feel the need to update some of the language in the book and workbook. First, I have removed any references to the "cycle of abuse" because experts now regard it as an out-of-date theory that is not representative of most cases of domestic abuse. In addition, feedback from support group participants over the past eight years has helped me see just how rampant spiritual abuse is in our churches. Although my husband used Scripture against me when I was in abuse, it was mild compared to the experiences so many other survivors have had. While I cannot predict all the possible Scriptures that have been used as weapons against survivors, I have reworded biblical concepts that have been used to oppress, particularly language that has been twisted to blame victims for the abuse they endured.

When I originally wrote the books, I made a few references to narcissism because people were starting to describe abusive behavior as narcissistic. In my mind, that simply meant self-centered behavior, but as the social media voices increased, I realized these people were talking about a psychological diagnosis rather than an attitude or belief system. The "narcissistic abuse" pundits usually attribute abusers' behavior to a clinical label rather than an individual choice, which removes personal responsibility. Experts in the field of domestic abuse and coercive control have come to recognize that this sort of abuse is not related to any specific diagnosis, but rather to individual choices that flow out of a warped belief system. People abuse because they see themselves as entitled, not because they have a personality disorder or a psychological diagnosis.

Reducing abusive behavior to a diagnostic label can be dangerous to victims as they blame their abusers' behavior on a diagnosis, which can blind them to potential lethality. I once heard a licensed therapist, and proponent of the narcissistic abuse paradigm, say that there were only two types of narcissistic abusers—the dangerous kind and the safe kind. These comments were the exact opposite of what experts on domestic abuse and coercive control teach. Numerous works in the field have given detailed descriptions of a multitude of abuser types,[2] and we are fully aware that nearly all of them can become deadly. Many, if not most, domestic violence related homicides happen after years of coercive control tactics, described on the Power and Control Wheel, that did not include physical assault of any kind. Through my ministry with victims, I have personally come to know many survivors of DA related attempted homicide, as well as family members of those who have been murdered. In the vast majority of cases, the victims never experienced physical harm at the hands of their abusers before they resorted to murderous actions.

Another problem with the clinical model is that it suggests that it is impossible for abusive men to change because of their diagnosis, rather than because of their beliefs and choices. While I recognize that it is rare for men who use power and control in their relationships to change, I have seen it happen more and more over my years of doing this work. I will never deny the power of the Gospel to redeem and restore those who yield to Him. I believe that saying that it is impossible because of a diagnostic label denies the power of the Gospel.[3] Scripture tells us that as a man "thinks in his heart, so is he" (Proverbs 23:7), and nothing could be more accurate when it comes to coercive control. There are people with many mental health diagnoses, including narcissistic personality disorder, who don't abuse their spouses, and research has shown that even in physically violent abusers the rate of mental illness is not high. Certainly, these issues can contribute to issues of power and control, but they do not cause them. The bottom line is that we must avoid models attributing coercive control to anything other than a warped belief system and selfish choices. Abusive behavior is not caused by mental illness, substance abuse, past trauma, anger, low self-esteem, or any of the other familiar excuses we hear, and those who promote teaching to encourage this sort of thinking simply perpetuate a host of myths surrounding the issue.

Addressing Recent Issues

Victim Related Issues

---

[2] One of the most descriptive books describing abuser typologies is *When Men Batter Women* by Drs. Neil Jacobson and John Gottman.

[3] While I have personally known abusive men who have overcome their abusive patterns, those counseling these situations must understand that this is rare, and unless those helping have very specific training on working with this issue, the potential for lasting change is far less likely. Abusive people are expert manipulators, and I have seen many counselors and pastors fooled by false repentance. Chris Moles' book *The Heart of Domestic Abuse,* his Men of Peace training, and Peaceworks University are great resources for those wanting to learn more about working with abusive men. Learn more at www.chrismoles.org. I did an interview with Chris on a process to help men who use power and control in their relationships overcome their abusive beliefs and behaviors. Access it at https://tinyurl.com/2ynzr763.

Since the "MeToo Movement," we now have an abundance of information on the dynamics, but it's become clear to me that while understanding the dynamics is incredibly validating for survivors of abuse, understanding alone does not lead to healing. In some cases, it merely leads to better-educated, yet very often angry, victims. There is no doubt that, for centuries, victims of DA and coercive control have been blamed for the abuse they endured, and in many twenty-first-century churches, they have been disciplined for leaving abusive situations. I have personally walked alongside hundreds of victims who experienced this, watched how it impacted their faith, and grieved as I've watched many of them leave the church altogether.

In recent years, we have seen extreme backlash against this sort of victim-blaming. Unfortunately, this backlash has progressed to the point that challenging victims to take responsibility for their healing is considered victim blaming. While it is never helpful to focus on the mistakes of those who have endured condemnation and abuse, there comes a point in the recovery process in which victims must become willing to honestly examine themselves if they want to move forward and truly heal. I constantly point survivors coming out of abuse to God's unconditional love, which is almost always obscured by abuse, and to the fact that He does not condemn them. Yet, we also know that His kindness leads us to repentance (Romans 2:4). At some point, we must be willing to allow the Holy Spirit to do His work in our lives by being open to His conviction. Those who teach otherwise do it under the guise of love but are not loving well at all. Instead, they create an enormous barrier to healing.

MINISTRY RELATED ISSUES

The good news about the latest wealth of knowledge is that victims of abuse can more easily identify what is happening to them. The bad news is that there are extreme views among the multitudes speaking out—from clearly angry advocates to ministry leaders who still choose to elevate marriages over the welfare of the oppressed. As a result, many who claim expertise on DA these days either leave victims stuck in their anger or heap greater condemnation on them. I pray that as time passes, we will see things balance out, but for now, I am grateful that we are hearing more genuinely helpful ministry voices. In the meantime, both abuse survivors and people helpers need to exercise discernment in choosing resources that are both biblically sound and trauma informed. As a biblical counselor, I have been pleased to find so many of my colleagues becoming educated and responding well to abuse-related issues. I have been honored to work with many who have developed expertise in the area and have cited many of their works in the *CTP* books.

When I first entered this work in 1997, I never could have imagined the abundance of biblically based information on domestic abuse that we are seeing today. Up until the past 5-6 years, those of us in the evangelical community had to utilize secular research and observation because there were few other resources available. In my own story, a secular observation tool, The Power and Control Wheel, finally showed me the truth of what I was experiencing and very likely saved my life. While I differ from the worldview of those who complied these observations, I cannot deny the accuracy of this tool. It was based on the experiences of over 200 victims of abuse, and it has proven true for the thousands of women I have worked with over the years. Of course, I could take the observations from the Wheel and reword it into a purely biblical framework, but I think it is important to honor the experiences of the women whose life experiences gave us the information in the first place.

To address the problem of coercive control well, listening to the experiences of those who can speak to the realities of it firsthand is crucial. While we believe Scripture is sufficient to speak to the problems of this life, there is no definitive case of domestic abuse in the Bible. Perhaps we could speculate that Abigail's husband Nabal was abusive, but there is no clear evidence of that. That being the case, it stands to reason that we must rely on observation to be able to define issues related to domestic abuse and coercive control. Obviously, those of us who base our lives on the ultimate truth of Scripture need to examine the conclusions of those observations in the light of biblical truth, but I believe that all truth is God's truth. Scripture itself points to observation as a valid way to discern truth (Job 12:7-8, Romans 1:20, Proverbs 6:6, Psalms 8:3, 42:20, Jeremiah 5:1). The bottom line is that to respond well to those suffering under the weight of marital oppression—that God abhors— we must listen to those who have experienced it and avail ourselves to knowledge of its dynamics and impacts, including research and observation. The discerning heart seeks knowledge (Proverbs 15:14b).

CHURCH RELATED ISSUES

When the *Called to Peace* books were written, abuse was not really an issue that was on the church's radar. In 2022, the Southern Baptist Convention (SBC) came under fire for mishandling or ignoring over 700 reports of sexual abuse perpetrated by pastors and other church-affiliated personnel within their churches. As I read the corresponding report from the SBC, I felt as though I was reliving a multitude of advocacy and counseling experiences I'd had with hundreds of Southern Baptist victims of domestic abuse. The responses they got from their churches closely mirrored what I was reading in the report. However, this issue is not unique to the SBC. For decades, I've watched church leaders from many denominations downplay and deny the reality of what was happening in their congregations. I was perplexed and upset at how the church was missing it until one day, as I was doing training at a church, I realized that as a victim, I missed it myself! I had been with my husband for over two decades before I finally recognized what I was experiencing was abuse and not just a marriage problem. How could I expect churches to see it more clearly than I did?

The good news is that the tide of abuse reports in the church has finally put abuse, particularly sexual abuse, on the church's radar, and many are learning how to recognize it and respond well. Coercive control is counterintuitive. Abusers often seem rational and charming, while traumatized victims can seem emotional and unstable. These dynamics make it particularly difficult for ministry leaders, who may only see an abuser a few times a week, to recognize what is truly going on behind closed doors. In addition, when there is an initial disclosure of problems in the home, most pastors and counselors tend to assume the issues presented indicate a marriage problem. In my experience, this is the number one mistake ministry leaders make. Once the problem is identified as a marital issue and joint counseling begins, things usually get much worse for the victim, as abusers tend to weaponize any counsel she's given.

Unfortunately, many of the women I have worked with have seen the church's past mishandling of abuse as a reason to give up on the church altogether. Yet, in recent years, I have been encouraged to see more churches seeking to understand and respond well to abuse. There are many biblically based resources available to help church leaders become more proficient on the issue of domestic abuse. Many of those resources are listed in Appendix G at the back of the workbook. In addition, our church partnership team at CTPM provides training, helpful resources, and mentoring to churches. This team consists of two on-staff pastors and nearly two dozen volunteers—pastors, counselors, and ministry leaders—who offer one-on-one consults to churches dealing with cases of coercive control in their congregations.

If your church or ministry is interested in learning more, please visit our website, www.calledtopeace.com, to request a consult with one of our church partnership liaisons. I am so grateful that God is shining a light on this critical issue so near to His heart. I pray that as you read this book, He will illuminate your heart to understand His great care for the oppressed and stir your spirit to help make a difference in the fight against domestic abuse.

CALLED TO PEACE

*A Survivor's Guide to Finding Peace
and Healing After Domestic Abuse*

Foreword by Chris Moles

Friends, I first wrote the following words in 2017, and since that time, we have witnessed tremendous growth in our work. Far more helpers have been welcomed in and engaged through partnerships and training opportunities such as weekend seminars and protect the flock trainings. Hundreds of survivors and helpers have attended the annual Called to Peace Ministries retreats and PeaceWorks Live conferences. Hundreds of men have received non-violence education through Men of Peace and G5. Thousands of hours have been spent mobilizing responses for victims and survivors, and the list goes on. I could celebrate this edition of *Called to Peace* with stories regarding the tremendous growth we have seen and while that could be justified, I believe we are well served by the original forward from 2017. You see, even though our movement has grown, there remains a great deal of work to do, and while we are a little larger, when compared to the gravity of the work, we long for more to lock arms with us. So, please view these paragraphs as an invitation and perhaps this book as your first or next step in the work to see the Church and the Christian home become the safest places on our planet. (12/2024)

I belong to a small tribe, at least at the time of this writing it is small. We have hope that more will join the cause. When it comes Christians who are engaged in the work of domestic violence prevention and intervention there is a small but growing number of us. So, as I became more committed to writing and speaking on the topic of domestic violence from a pastoral perspective it wasn't long before others in the movement began to reach out to me. Among the most memorable was Joy Forrest. A survivor herself she passionately advocates for others through a growing local ministry to victims and families. In addition to the common aspects of our work, Joy and I also hold similar graduate degrees in Biblical Counseling which means we shared something far more significant, a love for and commitment to the Sufficiency of Scripture. So, when she asked me to read Called to Peace I knew I was not only going to interact with her story and her knowledge, but the life changing truth of the Scripture.

Called to Peace is a story, but so much more. This book will illustrate to you how faith, family, and fear shaped the experiences of one victim of domestic violence. You will learn many of the tactics commonly used by abusers as you meet Doug, a charming and seemingly caring partner who at first uses subtlety to groom his victim which over time morphed into overt acts of coercive control. You will also gain tremendous insight into the life of a victim. Expect to see beyond just the incidents of abuse as Joy recounts the confusion, longings, and attempts to "fix" the problems in her relationship. The most pressing lesson from Joy's story, in my opinion, is that God cared for Joy and in fact He cares for all victims. He cares far more about the hurting, the oppressed, and the battered than our, sometimes misdirected, adherence to principles of headship, submission, and suffering. Joy's story is the story of a survivor of domestic violence, but it is also the story of God's faithfulness along the power and sufficiency of His word.

If you are a *victim*, please find hope in these pages. While your story will not be the same as Joy's story, the God of this story is unchanging. Yes, find comfort in knowing you are not alone, but embrace the hope of the gospel that you are loved, and pursued by a savior who has conquered evil.

If you are a *people helper*, please find insight into the families you will soon interact with. Perhaps some of the clients, counselees, and neighbors you interact with are experiencing the weight of domestic abuse. Glean what you can from this work as you pursue peace in your context.

If you are a pastor, prepare to be challenged. We are often the first place women go for help, but tend to be found the least helpful. Joy's words may sting, or challenge your assumptions. Please, as a fellow pastor read this work with an open heart and an open Bible, you may be surprised with what you find.

Called to Peace is a textbook. Throughout the book you will interact with truth regarding the nature of domestic abuse, but sections of the book will introduce you to concepts, terminology, and strategies for addressing the abuse in your life. If the story brings the realities of abuse to life, the teaching portions bring a practicality that is necessary to respond whether you are a victim or a helper.

Called to Peace a treasure. As Joy described the moment she said goodbye to her earthly treasures I was reminded of Joseph's words in Genesis 50:20, "What you meant for evil, God used for good." I wish this story was not true, but I am glad to say that we have it. God has taken a truly evil account and redeemed it for good. My prayer is that you will hear God's 'call to peace' through this work and who knows, maybe our little tribe will welcome one more to the cause.

Peace,
Rev. Chris Moles
2017

Author of *The Heart of Domestic Abuse: Gospel Solutions for Men Who Use Control and Violence in the Home*, and editor of *Caring for Families Caught in Domestic Abuse*

PREFACE

This book contains my own experiences with domestic violence, as well as stories from many precious survivors I have met over the years. In these accounts, names and identities have been changed except those of my children and the wonderful helpers God sent along the way. Without them, I am not sure we would have made it out, and I am forever grateful for their help.

Please note that my intention in writing this book is to help people better understand the dynamics of domestic violence, not to bash my ex-husband. These experienced happened over twenty-five years ago, and my children tell me he is different these days. The point of telling this story is to show how abuse progresses over time, and that God can and will redeem any situation. Also, it is not my intent to criticize pastors or counselors whose counsel I share in the book. I fully understand how easy it is to be fooled by these situations, and one goal of the book is to show how tricky dealing with domestic violence can be, especially for those without specialized training.

As you read, you will notice that I refer to victims and survivors as females and to perpetrators as males. Part of the reason for this is that my own experience has been almost exclusively with female victims. This is not to deny female against male abuse. However, when it comes to physical domestic violence and injuries reported, statistics reveal that nearly 90 percent of perpetrators are male. In addition, impacts on female victims tend to be more severe, especially when it comes to financial stability and post-traumatic-stress symptoms. Furthermore, when it comes to counseling within the church, gender is an important topic because so many abusers use Scripture as a tool to dominate their wives. In my case, misunderstanding Scripture kept me in a dangerous place for far too long, and I have seen many other women with the same struggle. This book is written primarily for women of faith who need to see God's heart for the oppressed and for those who desire to help them. For the sake of simplicity, and to focus on my intended audience, I will use male pronouns to refer to offenders and female pronouns to refer to victims/survivors

I think it is important to note that while my healing came primarily through meditating on Scripture and prayer, there were very few domestic abuse, trauma-informed resources available to me in the mid 1990's. By the time I separated from my ex-husband the final time, I had been a Christian for over twenty years and knew how to apply Scripture to my life. Still, it was an arduous path. My progress was slow and filled with dangerous mistakes, because of the lack of knowledge I faced. Women in these situations need wise, trauma/domestic abuse-informed helpers to help them navigate the multiple barriers and struggles they face. Two words of caution should apply when it comes to seeking counsel. First, it is crucial to find helpers with specific training in the dynamics of domestic abuse. People perish for lack of knowledge (Hosea 4:6). This is particularly true for an issue as complex as domestic abuse. Second, seek helpers who can encourage you with God's truth as revealed in Scripture. My father was a Freudian psychologist, and his approach to help left me filled with despair. There are many voices proclaiming expertise in abuse these days, but many do not acknowledge truths that both Scripture, and now neuroscience research, acknowledge— that God created us with an ability to heal. I often tell folks that God brought me through a supernatural process that some therapists have labeled cognitive behavioral therapy as He taught me to "take every thought captive to the obedience of Christ" (2 Corinthians 10:5). Living through abuse warps our thinking, so methods that focus on renewing our minds are most effective. Meditation on His Word is a powerful path to recovery after trauma.

Finally, I think I should mention that this book contains accounts of experiences that could be triggers for those struggling with PTSD. I considered leaving some of these stories out, but in the end, I felt it was important to share them to give readers— especially those unfamiliar with the dynamics of abuse— a more accurate picture of the malicious nature of domestic violence. Being able to see the truth clearly, even when it's ugly, is essential. While I know how unpleasant triggers can be, I don't believe avoiding them indefinitely is the solution. In our support groups, we teach our ladies to use triggers as opportunities to overcome faulty thinking patterns they have taken on as a result of abuse.

Typically, behind fear and panic, we find untrue beliefs heightening the problem. Identifying deceptive thoughts and replacing them with truth is crucial to moving forward. However, this does not usually happen overnight, but slowly as God gives grace. His way of transforming our minds is through a process (Romans 12:2). So, if you find yourself overwhelmed by emotion while reading, take frequent breaks. If you are worried about triggers, skip ahead to Chapter 12 on "Managing Your Emotions" and Lesson 5 in *The Called to Peace Workbook* "Healing from Trauma." Choose to apply truth to the negative thoughts and beliefs that consume you and continue to read gradually. In counseling, I often ask counselees to identify and write down the thoughts accompanying their intense emotions and then examine them in the light of Scripture. If it's an irrational fear, apply a Scripture that counters it. Say it out loud and repeat it often as the thought surfaces. Then claim His promises. There is a Scripture Database at the end of the book with numerous passages that were helpful to me as I was coming out of abuse. They can help you get started. Another powerful solution for overcoming fear is worship. When I was coming out of abuse I kept praise and worship music playing continually. I sang out loud when I felt especially overwhelmed. There is nothing more powerful than making Him bigger than your problems. Give Him your fears and your heart. He is entirely trustworthy and able to move you from victim to victor.

INTRODUCTION

My pastor looked at me apologetically as he handed me the business card for a local divorce attorney. His explanation caused an explosion of despair and anger in my heart. "I'm sorry, but I think this is your only option. I've tried everything I know, but things only seem to be getting worse."

I could not believe this man I'd reached out to for help was giving up and, even worse, was encouraging me to do the same! All I could think was, "Doesn't he know that God hates divorce and that nothing is impossible for God? How can he just wash his hands of the situation and give me a worldly solution?" I was too shocked to respond, but I decided then and there that I would seek help elsewhere. Over the months that followed, I exhausted every resource I could find, but the violence only grew deadlier. Ultimately, I came to the same sad conclusion as my pastor.

After finally leaving my abusive marriage, I began to realize how warped my thinking had become. Over time, I had become so rigid in my beliefs that my view of God actually worked against me. Although I never would have voiced it, as a conservative Christian, deep down, I had come to believe that God cared more about my marriage than my life. My own faulty thinking was constantly reinforced by my husband, who often quoted Scripture to remind me he was the head of our house. Looking back at myself during that time, I'm almost embarrassed to share this story. Those who have never lived with abuse will probably read this and shake their heads at the absurdity of my decisions. However, in the twenty-seven years that I have been out of abuse, I have worked with multitudes of domestic violence survivors and have found that most of them have struggled with the same sort of thinking. For me, the healing process required a complete overhaul in my thinking, and the same is true for nearly everyone coming out of abuse.

If you are currently in or have been in an abusive relationship, this book is especially for you. It is also for anyone who wants to help and support you. There are numerous resources for those who want to learn more about the dynamics of domestic abuse and how to get safe and respond wisely to abusive people.[4]

However, my goal with this book is not to address those issues. Neither is it my intention to debate whether abusive relationships can be saved.[5] My prayer is that this book will help you heal spiritually and emotionally, and help you see that God's heart is for you— regardless of what people tell you. His

---

[4] For a list of recommended resources visit https://www.calledtopeace.org/resources/

[5] For the record, I do believe these relationships can be saved. To believe otherwise would be contrary to the gospel. Still, I have found it to be quite rare. Most studies find that abusive men are usually unaffected by intervention and

heart is always for the oppressed, and He holds the keys to your healing. Our Redeemer can turn your ashes into beauty. He loves you with an everlasting love and calls you from violence to peace.

---

prone to recidivism (See https://ojp.gov/pdffiles1/nij/195079.pdf). Chris Moles' Men of Peace training and book, *The Heart of Domestic Abuse,* are great resources for those wanting to learn more about working with abusive men. I also did an interview with Chris on the steps that should be taken in order for them to overcome abusive beliefs and behaviors. Access it at https://tinyurl.com/2ynzr763

PART ONE

A Story of Abuse

My companion attacks his friend; he violates his covenant.
His talk is smooth as butter, yet war is in his heart;
his words are more soothing than oil, yet they are drawn swords.
Cast your cares on the LORD and He will sustain you;
He will never let the righteous be shaken.

~ Psalm 55:20–22

Chapter 1

A Fragile Foundation

Unless the Lord builds the house, the builders labor in vain.
~ Psalm 127:1a

I did not grow up with abuse. As a matter of fact, in my family, I never heard harsh words or raised voices. In my early years, my father was a pastor. His theological training led him to question the authority of Scripture and suggested that God was uninvolved in the affairs of humanity. Like most children, I admired my dad and naturally absorbed his beliefs. His teachings led me to believe Jesus's sole purpose on earth was to challenge injustice, while His redemptive work on the cross was never explained to me. I very much appreciate the brave stand my parents took against racism in a small Southern town in the 1960s. My dad eventually preached a sermon in favor of civil rights one Sunday and, almost immediately, the backlash began. Within days, Klansmen *in our congregation* had burned a cross in the churchyard leaving Daddy with little choice but to resign.

After leaving the ministry, Daddy went into psychology, but his change in vocation was more like a change in religion as he traded postmodern theology for the futility of Freudian psychology. As soon as he helped us find a church, he stopped attending. In the meantime, we were introduced to a new concept—the family meeting. Daddy would bring up a problem issue and then encourage us to express our feelings on the subject. The whole point seemed to be emotional venting rather than finding solutions. It never made much sense to me and never appeared to accomplish anything. As I visited my father at work, I learned that our family meetings mirrored group therapy. I guess those meetings were his attempts to help his family; however, they simply deepened my already growing sense of despair.

Both ideologies I had learned from my father rejected absolute truth, and I became an extremely confused and empty teenager. I was angry about the way the church had treated my dad, so Christianity wasn't an option for me. Eventually, I became a hippie and began to search elsewhere for answers, studying everything from Buddhism to New Age. I even ended up practicing witchcraft and the occult. As I began to spin out of control, my parents' marriage began to teeter on the verge of collapse. I chose to escape the unspoken strain by running away from home a few months before my 15th birthday.

My dad stopped everything to find his runaway daughter. When he found me two weeks later, I was numb from drugs and angry that I had to return home. I certainly didn't care about the pain I had caused my parents. However, my drastic action caused an equally drastic reaction on their part. I was reeled in and introduced to discipline unlike any I had ever known. I was grounded and only allowed to go to school and church. Within a few months, I went off to summer camp. The pastor of our church gave me a copy of the New Testament. Although I believed that Jesus was divine and good, I had never really understood that the God of the universe wanted to have a personal relationship with me. My sinful path had left me empty and miserable, but by the end of that week at summer camp, I had surrendered my life to Jesus. The change was dramatic. I was a new person, and the emptiness was gone.

Regardless of the obvious change in my life, my parents continued to grow apart. My mother eventually returned to the faith of her youth, but Daddy held on to his faith in empty philosophies. One day during my junior year of high school, he called a family meeting and politely announced his intention to leave our family. My mother and younger sister remained calm, but I was devastated. And even though he assured us that we would see him regularly, his visits became increasingly sporadic. By the time I reached my sophomore year in college, I had not seen or heard from my father in over a year. The father I had so deeply admired as a child seemed to have rejected me completely.[6] I found comfort from my Heavenly Father, but still, my parents' divorce profoundly affected me.

---

[6] While there's no room for it in this account, I do not want to let the last mention of my father here be a negative one. My dad eventually came back to God, and we were reconciled. He passed away six years before I finally left Doug for good, but I know he saw the signs of abuse before anyone else did because he often tried to warn me.

Chapter 2

Becoming a Victim

*Do not make friends with a hot-tempered person, do not associate with
one easily angered, or you may learn their ways and get yourself ensnared.
~ Proverbs 22:24–25*

During my tumultuous high school years, I met a young man three years my senior. He was handsome and charming. Frankly, I was surprised that he even took an interest in me. Even more amazing was that he seemed to care about every little detail of my life. He called me often and usually knew where I was and what I was doing at any given time of day. I thought, indeed, this kind of attention represented real love. As a middle child in a family of four children, I was unaccustomed to being the object of so much attention and found it extremely flattering.

One day, after a few months of dating "Doug," he began asking questions about my past. He did not like my answers about prior boyfriends and blew up at me with a fury, unlike anything I had ever experienced. We were driving at the time, so he slammed on the brakes and ordered me out of the car nearly five miles from my home. I quickly obeyed his command, and he drove off. He soon returned, ordered me back into the car, and drove me home without a word. The whole incident was quite confusing, and I couldn't figure out why he had become so angry. However, I assumed I must have deserved it.

He did not call for several days, but when he finally did, he apologized, explained how I had hurt him, and said that he just couldn't handle it. He seemed so sincere that I felt truly sorry for him and was sorry I had caused him such trauma. So ended lesson number one in a relationship that eventually distorted my thinking and nearly cost me my life. While nothing I did could affect the father who raised me, everything I did affected Doug. I became even more convinced that he must really love me because I had the power to hurt and upset him so deeply. I also began to believe that he could not help himself when he blew up. I felt sorry for him because he'd had such a hard life. It seemed he had always been the victim somewhere. I thought that if I left him, he might completely fall apart. I did leave once, but he suddenly converted to Jesus and changed his behavior for a while, so I stayed.

Doug and I dated for eight years before we got married. During that time, I got used to the ups and downs. We had some wonderful times, but I never knew when something minor might set him off. He either treated me like a princess or like a slave. Just when I would begin to get fed up enough to leave, the sweet temperament I had fallen in love with would return. Over the years, I learned to "tiptoe" to avoid his explosions. Yet there were times when they blindsided me. I couldn't always predict what might set him off. It could be as simple as a lost item or my choice of clothing, but it could also be related to his erroneous interpretation of my thoughts or motives.

One day, we were enjoying a pleasant meal when suddenly, Doug's demeanor changed. I could tell he was angry but couldn't figure out why for the life of me. After we left the restaurant, I asked him what was wrong. He just glared at me, inferring that I must know the reason. I knew I had done nothing wrong, so I continued to press until he finally told me what was bothering him. It seems he thought I was staring at a man across the restaurant, although I had never noticed the man he described. Throughout our eight years of dating, there were numerous situations of extreme jealousy. Even though our relationship was emotionally painful at times, I told myself that leaving meant I would be wasting all the years I'd been with him, and I also knew that God could make it work. Besides, Doug had never physically harmed me. He had seen his father abuse his mother and had hated it with a passion, so I figured I would never have to worry about that.

The bottom line was that I made excuse after excuse to justify staying in a relationship that I intrinsically knew was not honoring to God. The worst part was that Doug became the center of my universe, and God took second place in my life. As a result, the focus of my life was trying to please a man who constantly changed his demands. Regardless of my spiritual compromise, I prayed for the Lord to bless our relationship and believed He would certainly answer my prayers. After all, we both claimed His name. During a period of backsliding and severe depression on my part, Doug and I married. I attempted to return to God and asked Him to bless our marriage, but I had no peace about it.

Chapter 3

Perishing

*Be gracious to me O God, for man tramples on me;
all day long an attacker oppresses me...
~ Psalm 56:1 (ESV)*

There was never a honeymoon stage in our marriage. Within a month of the wedding, Doug's behavior became increasingly unbearable. One weekend, my brother came to visit us. He went to bed, leaving his socks on the floor and an apple core on the table. I had gone to bed earlier, but Doug was still awake. Around 3:00 a.m., he entered our bedroom, turned on the overhead lights, and yanked the covers off of me. He got right in my face and angrily hissed, "Get in there and clean up your brother's mess!" I was hardly coherent but was utterly stunned that something so minor would upset him this much. While I had already learned to be careful about what I said and did around Doug, this experience added a whole new dimension of fear for me. The anger I saw in his eyes that night seemed dangerous, and I felt that if I didn't obey him, he would have physically hurt me.

Doug had graduated from college a month before our wedding but hadn't been able to find a steady job during the first two years of our marriage. Somewhere along the line, he'd read a book by a famous faith teacher that gave him the impression that God was bound to answer any of his prayers if he claimed the answers by faith. Doug thought he could believe himself into any job he wanted and refused to take anything less than the best. When he was still unemployed a month later, he began to blame God, and his temper seemed to worsen daily. Shortly afterward, we both were accepted into master's degree programs at a nearby university, and his anger subsided briefly. However, by the end of the first semester, he mentioned he was having some problems in his program. When I prompted him further, he said he had simply had a personality conflict with the program director. As a result, Doug ended up leaving school. On the other hand, I took quite well to my program and remained in it. Unfortunately, Doug was upset with my success.

As Doug's problems in school increased, so did his rage at home. The verbal abuse was horrendous. I had never heard such language and had never felt so hated. There were times when he would scream at me into the early hours of the morning, refusing to let me sleep or study. He belittled me, called me names, and implied that I was stupid and worthless. He often blocked the door to our room and held me hostage as the verbal assaults continued. During these rampages, he often threw things, punched the walls, and destroyed my property. Although he had never actually hit me, I truly feared for my safety. Even though I'd tried everything to encourage him and let him know I wanted only the best for him, Doug saw all of his problems as my fault. His perspective on life was warped, and he did not trust anyone, especially not me. It seemed he couldn't believe that anyone could love him unconditionally. No matter what I did or said, he judged my motives as evil. In my heart, hopelessness and despair began to set in and, deep inside, I found myself disappointed with God. Although I had never prayed for His will before entering marriage, I expected Him to make it work. Surely, I thought, He would be bound to bless the covenant we made before Him and work out all the kinks. Contrary to my expectations, and despite of my prayers, the problems only amplified as time passed.

Over time, I began to dread leaving my friends at school and entering my dreary, lifeless home. I was free to be myself at school, but at home, I could show no joy. Doug's misery was thrown in my face anytime I showed any happiness. How dare I be happy when he was so miserable? Every conversation was focused on him, and I did my best to encourage him. However, Doug said I had no right to try to cheer him up since I had no idea what his life was like. Most attempts to support him ended with him calling me a naïve idiot. He criticized me so much that I was convinced he couldn't really love me.

Although Doug had never physically hurt me, the angry outbursts at home continued to worsen until I felt I could no longer bear it. I shared my predicament with a friend at work who encouraged me to leave Doug. This support gave me hope, and I began to plan my escape. My newfound hope must have caused my demeanor to change because Doug seemed to suspect I was planning to leave. One night, he began to press me for information. He asked if I was planning on leaving or if I wanted out of the marriage. I was terrified but did not want to lie. I told him we didn't have a real marriage and that I was miserable. He flipped out, and suddenly I was up against a wall as he kicked my abdomen repeatedly. The verbal cruelty I had endured for eleven years had finally become physical. I do not remember how I got through that night, but I know that I packed up and left the next day. We had no car, so a friend drove me to my mother's house about twenty miles away. Doug ended up spending a night in jail for communicating a threat to my friend, but his parents came the following day, bailed him out, and took him back to their home a few hours away. At first, I was terrified that Doug would come back and hurt me, so another friend offered me lodging in her apartment. I wasted no time getting a formal separation that included a protective order. My stomach seemed to be doing flip-flops, and I was nauseated daily.

Two weeks later, I discovered my stomach issues were not merely from nerves, but I was pregnant! This caused me to do a lot of soul-searching. I knew I had failed to seek God's path for my life and marriage. How sobering it was to think I was going to be responsible for another life when I couldn't even handle my own. I was completely broken before God and felt a profound sense of sorrow. I had strayed from His path and wanted to get back on it. I began to wonder if I had given up on my marriage too soon.

I faced the beginning of my pregnancy alone. Financially, things were bleak. I had a part-time job and financial aid, but these were, at best, temporary and insufficient means of income. Worst of all, I had no health insurance. It was a scary place to be in life, and there were no easy answers. In the meantime, I stayed in touch with my sister-in-law. She was a good friend and kept me informed about Doug. It seemed, contrary to his picky nature, he had taken a low-wage job and was going to church regularly. He was even counseling with the pastor there, so I began to find hope for reconciliation. Sometime in my second trimester of pregnancy, I got up the nerve to pick up the phone and call him. When I told him I was pregnant, he began to cry. After asking if the baby was his, he told me God had answered his prayers. He regretted our separation and was longing for a family. I told him I was also grieved over the loss of our marriage but was afraid of what he might do to me if we reconciled.

Over the next few weeks, Doug did everything in his power to win me back. I thought I saw an overall improvement in his temperament. Since the prospect of being a single mom did not appeal to me, I decided to ignore any remaining doubts I had about safety and consented to a reconciliation. Within weeks of our reunion, the fear was back. During my seventh month of pregnancy, Doug went into a rage while driving. We were in a downtown area when he began to speed through red lights, weave in and out of lanes, and dodge cars. I was sure we were going to die. Terrified, I begged him to slow down. After numerous pleas, he finally screeched to a halt. I knew then that there had been no real change in him. He had only put on an act to get his way.

During the final stages of my pregnancy, I had to stop working and became entirely dependent on Doug for financial support. He had finally gotten a decent job with health insurance and that seemed to improve his attitude around the house. Every time there was a lapse in his anger, this man and my dream of an ideal marriage became the center of my universe. I continued to believe that God would heal us, and our child would be raised in a wonderful Christian home.

Our daughter Haley was born via emergency C-section after twenty-seven hours of labor. Her heart rate showed she was in distress, so there was no other option. Doug got angry with my doctor, called her incompetent, and stormed out. I was about to give birth to my first child and went into surgery with no idea of where my husband was.

Chapter 4

Hope Deferred

Hope deferred makes the heart sick, but a longing fulfilled is a tree of life.
~ *Proverbs 13:12*

My dreams of an ideal Christian family never materialized. Doug soon lost his job and became increasingly bitter. He reminded me of the book he had read a few years earlier, stating that God would answer any prayer claimed in faith. He had prayed and believed for a new job, but nothing had happened. Since the faith teachers guaranteed he could pray for and receive any job he wanted, he decided that God was nothing but a liar who played favorites. He also thought that since I seemed to have better luck with jobs and schooling, I was clearly one of God's favorites. Doug saw himself as a miserable victim of circumstances and felt that God was responsible for his misery. His response was to turn his back on God. He ordered me to quit going to church, and insisted I give up my faith because he saw God as an enemy. My allegiance to Him was seen as betrayal. Even though I tried to encourage him and assure him that both God and I were on his side, he could not be persuaded. Violence soon became a regular occurrence in our home. On one occasion, Doug held a pocketknife to my throat and told me I could either deny God or prepare to meet Him immediately. We struggled until I was able to break free and run next door. The next-door neighbors in our townhouse apartment couldn't help but hear what had been happening. They were Christians, and they tried to encourage me to leave, but I rejected their advice as clearly unbiblical.

The morning after the knife incident was a Sunday. As the baby and I were leaving for church, Doug ran out of the house and ordered me back inside. He reached into my car, grabbed my Bible, tried to tear it apart, and then threw it to the ground and stomped on it. I was afraid I would be next, so I drove off. He followed on foot until I could get past the speed bumps in our apartment complex and gain enough speed to escape him. At church that morning, I was completely overwhelmed and confused as I poured my heart out to the Lord. As a young Christian, we had attended an ultra-conservative church where women had to wear head coverings and were taught to submit to their husbands in every circumstance—no exceptions! This created a real struggle within my spirit. After the service, I told our pastor and his wife what had happened the night before and asked for prayer. I explained that I knew I was supposed to submit, but I was terrified to go home.

Pastor Rick calmly listened and simply stated, "The Bible says to submit as is fitting in the Lord, and this isn't fitting!" I was shocked he didn't try to send me home to that angry man. Based on my understanding, or misunderstanding, of Scripture, I thought the Lord wanted me to submit, regardless of the situation. How amazing it was to catch a glimpse of His amazing grace. Through my pastor's simple statement, I understood that my Heavenly Father cared more about me than my submission. Tears began to flow as I was reintroduced to His marvelous love. It was that love that had drawn me in the first place, but over the years, it had become obscured as fear of man had replaced my worship of Him.

For the next few years, Doug and I separated and reunited numerous times. Each time I left, Doug eventually calmed down and seemed repentant. He went to great lengths to win me back and said all the right things in counseling. We tried numerous counselors—pastors, Christian counselors, and even secular mental health professionals. In most cases, the focus of counseling became what I could do to keep Doug from becoming so angry. After all, why would anyone be angry without being provoked? One psychiatrist suggested Doug had the lowest self-esteem of anyone he had ever seen and thought I should do everything I could to boost his self-worth. His advice was not contrary to what I was already doing. In an effort to keep things from getting out of hand, I usually did everything in my power to encourage and build Doug up, but my attempts were met with very little success. The doctor's prescription had already failed before he'd even prescribed it to us.

Despite my never-failing optimism, Doug's violent attacks against me continued. It was like a roller-coaster ride—a never-ending cycle that seemed impossible to break. Finally, somebody gave me a copy of *Love Must Be Tough* by James Dobson. This book opened my eyes to a whole new concept. Perhaps rolling over and taking the abuse wasn't the most loving thing I could do. I was fed up with the violence and determined to take a strong stand against it. Eventually, Doug learned that any aggression on his part would result in a call to the police on my part, and I began to see some positive changes, although he never seemed very happy.

In his never-ending search for significance, Doug decided to apply for medical school. We drove to West Virginia and Pennsylvania for interviews, but he returned convinced he would never be accepted. However, both schools offered him a spot. Just before we were ready to move, I found out I was pregnant again. Doug thought this meant he would not be able to attend medical school since I would have to be the primary breadwinner. As it turned out, we were able to go anyway because his father offered us financial assistance. Our second daughter, Hannah, was born just after Doug's first semester. This time, I had elected to have a scheduled C-section. At the time, he was angry with his school—convinced he had flunked the first semester—so he sat in the operating room as the doctor was doing the surgery and made critical remarks about the school the whole time. It was awful; I felt exposed in every way possible.

After Hannah was born, it turned out that Doug's pessimistic predictions were wrong, and by the second year of school, life seemed to improve. Although things were stressful for me with a full-time job and two small children, it seemed the violence had become a distant memory. Doug was finally realizing his lifelong goal of becoming a doctor, which seemed to improve his disposition somewhat. There was no true joy in our relationship, and he was often critical of the kids and me, but his concentration on school and fear of negative consequences helped to maintain the peace. I also believe that my role as the main wage earner helped Doug to control his temper. He seemed to try to avoid upsetting me too much for fear I would quit my job or leave, in which case he would lose his source of income. Consequently, those four years were the most stable years our marriage ever knew.

Chapter 5

Losing Ground

A hot-tempered person must pay the penalty;
rescue them, and you will have to do it again.
~ Proverbs 19:19

Perhaps the four years of relative peace lulled me back into complacency. I seemed to have forgotten how taking a firm stand had finally stopped the violence before. After Doug graduated from medical school, our stability quickly became a memory. We moved from Philadelphia to Atlanta, and I decided to try staying home with the children for a while. I felt like I had missed so much of their lives by working full-time while Doug was in school. This decision was vitally important to me, and I believed any financial sacrifice was worth it. Perhaps that decision also influenced my increased willingness to tolerate increasingly problematic behavior from Doug. Working untold hours as an intern, and the pressure of having full responsibility for our financial well-being, seemed to weigh heavily on him.

As we became acquainted with the demanding life of a medical intern, we became reacquainted with our old relationship patterns. Doug would become stressed about something that happened at work, then come home and take his frustration out on the girls and me. Although he didn't physically harm us, his fits of rage were terrifying. I had to take the children and leave the house several times. One time, we had to stay in a hotel for two days to escape his wrath. Our credit card reached its limit on the third day, and we had to return home even though Doug was still quite angry. Fortunately, his long hours at the hospital kept him away for another day or so and tired him out enough to prevent another crisis once he came home.

While things were back to "normal" on the home front, things did not go smoothly for Doug at work. One day, he overreacted to a scheduling change and threw a lamp. He was immediately suspended from work without pay and was forced to seek a psychiatric evaluation. He was required to complete any prescribed treatment before returning to work. During his suspension, I called the chief of the residency program and tried to explain Doug's behavior while begging for leniency. I explained that our family was dependent on Doug's income and that he was probably suffering from a severe lack of sleep when he threw the lamp. As had become my habit, I took responsibility for his life and did my best to clean up his mess. My efforts were met with success as I was able to convince the chief to bring him back earlier than the original suspension required.

Things went quite well for the two to three weeks Doug was home during his suspension. He started attending church and praying with me. It seemed that a crisis always brought him to his knees. However, it appeared that even as Doug was seeking the Lord, he was also seeking to maintain a degree of control during the crisis. He didn't like the diagnosis he received from the first psychiatrist he had seen and eventually settled on a counselor from a prominent Christian counseling center. I even went with him to present his case to the counselor because I was just as determined as Doug was to present a sanitized version of our problems. As a result of our efforts, the counselor simply prescribed a course of anger management. This allowed him to return to work, and within a few months, the counselor sent the hospital a letter stating Doug had successfully completed anger management—as if to say he was fixed. I chose to believe that the course had changed him because the truth was too painful to accept.

In the years that followed, lies and denial continued to be our standard. I went with Doug to his counseling sessions occasionally and found that he rarely told the counselors the truth. But I was afraid to call his bluff, so I sat silently and let the deception flow. I knew I would surely face his anger at home if I said anything, and I guess I knew that exposing his dishonesty would also shine a light on my own unhealthy condition. After all, I had supported him and smoothed his path for years. How stupid would it make me look if people knew the real story? As Doug finished his training years, our social standing in the community improved, making the thought of exposure even more dreadful to me. We moved to a small town in Virginia and portrayed the all-American family to the community. To use Jesus's analogy, our family was nothing more than a whitewashed tomb: beautiful on the outside but dark, dank, and rotten on the inside. However, we serve a Lord who is a specialist at rolling away tombstones, and His light would soon shine into our darkness.

Chapter 6

The Tempest

*I said, "Oh that I had the wings of a dove! I would fly away and be at rest...
I would hurry to my place of shelter, far from the tempest and storm."*
~ Psalm 55:6 & 8

While I made every effort to conceal the true nature of our family from the world, I continued to cry out to God for healing. My heart longed for an easy answer, but my Great Physician knew surgery would be required. He gently began to prepare me for the pain that was to come. I found a few like-minded homeschooling moms shortly after I arrived in Virginia. My dear friend Susan had been involved in several of Kay Arthur's Precepts Bible studies in Florida and suggested that we start with one of Kay's Lord Series books. The title chosen was *Lord, Where Are You When Bad Things Happen?* One of the members of our group expressed reluctance to do the study. She said God always used her studies to prepare her for life circumstances, and she was not in the mood for tragedy. I just laughed at her and proceeded to sign up for the class.

I had been a Christian for over twenty years and was finally about to learn how to genuinely study and apply the Bible. Our study of the book of Habakkuk focused on the sovereignty of God. The idea that God would use tragic situations for good was not new to me. However, the thought that He was still in control, even during the worst of circumstances, was something I had never really pondered. In the videos accompanying the book, I remember Kay Arthur speaking of bad circumstances as being "sifted through His fingers of love." She gave examples of horrific tragedy and demonstrated God's goodness during those situations. To this day, my limited mind can't fully grasp the tension between the existence of evil and our sovereign God's goodness, but soon after completing that study, circumstances would help me experience it. My world was about to change completely.

Toward the end of his residency, Doug discovered he could make incredible money by moonlighting in community hospital ERs on the weekends. Suddenly, our financial problems were a thing of the past. As his income became abundant, our time together became scarce. Doug worked back-to-back shifts so often that he did not make it home most weekends. Even after he finished his residency and began his first job as a staff physician at a hospital fifty miles away, he continued to moonlight on weekends. Often he worked 14-hour shifts at his new job and just spent the night at the hospital to avoid two hours of travel time back and forth. When he did come home during the week, he was tired and irritable. Frankly, it got to the point that I was usually relieved to see him go back to work. His temper seemed to be getting worse and worse. Violence subtly began to creep back into our marriage.

One day, Doug came home in a terrible mood. I was homeschooling Haley at the time, and he decided I wasn't doing a good job. He asked her how to spell a word. Spelling had always been her weakness, and she misspelled it. That sent him over the edge. He then asked her how to spell "belt" and threatened that if she didn't get it right, he would spank her with his belt. Haley became so afraid that she clammed up, and he began to scream even louder. When I tried to calm him down, he grabbed my arm and attempted to throw me down our basement stairs. I sat down and resisted as much as possible, but we struggled for quite a while. After this incident, I took the kids and left the house for a few days. Things soon calmed down, though, and once again we returned home. There were several months of relative calm, but as usual, the holidays added stress which led to problems.

That Christmas Haley had asked for a guitar, but I had not been able to find one that fit the budget I was given, so I got her a keyboard instead. It was apparent from her facial expression that she was disappointed, but she didn't vocalize it. Doug was furious when he saw her face. He told her that if she didn't like what she got, she could just say goodbye to all her Christmas presents. He went to the kitchen, got a large trash bag, and proceeded to throw all her presents into the bag while yelling, "No Christmas for you this year!" She begged and pleaded for him to stop, but he pulled her hair, pushed her toward the stairs, and told her to go to her room. Hannah and I were so afraid that we went with her into her room and locked the door.

That was the first time he had crossed the line of violence with one of the children. I wanted to run as far away as I could. We sat on Haley's bed crying. Her response hurt just as badly as his outburst. "Why does he have to be my dad?" she asked. What was happening to my children? When the violence was directed at me, I could handle it, but this was a whole new level of pain. I would have left that day, but we had his family coming in from out of town, so we waited upstairs for a few hours until he calmed down. Then, we did what we had learned to do so well; we continued the day as though nothing had ever happened. Haley even got her gifts back. His anger was gone, and the day ended pleasantly. It seemed ridiculous to leave on Christmas after things had turned around so nicely.

Over time, the never-ending progression of violence became a downward spiral. I was so weary and begged the Lord for relief. The events in the months after the Christmas episode gave me more courage to confront the truth, regardless of my fear of Doug. As I prayed, I began to realize that Doug was rarely honest with me, and I couldn't live with lies any longer. Each time I would confront him about things, he managed to turn everything back on me and make me believe I was imagining things. He had always been a great actor and, in addition to acting completely innocent, he made me think I was crazy for ever doubting him. However, I had been keeping a journal over the years, and as I read it, I began to recognize his pattern of lies. I could not let it rest any longer. Still, I wanted to do things God's way and thought I should confess my sins even as I confronted his. As soon as I confessed to Doug, he knocked me to the floor in front of the girls. He stormed out of the room, and I could hear him rampaging through the house, destroying things. I heard a loud bang in the kitchen, which I later learned was our brand-new microwave hitting the floor. I knew time was short before his return and reached for the phone.

Too embarrassed to have the police show up, I called the home of a dear couple from my church. They had given us refuge earlier that year when Doug had blown up. Ellis didn't even recognize my voice because I was so upset. I explained the situation to him, and he got into his car to get us. I gathered the girls and my purse and then ran outside to wait. Doug was still upstairs tearing things up, so we were able to get away. Doug did not know where my friends lived, but he did know their phone number and used it repeatedly that night, though they never told him we were there. The next day, I decided we needed to go back to the house and get some things because we had left with nothing but the clothes on our backs and my purse. My friend Ellis was bigger than Doug, so he came with me for protection. As soon as we entered the house, we noticed an ax sitting on the couch. Doug quickly grabbed my purse and cleared out all my bank cards. Ellis tried to convince him to be reasonable and let me get some things, but Doug just picked up the ax. He told us to leave and filled our ears with profanity. As we left, Doug followed us outside, waving the ax and cursing all the way. When we got into Ellis's van and started backing out of the driveway, Doug threw the ax at us. It was clear I would not be able to get any necessities from home anytime soon, so Ellis drove me to the bank. After some discussion with the teller, I was able to empty half of our savings account.

Chapter 7

Light in the Darkness

The light shines in the darkness, and the darkness has not overcome it.
~ *John 1:5*

As we drove back to Ellis and Karen's house, I realized we would no longer be able to stay with them; Doug had threatened them too many times. One of the ladies from my Bible study came to the rescue and offered us refuge with her family. During my stay there, I spent much time in the Word and prayer. The Lord was faithful to speak to my aching heart. Two Scriptures seemed to jump off the page and land straight into my heart. When I stumbled onto Jeremiah 29:11, in which God promises His children hope and a future, I knew it was God's word for me. Just before I found it, I had been crying out to God how life seemed hopeless and how I had no future. He also reminded me of the promise in Romans 8:28 that He would somehow use what I was experiencing for good.

The day after the Lord showed me these Scriptures, I visited my friend Dee. Her pastor's wife was there, and Dee explained my plight to her. As she listened, she picked up her Bible and looked me straight in the eye. She said, "I believe the Lord would have me share two passages with you." The first was Jeremiah 29:11, and the second was Romans 8:28. Even in the darkest days of my life, our wonderful Lord reached down to confirm His great love for me, and He would continue to speak His words of comfort into my life. However, circumstances only continued to worsen.

One morning, I woke with Jesus's words on my mind: "Lay not up for yourselves treasures upon the earth, where moth and rust consume, and where thieves break through and steal, but lay up for yourselves treasures in heaven…" (Mt. 6:19). Deep inside, I knew I was about to lose most of my earthly treasures. Doug had destroyed some of my clothes the first time we separated, and I believed this time he would do worse. It wasn't long before that belief was confirmed. I had inherited many beautiful antiques from my grandmother, so Doug decided that if he couldn't get to me, he would destroy the things I loved. Still, the message from God was clear, and my heart was prepared. Soon afterward, I learned Doug had taken his ax to my beloved antiques.

My mother was the one who informed me of Doug's destructive rampage. Not only had he chopped and burned furniture, but he had also bagged up all my clothes and personal belongings. He called my mom and told her he had destroyed many of our family heirlooms, and the rest of my stuff would be going into the dumpster if I didn't come home and "face my punishment." I contacted the police to try and stop the destruction. They asked many questions about how dangerous Doug might be, whether he owned a gun, and whether he might attack any officers who might visit the house. They told me there was nothing they could do to stop him from destroying the furniture. Even though I brought it into the marriage, it had become marital property, so he could do whatever he wanted with it. Despite their reluctance to deal with this issue, I finally convinced them to go talk to him. When the officers arrived at the house, they found him holding an ax and burning furniture. They couldn't convince him to stop the destruction, but they were able to get a key to one of our cars for me. However, they told me he had let the air out of all the tires.

The following day I learned that Doug had taken many of my belongings to the town dumpster, so I decided to go and try to retrieve what was left of my things. Some ladies from my Bible study volunteered their husbands to accompany me. It was nearly dusk when I climbed down into the rubbish. I saw so many of my precious belongings strewn over mounds of garbage. He had poured ink over my most expensive clothes. Some items were in trash bags, so I opened bags as I went and handed things up to the men outside. It seemed as if every personal item I owned was in that dumpster: jewelry, shoes, antique silver, houseplants, clothing, lamps, toiletries, makeup, curling irons, books and more books—even my Bible! Some trash bags contained my things, and others just had garbage. Before long, I was up to my thighs in dirty diapers and rotten food.

Suddenly, I heard shouting outside. Doug was back and yelling at the men helping me. He ordered them to stop taking my things out and told them he was burning all the furniture at home. It was getting dark outside, so I turned off my flashlight and prayed he would not see me. He didn't, but he began throwing items back into the dumpster. First, he threw a lamp, which barely missed my head, and then a large bag that knocked me over into the debris below. I just sat there and prayed until he left. As I stood up, I found myself saying, "Lord, nobody has ever been through this before! Nobody knows what I'm going through!" As soon as I uttered those words, something amazing happened. His supernatural peace flooded my soul. In my spirit, I could hear Somebody gently saying, "I have. I know." God was with me, and everything on earth faded in His presence. Words cannot adequately describe what happened to me that day as I had a revelation of His love, unlike anything I had ever experienced. He knew the betrayal I was suffering. He had been betrayed by an intimate friend and was beaten and shamed by those He loved. Although I had known Him for over twenty years, I had never experienced the depths of His love like I did in that moment. He had endured the cross because He knew sin would cause me to suffer, and He chose to share in my suffering. In the darkest moment of my life, His amazing light came shining through.

I often tell people that day was both the worst and best of my life because my eyes were opened wider to the depths of His great love for me. Paul's words seemed to sum up my feelings perfectly: "I count all things to be loss in view of the surpassing value of knowing Christ Jesus my Lord, for whom I have suffered the loss of all things and count them but rubbish so that I may gain Christ" (Phil. 3:8). I would never have chosen the suffering I was experiencing, but Jesus chose to endure something far worse because of His great love for me. The thought was overwhelming, so I stood in that dumpster and thanked Him for His amazing love. I knew that a God who loved me that much would never let me go, and I vowed I would not let go of Him either.

In the days following my experience at the dumpster, I tried to reach out to people for help saving our marriage. I called our pastor to let him know what had happened, and he arranged to have us meet in his office for counseling. Apparently, he had already visited Doug and had gotten the story from him. Doug had told him that I had caused him to "lose it." Our pastor's tone indicated that he didn't think anyone would go that crazy unless they were provoked. I was astounded that, once again, I was being blamed for Doug's anger. Even though I had been so faithful to this church that Doug attended only once or twice a year, my pastor seemed to believe him instead of me. No matter how many times I explained that he was angry when I met him, the burden for his behavior always seemed to fall on me.

I got to the counseling session early and stayed close to the pastor. Doug's jaw was clenched tight as he sat and listened to the pastor tell us what he thought needed to happen for us to be able to reconcile. Once the pastor finished speaking, Doug decided to give his take on the situation, and his prescription for saving the marriage. As far as he was concerned, I needed to get down on my knees and beg him to take me back. Doug also accused me of putting on a holy front before the pastor, and this angered me immensely because he always missed my true heart's motives. After years of living with a quick-tempered man, I had learned his ways and responded by showing the pastor just how unholy I could be with words. I let them both know, in no uncertain terms, that I really didn't care about what the pastor thought—I just wanted our marriage to work. In the meantime, Doug's insistence that I get down on my knees and beg for forgiveness intensified. He grabbed a large rock off the pastor's bookshelf and raised it toward me, demanding an apology. The pastor quickly intervened, put the rock away, and the counseling session ended, having done more harm than good.

It was clear we were not going to find a peaceable solution to our problems. Doug continued to call friends and relatives to relay threats to me, and he persisted in chopping and burning my grandmother's antiques. One day, while he was at work, I was able to get into the house and recover a few of the things he had not yet destroyed. He had not damaged the china cabinet yet, but had begun to empty it. One of our outside garbage cans had been pulled into the middle of the dining room. I looked inside to find it filled with broken china, glass, and many other family treasures. I took as many remaining items as I could from the cabinet and began searching for family photos. I was nervous and didn't want to stay long, so I only found a few of our photo albums. It was hard to lose so much family history, but God's comfort was ever-present, assuring me of greater treasures.

A few weeks after our first counseling experience, I tried to talk with my pastor about what could be done to save our marriage. He had made a few attempts to speak with Doug since the session in his office, but he decided our problems were beyond his abilities. He also suggested that separation and divorce were inevitable and gave me the card of a divorce attorney. I couldn't believe it; he was just giving up. It seemed like everyone thought nothing could be done, and nobody even tried to stop Doug's rampages—neither the police nor the church. It was devastating to me because I knew that nothing is impossible with God. Still, even though I wanted to restore our marriage, I knew my main priority had to be safety.

Doug's threats worsened daily. He did not know where the girls and I were, so he harassed friends and family members incessantly. If they didn't take their phones off the hook, he would call them in the middle of the night to make threats and rant about my faults. It became unbearable to everyone involved, so I decided something had to be done. One of my friends was married to a deputy, and I sought his advice. He suggested I file a warrant and have Doug arrested for domestic assault. I went to the courthouse and filled out the paperwork. The magistrate was sympathetic and granted the warrant. However, it turned out to be more harmful than helpful. Doug was not home when law enforcement tried to serve it, so they just taped it to the door. The warrant simply stated that he needed to appear in court in a month, which only increased his rage, and his threats intensified. I knew that if Doug ever found me, I would be severely injured or even killed. It wasn't long before I was faced with that possibility.

One Sunday morning, the girls and I got up early to attend a friend's church in Richmond. As we were driving home, I spotted Doug's car on the opposite side of the road. He recognized us and crossed the centerline into our path at about 60 mph. I slammed on the brakes and swerved off the road just in time to avoid a collision. Apparently, he was on his way to work and did not turn around to pursue us. The effect on the kids was the worst of it. They had seen the whole thing and were crying and screaming. Hannah had bumped her head and, with all the wisdom of a six-year-old, announced that daddies were not supposed to do such things to their children. It broke my heart. I could endure his violence toward me, but seeing how he continued to hurt them was worse than anything he had ever done to me.

About a month after our separation, I was able to rent a small house about twenty minutes outside of town. I had been able to retrieve some of my remaining furniture from the house while Doug was at work. When we first moved in, Doug had no idea of our whereabouts, but within just a few months, our fragile security there was threatened too.

Through all of the turmoil, I had never given up on the idea of reconciliation. After all, my parents' divorce had caused me to believe that people who divorced just didn't try hard enough. Besides, God had miraculously changed my heart; surely, He could also redeem our marriage. After things had calmed down for a few months, I contacted Doug and asked him if he would be willing to go for counseling again. He wept and indicated a strong desire to save the marriage too. I decided not to tell him where we were living, and we went to counseling a few times.

I tried to proceed with caution, but my desire for reconciliation was greater than my ability to discern the truth. I confronted Doug, and he seemed genuinely repentant. After a while, he convinced me the violence was a thing of the past and it was ridiculous to keep my address a secret. One day, I let him follow me home, and it did not take long to realize I had made a grave mistake. At first, he tried to convince me to move back home with him, but when I told him I didn't feel comfortable with that, he began to make threats. He called me constantly, and most conversations ended with one of us hanging up. I was afraid to keep the phone off the hook because I was sure it would provoke him to come out to the house. Often, I just held the phone away from my ear and let him yell. Sometimes he would threaten to come out and kill us all. In those cases, I would load the girls into the car and head for a hotel. At times, I had to wake them in the middle of the night to flee, and since we lived in a small town, the only option was to drive an hour to get to a hotel.

One morning, Doug showed up at the house screaming and pounding the window on the side door with a nightstick. He ordered me to come out, but instead, I dialed 911. I guess he was afraid the police were on the way because he merely yelled a few obscenities and then returned to his car. That wasn't the end of it though. He took his car, rammed the side of mine, backed up, and then rammed it two or three more times before he finally drove off. Miraculously, there was not a single dent in my car. I sat and waited for the police to come, but they never showed up. This pattern continued for several months until it became obvious that the law was not going to protect me. I grew tired of running and eventually borrowed a gun from a friend. However, I decided I would not aim to kill if I ever had to use it.

The months following our initial separation were like a roller-coaster ride. As crazy as it sounds, every time we had a month or two of calm, my intense hatred of divorce would kick in, and I would reach out to Doug hoping for reconciliation, although he had never shown any evidence of true heart change. My own parents' divorce had hurt me so much, and I wanted to protect my children from the same hurt. However, Haley begged me to divorce him, saying if I didn't get away, he would surely kill me. Sadly, years of abuse, along with my own misinterpretation of Scripture, had left my belief system completely warped! My marriage had become an idol, and I was determined to work it out regardless of the ugly truth. The phrase from Malachi 2:16, "God hates divorce," haunted me, and the idea of divorce was almost more painful than living with abuse, so I refused to give up. If only I had studied the true intent of that passage, I might have saved my children and myself from a world of pain and sorrow.[7]

Although I didn't believe divorce was an option, I did try to stay safe. One day, I went to Doug's house to drop something off but I decided not to get out of the car or go inside. He became angry when I told him I wasn't coming in and that I didn't see much hope for our relationship. He reached into the open window of my car, grabbed the hair on the back of my head, and began to pound my head against the steering wheel for what seemed like a couple of minutes. Haley was in the passenger's seat and reached over me to try to fight him off, scratching his neck in the process and leaving a long, deep gash. I suppose the pain finally caused him to let go. When I escaped, I found he had created a bald spot on my head, a knot on my forehead, and a few days later, I developed a noticeable black eye. That was a first. In the previous years, he always managed to kick or grab me in ways that left no visible bruises.

---

[7] This passage was written to address a specific problem in Israel that was harming women and was never meant to entrap them under oppression. To learn more, see chapter 3 in *Divorce and Remarriage in the Church: Biblical Solutions for Pastoral Realities* by David Instone-Brewer, IVP Books, Downers Grove, Illinois, 2006.

Chapter 8

Facing the Truth

Then you will know the truth, and the truth will set you free.
~ *John 8:32*

After I received the black eye, things calmed down again. However, I was determined I would not get close to Doug again unless we could find some real help. As usual, he softened and seemed repentant, but I was too afraid to attempt reconciliation again. His kindness toward me continued for a few months, so I thought that maybe if I could find some expert on domestic violence, he'd be open to get help (I had finally begun to admit it was abuse). I asked him if he'd be willing to do whatever it took to achieve reconciliation, and he said he would. Considering that, I called Focus on the Family, suggested they should do a show on domestic violence, and explained what was happening with us. They were quick to let me know they had already done a few shows on the subject and graciously sent me the tapes free of charge.

When I listened to the Focus on the Family tapes, hope began to rise in my heart. Paul Hegstrom, founder of Life Skills International, was the guest. His program claimed a high success rate with abusive men, while most secular DV programs indicated a very small percentage (3–5%) of abusers ever overcome their abusive patterns. Paul also told his own story of abuse. As an active pastor, he regularly used to beat his wife, Judy, until the day he finally decided to leave her and the ministry. After they separated, he moved in with another woman and began to abuse her as well. One night, he threw her down a flight of stairs, and the following day she had him arrested. Hegstrom lived in Minnesota, which, at the time, was one of the few states in the nation with domestic violence laws on the books. The only way for him to avoid jail time was to enter a program for abusers, which placed him in a group of batterers who were all making excuses and rationalizing their behavior. Hegstrom said he was quickly able to see just how ridiculous those excuses were because they were so familiar to him. Over time, he realized he was just as guilty as the other men in that group.

As this realization hit him, Paul spent a night in prayer before the Lord, asking Him to please change him. He felt hopeless after years of therapy and counseling and asked the Lord why he couldn't change. After a night of crying out to the Lord, Hegstrom said it was as if the still, small voice of God answered and told him the reason he had never changed was because he'd never had a teachable spirit.

This was the turning point he needed. After that, he was determined to learn everything he could about DV and to be teachable. Eventually, he remarried his wife Judy, and they founded Life Skills.

By the time I called Life Skills, Doug and I had been separated for nearly a year. I spoke to Judy, and she told me there weren't any programs near us. They could only suggest an intensive week with an affiliated psychologist in Omaha. I convinced Doug to pay the $3,000 required, and we made the reservation. It was scary to have to get into a car and drive to the airport with Doug—even scarier to spend a week with him in a hotel in Omaha, but I was willing to give it one more try. On the first day, we were taken into a training room with a video player and numerous Paul Hegstrom training tapes. We were also given various handouts on domestic violence, many coming from the Domestic Abuse Intervention Project out of Duluth, Minnesota.

For the first time ever, we had found someone who understood what was happening in our home, and for the first time ever, I was told that I was not responsible for the abuse! I was amazed to find our situation was not uncommon, and that there was a whole body of research on domestic abuse. Abusers don't just suddenly go crazy, lose control, and start hitting. Rather, physical abuse is just part of an overall pattern of behaviors that perpetrators use to maintain control over their victims. When I saw the Power and Control Wheel,[8] I began to cry at the overwhelming reality before me. It was as if someone had been observing and taking notes for our entire marriage. Even before Doug delivered the first physical blow eleven years into our relationship, he had been using many of the control tactics on the Wheel since the day we met. By this twenty-third year of our relationship, I had experienced nearly every type of abuse shown on that diagram. Over the years, his control of me had grown to the point where I filtered nearly every thought through his possible reaction. It was idolatry[9] of the worst sort, and the resulting bondage was unbearable.

The first day of the Life Skills training was incredibly eye-opening. Over the years, despite all that had happened, I had never considered myself an abused wife. I just thought something had snapped in my husband. I thought some odd combination of events, along with his dysfunctional upbringing, had caused him to lose control. Suddenly, I was learning that his whole history with me had been about gaining and maintaining control. In one of the videos, Hegstrom pointed out that when abusers start destroying property, it's never their own. Generally, they choose to destroy things that are valuable to their partners. If it were a complete loss of control, nothing would be exempt from their rampages. As I sat and listened, my heart began to grieve all the lies I had believed. I had basically given my whole

---

[8] See Appendix B. The Power and Control Wheel is a tool developed by the Duluth Model, based on interviews with over 200 victims of DV, describes typical traits of abusive behavior, which I have found present in every case of abuse I've seen (3000+ as of 2024). Much to my surprise, most of these tactics do not involve physical violence. To learn more, visit https://www.theduluthmodel.org/wheels/. While some in our circles deny the value of this tool and see it as unbiblical based on the worldview of those who collected the information, I believe it is important to honor the experiences of the victims who participated in the study as well as those who have benefitted from it over the last 4 decades.

[9] When I say idolatry, I do not mean that I worshipped my husband or even my marriage. I mean that in fear I unconsciously gave him lordship of my life, as in, my goal in life was to please him more than it was to please God. Many victims of abuse have had idolatry language used against them and have found my idolatry terminology shaming. Please know that this is in no way meant to condemn. For me, it was a major realization that began my path to freedom.

life to support and protect a man who had willfully chosen his selfish desire to control the girls and me. I had foolishly believed he was the victim and that I needed to help him. Even more eye-opening was the fact that the information presented suggested my response to the abuse may have contributed to its escalation over time. While I did nothing to cause the violence, my compliant attitude had certainly empowered Doug's abusive mindset. I thought I was being a good, submissive wife, but the more I gave in to his demands and threats, the worse things got.

The information we received at Life Skills directly challenged the wisdom of my broken responses, and suggested that accountability, rather than compliance, is crucial for abusive men. The problem is that, most often, victims alone cannot provide the accountability needed, and any attempt on their part to do so can put them in greater danger. Even so, it was helpful to hear that a fear of consequences could deter some abusers from further violence. That was the theory I had tested and proven after reading *Love Must Be Tough* over a decade ago. However, this time around, I hadn't been able to get the help needed to hold him accountable. The church had backed out of the situation, and law enforcement rarely responded to my calls. Even when I filed for a protective order, there was no indication there would be consequences if he violated it. It seemed like the whole system was in his favor.

If I thought my inability to hold Doug accountable was discouraging, the final portions of the Life Skills training left me baffled and even more dismayed. In addition to the illuminating materials developed by DV programs, the Life Skills curriculum focused heavily on past trauma, citing it as the driving force behind abusive behavior. Hegstrom stated that all the abusers he had ever met had experienced trauma as children, which had arrested their emotional development. The key to healing for the abuser was to go back into his past to identify the traumas (particularly the first one) that had hindered his maturity. Somehow, in reliving the hurts of the past, healing would come. Even more enigmatic was the possibility that some of those traumas might only be carried in the subconscious and may not come to the surface for years. Doug had definitely experienced a tumultuous childhood, but he had no problem remembering it and reminding me of how he had been a victim most of his life. Still, the suggestion that his past was possibly worse than he remembered was not at all appealing to him, and this only added to my fear that we could not be restored.[10]

As much as I wanted to apply what we had learned from Life Skills, it did not take long for the violence to return. As soon as we returned home, Doug decided it was too expensive to maintain separate houses, and since he had complied with my desire to go to Omaha, I needed to come back home immediately. I reminded him that making demands was not the way to win back my trust, but the situation quickly deteriorated. I called Life Skills and spoke to Judy Hegstrom again. She told me that if Doug wasn't willing to change, I needed to be willing to move on without him. It appeared that all hope was gone, and as much as I hated the idea of divorce, I was starting to see that a marriage couldn't be saved if only one person was trying. I also realized that safety had to be my number one concern, but it was not so easily achieved.

---

[10] While I agree that traumatic childhood experiences can and do influence behavior, I do not agree with that they cause it. I have met many abuse survivors who are not abusive, and I have known many abusive men who did not experience abuse and neglect as children. The bottom line is that abuse is a choice that stems from attitudes of entitlement and arrogance. Of course, abusers who have experienced trauma may benefit from dealing with those issues, but without working on the underlying beliefs behind the abuse, change is unlikely.

On his birthday in July, Doug asked if he could see the kids after church. Haley had gone home with a friend, so I told him that. He responded that he didn't want to spend the day alone. I resisted his pleas, but he countered all my concerns about safety with promises of being on his best behavior as he cried about how lonely he was. Finally, I gave in and drove over to his house. I told him I would leave Hannah and come back later, but he begged and pleaded for me to come inside. After all, nobody should have to spend their birthday alone wallowing in self-pity. Once again, he managed to persuade me to go against my instincts. As soon as we got inside, it was clear that seeing Hannah was not his priority. He began to beg me to take him back and then begged me to have sex with him—even with Hannah sitting right there! When I refused his request, he suddenly turned from cajoling and sad to fierce and demanding. He grabbed me and began to drag me upstairs, all the while muttering something about rape. He managed to get me upstairs and we struggled there for a while.

I was eventually able to break away and get back downstairs, but he was right behind me. I told Hannah to get up, but she didn't move—she appeared to be frozen in fear. Suddenly, Doug got behind me, put his arm around my neck, and began to apply pressure. He said, "Let's just end it right here!" I could feel the air being cut off as he jerked my body up. All I could think about was that he was going to kill me right in front of Hannah. I couldn't let that happen, so I tried to tell her to call 911 whenever I was able to speak each time he let my body down. My vision started to blur, and all I could do was pray for deliverance. Somehow, I thought to turn my head sideways and was able to slide my head down under his arm when he let me down again. I fell to the floor, and he went and sat by Hannah on the couch. He began crying, hugged her, and apologized over and over. Since he seemed broken, I was able to get her to come to the car with me. For days afterward, my voice was hoarse and my whole neck hurt. Yet, from the outside, I looked completely unscathed.

That strangulation attempt was the final straw for me. I realized that having any contact with Doug was far too dangerous, and I knew that I needed to move away. I was from North Carolina, so I began to search for a job closer to my family there. Haley, Hannah, and I moved away just a few months later. I gave Doug only a cell phone number and a P.O. address so he could send child support checks. The cell phone was a bad idea because airtime was expensive back then, and he called scores of times each day. Sometimes, he hung up, and other times he left threatening messages, but either way, he used up so much airtime that the first month's bill was as high as my rent.

Chapter 9

New Beginning

*See, I am doing a new thing! Now it springs up; do you not perceive it?
I am making a way in the wilderness, and streams in the wasteland.
~ Isaiah 43:19*

Amid all the turmoil, God was ever gracious. At my new job, there were several other Believers who held me up in prayer over the difficult months that followed. Twice, I had to take off work and drive all the way to Virginia for domestic court, only to find that Doug had his attorney continue our case. I continued to struggle with the thought of divorce, but one day, as I was reading 1 Corinthians 7, verse 15 seemed to jump off the page at me. Paul said if separation occurred because an unbelieving spouse left the marriage, the believing spouse was not under bondage because "God has called you to peace." Before, I had always focused on the instructions in these verses rather than the heart of God in them. Suddenly, I was struck with an overwhelming realization that I had not had peace in over twenty-three years! I had lived in torment for over two decades, and in that moment, I sensed His gentle Spirit assuring me that I was not called to torment but to peace.

While I tried to establish a more peaceful life, turmoil seemed to follow us. Four months after we moved, Doug found my house and burst in while my mom and brother were visiting. He threatened to kill us all, but my brother was eventually able to get him out. That week, I went and filed for another protective order. Even after the order was granted, he continued to instill fear in me from a hundred miles away. I had all the signs of post-traumatic-stress (PTS) and often woke up with nightmares of him coming at me with a gun or a knife. I was always on guard and filled with anxiety, but that only caused me to press in and seek the Lord more fully. I knew only His grace and mercy would enable me to overcome the aftershocks that continued to plague me.

Oddly enough, as I settled into my new home, I often found myself longing to be back with Doug. To be fair, I was grieving the loss of my marriage, but it was also like breaking an addiction.[11] For over

---

[11] In recent years, behavioral scientists have come to call this dynamic trauma bonding. A traumatic bond is created through a series of highs and lows that cause the victim to feel sympathy and affection towards her abuser. To the untrained eye this dynamic may look very much like co-dependence. However, it is actually a common response to trauma.

two decades my entire existence had revolved around pleasing him. I conformed my thinking to his and adhered to his preferences and prejudices, even when I disagreed inwardly. It was as if I had been brainwashed. Trauma makes us think we cannot survive without our abusers, and it takes time to untangle all the lies we have come to believe. After primarily living to please Doug for so long, I didn't know how to live on my own. My emotions were erratic, but I was learning that I could not allow them to control me. Instead, I chose to believe God's truth, even when I didn't feel like it was true. After our separation, I had found that writing out passages of Scripture and posting them in conspicuous locations helped me to counter untrue thoughts and overwhelming emotions. God was also faithful to place appropriate studies in my life at just the right times.

A few months before I had left Virginia, our ladies' group did another Kay Arthur study. The title of this study was *Lord, Heal My Hurts*. When I first picked up the book, I saw references to forgiveness and asked the Lord, "How can I forgive him?" However, by the time I moved to North Carolina and finished that powerful study from the books of Jeremiah and Matthew, I knew I could not possibly withhold forgiveness. When I finally forgave Doug, it was as though I had been set free. I hadn't realized how horribly anger and unforgiveness had been affecting my life, but when I was able to forgive, the change in me was incredible. Forgiveness did not lead to reconciliation, and it did not restore my trust in Doug, but it did completely release me from the bondage.

Another powerful truth Arthur's book reinforced that God's truth trumped man's wisdom. My father had introduced me to Freudian psychology at an early age, and even though I couldn't find much hope in it, I believed the basic tenets. One such tenet said that trauma, such as abuse, left victims permanently scarred with little hope for healing. I thought this meant the children and I were doomed to a future filled with pain and grief. However, *Lord, Heal My Hurts* showed me that Scripture counters that belief. Arthur compared the philosophies of men to Jeremiah's empty cisterns that couldn't hold water or satisfy (Jeremiah 2:13). Rather than the lie that my children and I would always be victims, I chose to believe God's truth.

In the years that followed, God persistently and gently continued to show me His freeing truth. If He had shown it all at one time, I never could have handled it, but He was faithful to give me just what I could bear. Part of the truth I had to face was my own sin. I had given God's glory to a man, and the result was an unholy, sinful fear that made Doug bigger than Him. Such fear thrives on lies. I believed lies, told lies, and lived a lie. By the time Doug and I separated, we had been together for over twenty-three years. For over half my life, I had chosen deception over truth. Overcoming that took time. Sometimes, it seemed as though each new day brought a revelation of truth that I had suppressed, but through personal quiet time and group Bible studies, God's truth continued to challenge my faulty thinking. Over time, I realized the worst distortion in my thinking related to my view of God. Even though I knew He was loving, I viewed him as rigid and demanding—just as Doug had been with me. It was as if I had remade Him into Doug's image. Although I knew what grace meant, I surely didn't live by it or extend it to other people. I was hard on myself and others—especially when it came to divorce. I was judgmental and thought I was representing Him when I disapproved of all divorce, no matter the cause. However, losing everything has a strange way of helping you see your desperation for His grace, and once you receive it, you can't help but want to extend it to others.

Even though I would have never chosen to suffer as I did, I came to realize that suffering had done something beautiful in my life. Before, I said I trusted God but lived in constant fear. After my trials brought me to the end of every human resource, I found Him to be entirely trustworthy and was able to joyfully surrender my life to His loving care. I often tell people I would never have chosen that path of suffering, but I am so grateful for it because if I hadn't experienced it, I wouldn't know Him the way I do now. Nothing in this world is more precious than knowing Him! The more I came to know Him and His truth, the freer I became. Over time, it felt as though I had been released from prison!

Along with my newfound freedom, I had the assurance of God's presence and provision. Isaiah 54:6, in which the Lord promised to be a husband to His people, became especially precious to me. As I learned to trust Him fully, He proved to be truly wonderful and faithful. In time, I realized that rather than being a victim for the rest of my life, I had become victorious, and God wanted to use my experience for good. When I was in the abuse, I realized that without help, it is nearly impossible to get out, so I promised the Lord that if I survived, I would help other women in similar situations. A few years after I came back to North Carolina, He gave me the first opportunity to keep that promise, and as time went on, more and more opportunities arose.

Chapter 10

Reaching Back

> Praise be to the God and Father of our Lord Jesus Christ, the
> Father of compassion and the God of all comfort, who comforts
> us in all our troubles, so that we can comfort those in
> any trouble with the comfort we ourselves receive from God.
> ~ *2 Corinthians 1:3–4*

At one point, a lady and her three small children came to stay with me after reporting a strangulation incident that had happened at the breakfast table before coming to church that morning. On Sunday, our pastor seemed supportive, but on Monday he called to let me know the church really couldn't get involved because he'd received a call countering her claims of abuse and "in these cases, it's just too hard to tell who is telling the truth." I told him what the children had told me, which backed up their mother's claims, and in response he told me to do what I thought was right, but since the truth was so unclear, he believed the church should stay out of it. He also let my friend's husband's family know that she was staying with me, and her husband showed up a few days later making threats. In the end, I had to drive my friend to the nearest domestic violence shelter, Safe Space, for help. They helped her obtain a protective order, housing, and financial assistance. While I was there, I told them parts of my own story and indicated that I would love to become a volunteer.

Weeks later, someone from the shelter called and asked if I would give a brief testimony at an upcoming vigil to remember victims of domestic homicide. Even though I had always been terrified of speaking in public, I realized that God had not brought me this far just to have me hide my light, and I reminded myself that I could do all things through His strength. When the night of the vigil arrived, I was extremely nervous but asked the Lord to calm my heart. As I opened my mouth, He answered that prayer, and I was able to testify of His goodness and truth, which had set me free. When I finished speaking, one of the board members stood up and hugged me. A few weeks later, they called to offer me a job as their Community Educator—basically, their spokesperson! For over a year, I had to speak in public almost weekly. I provided training for law enforcement, educators, and civic groups, but the church was conspicuously absent. It grieved my heart that the Body of Christ was missing the opportunity to minister to so many hurting families.

Although Safe Space had hired me to be the Community Educator, I believe the Lord placed me there also to be educated myself. I learned that the statistics related to domestic violence are just as high in the church as they are in society in general, and I met scores of precious Christian women who verified those numbers. In fact, it seemed their abusers regularly used their faith to keep them in line, just as Doug had always used my belief in Scripture against me. He often reminded me of his headship over me and demanded that I submit. At the shelter, I heard the same story repeatedly, and everyone seemed baffled about the church's lack of response. Within a few months, I decided I would reach out to churches in the area and offer training. I wrote a letter and sent it to every church I could locate in our rural county. The letter included a survey about DV within their congregations, and a self-addressed, stamped envelope to return it. Out of over two hundred surveys mailed out, only ten were returned, and over half of those had been completed by women in various ministry positions.

Safe Space arranged a call-in radio show appearance to promote our training for churches. The first call I answered was a lady asking me why her pastor kept sending her back to an abusive man. The second caller asked me why the church refused to believe her, and on it went. It was clear to me that we had touched a nerve. Later, I did a call-in television show on a local public access channel. The results were similar, and there were far too many callers to respond to them all. The host said they had never received so many calls in one show.

When the day for our church training came, only five of the two hundred churches we contacted were represented. Safe Space allowed me to openly proclaim my faith since it was part of my story, and we asked a few local pastors to lead prayers or speak on related biblical topics. Besides those participating pastors, only one pastor showed up. Other church representatives ranged from ministers of education to youth ministers to women's ministry leaders, and three out of five were women. It was all rather disheartening. After our attempt to train local pastors, I reached out to counseling professors at nearby Southeastern Baptist Theological Seminary (SEBTS). As a fellow Southern Baptist, I thought they might be more responsive to me.

One of the professors agreed to meet with me. I shared my story and asked if he would consider allowing me to speak in his classes. He seemed genuinely interested in doing something to help. When I called the other professor, he was not open to meeting but was willing to talk over the phone. I asked him about his strategy in domestic violence cases and was pleased to hear he had one. This professor told me that when he'd faced domestic violence in his church, he'd confronted it, made sure the church provided housing for either the husband or wife, and continued to work with both spouses until they could be brought back together. This was done slowly and gradually, beginning with dates in public and eventually bringing the abuser back into the home for limited periods of time. I thought it could work, even though the DV shelter statistics for long-term reconciliation were pretty dismal (only 2–3 percent). Several years later, this professor ended up coming to my church to launch a biblical counseling ministry, and we would have the opportunity to test his plan.

In 2001, I quit Safe Space to spend more time with my new husband and our four teenagers, and in 2004, God very clearly called me to SEBTS to study counseling. When I enrolled, I did not realize the counseling program there was a biblical counseling program. The basic premise was that proper application of God's Word and His Spirit are the most powerful means of achieving emotional and spiritual well-being. Though I felt that some early proponents of the biblical counseling movement were harsh in their application of Scripture, I agreed with the overall concept. After all, it was

God's Word and truth that had healed me. As Believers, Scripture should always be our standard, and we should reject psychological models that do not align with His truth.

My training in biblical counseling was quickly put to use in my own church as the professor mentioned earlier came and launched a counseling ministry. For the first 3-4 years, I was the only female counselor in a congregation of over 2000 members, and very quickly, abuse cases began to surface. Eventually, my professor and I worked a case together, implementing his coordinated plan for reconciliation. Unfortunately, it did not turn out so well, and I fully acknowledge that my own lack of knowledge contributed to the negative outcome. Despite my training at Safe Space, I lacked an understanding of the dynamics of abuser intervention. We prayerfully and strategically worked with the couple and helped them reconcile after fifteen months of separation.[12] Within months, the violence returned, and the couple soon left the church. A few years later, their daughter admitted her father had been abusive towards her too. As a teen, she developed life-threatening anxiety and depression with severe suicidality. Sadly, old habits die hard, and there had been a part of me that still thought marital restoration needed to be the main goal in DV intervention, but this case made me realize that the welfare of individuals must always be the primary objective. Jesus consistently esteemed people above institutions. He told the Pharisees that the Sabbath was made for man and not man for the Sabbath. I believe the same is true of marriage. God established marriage on the principle that it is not good for man to be alone. He never intended it to be a haven for oppression. I am not saying we should not ever attempt to save an abusive marriage when both the husband and wife are willing, but instead that we should prioritize the safety and wellbeing of each family member over the marriage."

Over time, I branched out from counseling at church alone. Professors at my seminary began to invite me to speak on domestic abuse in their classes, and the counseling professors began to refer women struggling under the weight of domestic abuse to me. Based on these experiences over the years, I noticed some common themes in church counseling that tended to worsen matters. I saw pastors and counselors at a loss for how to handle the complexities that nearly always came up. Often, churches become ineffective to help as they get caught up in trying to figure out who is telling the truth, and generally, abusers tend to win that competition.

Without an understanding of the dynamics of domestic violence, it is easy to mishandle this issue. By its very nature, it is counterintuitive. As a victim of abuse, I was always perplexed about what was happening in our home. I erroneously believed our problems could be alleviated through marriage counseling and that if I could just be a better wife, my husband would come around. My view of headship and submission worked against me. It is similar in many evangelical churches; women are encouraged to submit to their abusers as long as they are not requiring them to sin.[13] The unintentional

---

[12] In recent years, research is showing that a coordinated community response is most successful in helping abusive men change. See https://vawnet.org/material/evaluating-coordinated-community-responses-domestic-violence for more information. An expert in the field told me they are finding that successful intervention with perpetrators of abuse generally takes 3-5 years.

[13] Many Christian women believe they have to submit to just about anything their abusive husbands demand, but that only serves to promote sin. I wrote a blogpost about marital submission and abuse at https://joyforrest.wordpress.com/2014/02/26/biblical-headship-and- submission-in-emotionally-abusive-marriages/. This article was based on a paper I did in seminary and approaches the subject from a traditional, complementarian perspective. I believe that even those who hold this perspective should understand that Scripture does not command wives to submit to husbands who are using submission to harm them.

consequence of this counsel most often emboldens abusers' sinful heart motives. Women who have received this sort of counsel from their churches have told me they felt doubly abused: first by their husbands and then by the church. Some women I have worked with have even faced church discipline for failure to submit. On the flip side, I have seen very little accountability required from the abusers, and churches unwittingly end up perpetuating the abuse.

Over the years, I have seen this dynamic play out repeatedly, and my desire to help has intensified every time. Ultimately, this desire led to the founding of a nonprofit parachurch ministry to help families affected by domestic violence. Called to Peace Ministries (CTPM) was established in 2015 to provide practical assistance, counsel, and support groups for victims of domestic abuse and coercive control. In addition, providing education for churches and people helpers has been a major emphasis of the ministry since its inception.

After spending over a decade counseling within the church, I saw how detrimental couples' counseling is in these cases and how limited resources are for victims. Secular DV shelters do a great job of helping victims get safe, but most only allow them to stay for 2–3 months. For the majority of victims, I've met, that just isn't enough time to get a life together. Called to Peace Ministries strives to fill many of the gaps in services by meeting the multiple needs of victims and their children. However, we believe that victims need the church. Our ministry simply cannot, and should not, provide for all the needs of families impacted by domestic abuse. God established the church to reflect His character and love to the world, especially by caring for the "widows and orphans" among us (James 1:27, Isaiah 1:17, 58:7 Psalms 82:3-4, Acts 2:45-46).

When I worked at Safe Space, I was often grieved to watch unbelieving co-workers listen to stories of women who had been urged to stay in abuse or were kicked out of their churches for leaving their abusers. The director of our program told me she had no interest in Christianity because she saw it as a patriarchal, anti-woman religion. The way our churches treat the abused can either honor or dishonor His reputation. I believe that failing to take a stand against abuse and oppression dishonors it and diminishes the church's witness before a watching world. In recent years, most evangelical denominations have come under fire for mishandling abuse, and I know this grieves God's heart. However, I have been encouraged to see more and more churches begin to humbly recognize their need to better respond to all forms of abuse.

People are destroyed by a lack of knowledge (Hosea 4:6), especially when it comes to domestic violence. CTPM desires to provide knowledge that will help free families from its devastating effects. If you are living with domestic violence, I want you to know that God is more than able to turn your ashes into beauty (Isaiah 61:3). He holds the keys to healing. I know firsthand because He has healed me, and many other survivors I know. Over the years, I have had many chances to listen to the stories of women who have struggled with this disturbing issue. I have been shocked by the brutality of the abuses but amazed by God's ability to use pain and suffering to mold His children into His likeness. What a wonderful Redeemer we serve! He is able to heal completely and redeem every sorrow. He loves you dearly, dear sister, and calls you from violence to peace.

PART TWO

Keys to Finding Peace & Healing

*Heal me, LORD, and I will be healed;
save me and I will be saved,
for You are the One I praise.
~ Jeremiah 17:14*

Chapter 11

Education & Truth

"My people are destroyed from a lack of knowledge..."
~ *Hosea 4:6*

One fine day in the spring of 1996, I lied to a judge. This happened shortly after taking an oath to tell the truth, the whole truth, and nothing but the truth. Oddly enough, I didn't feel even a twinge of guilt because, at the time, I didn't believe I was lying. I testified to the judge that my marriage of fourteen years had not been abusive at all. Rather, some recent stress had caused my husband to snap and act completely out of character. It was a story I wholeheartedly embraced because I had been telling it to myself for so many years. I was there to have him convicted of assault, but I told myself it was the result of some sort of nervous breakdown rather than Doug's conscious choice. Up until that point, there had been numerous incidences of violence, but they didn't happen on a regular basis. In fact, the majority of the years we were married, did not involve incidents of physical harm.

Perhaps another reason I did not think I was abused was the image I had conjured up in my mind about abuse victims. When I thought about domestic violence, the term that came to my mind was "battered," and I was certainly not battered. In the entire length of our relationship, he had never once punched me with his fists. Our rare physical altercations usually began with something like a shove or being jerked by the arm. Once, I had my fingers slammed into a drawer, and once I was kicked. Oh yes, and there was that time when he held a knife to my throat, but no, I wasn't battered. Maybe believing lies was my way of trying to convince myself that things really weren't that bad. So, when I finally did have to admit I had been in an abusive relationship, I felt like a complete fool. I had always considered myself an intelligent woman, but facing the truth challenged that belief. The truth also challenged my idealistic concept of my husband's opinion of me. I believed my ability to elicit such great emotion from him meant he truly loved me. It didn't matter that his actions toward me were the exact opposite of the biblical description of love: Love is patient and kind; love does not envy or boast; it is not arrogant or rude. It does not insist on its own way; it is not irritable or resentful; it does not rejoice at wrongdoing but rejoices with the truth. Love bears all things, believes all things, hopes all things, endures all things"– 1 Corinthians 13:4–7 (ESV).

Whenever I came across this passage in my quiet times, I couldn't help but notice that my husband's actions toward me were nearly always the reverse. It didn't take much for him to lose his patience with me, and within my first month of knowing him, jealously reared its ugly head several times. I can't tell you how many times he embarrassed me in public by making rude comments toward others, the kids, or me. I felt so vulnerable when I was with him—certainly not protected. It was his way or no way and lies were the foundation of our relationship. Perhaps the most blatant contrast between godly love and my relationship was found in verse 5, which states that "love is not easily angered." There were times when I couldn't believe how seemingly insignificant circumstances could enrage my husband, and over the years, I've heard countless stories from other victims of abuse who suddenly found themselves the object of wrath when a small detail set off a reaction of atomic proportions.

One dear lady told me she received a horrible beating simply because she left hamburger meat in the sink to thaw, while another was belittled to the point of tears in front of her children because she failed to fold and stack her towels in the "correct" manner. On one occasion, Doug rampaged through the house, throwing things against the walls and sweeping the contents of counters onto the floor as he went through each room. The trigger was that one of our children had moved his hairbrush from its prescribed resting place in the master bath. In recent years, a friend told me that just leaving a single cup in the kitchen sink resulted in brutal criticism from her husband as he berated her and called her a worthless wife. I would call that being "easily angered," and it took me years to realize that true love does not act that way.

It takes a lot for most of us to realize and admit the truth. We tend to lie to ourselves because the truth is almost more painful than the abuse. It means acknowledging that our partners' actions do not equate to love at all, so most of us make excuses for them and convince ourselves that they have little control over their actions. I honestly thought my husband was not in control when he blew up, and that I needed to try to hold things together so he wouldn't have a reason to lose his temper. I thought my job as his helpmate was to build my life around making things go as smoothly as possible for him. I realize this is probably contrary to common stereotypes about domestic violence. Some people who are unfamiliar with the dynamics of coercive control believe domestic abuse is the result of heated arguments, which either party could have started. Certainly, no man would blow up or harm his wife unless she had done something to provoke him, right? It seems like a logical conclusion, but in the vast majority of cases, it's a faulty one. Abusive people are self-seeking, easily angered, and impatient, along with all the other contradictions to God's love listed in 1 Corinthians 13:4-7. In fact, the reason they abuse is not anger at all, but an attitude of entitlement that "insists on its own way."

Research suggests that an abuser rarely engages in actions that he himself considers to be morally wrong or unacceptable. While he might deliberately conceal his behavior, fearing disapproval or judgment from others, he often rationalizes his actions internally, constructing justifications that make him feel his choices and behaviors are reasonable or even necessary. After working with victims and abusers for over two decades, I'd have to say this assessment is spot-on. Unfortunately, it is not something most of us would like to admit. It is so much easier for us to believe our partners are abusing us because they are wounded inside or because they lack coping skills due to emotional problems, substance abuse, or a myriad of other excuses, than to admit they are actively choosing to hurt us.

Coming to terms with the truth was almost too much for me to bear, so I lied to myself until the day somebody placed a tool called the Power and Control Wheel into my hands.[14]

The Power and Control Wheel was generated by the Domestic Abuse Intervention Project of Duluth, Minnesota, in 1984 and is based on observations of focus groups of women who had been physically abused. When project personnel began interviewing these women, they discovered patterns of control and manipulation that seemed to exist almost universally within the groups. As they began to document these common behaviors or tactics, the result was a tool victims' advocates have used for over three decades. The first time I laid eyes on a Power and Control Wheel, I cried, as have numerous victims with whom I have shared it over the years. It's easy to deny a relationship is abusive until someone puts a detailed description of your life right in front of your eyes! For years I suffered in silence, thinking nobody knew what I was going through. However, when I picked up the Wheel, it seemed as though somebody had been a silent observer of my life for over two decades. I was also amazed to find I was not alone and that as many as one in three women will experience physical abuse from an intimate partner within their lifetime.[15]

One thing that stands out to most observers is that most behaviors listed on the Power and Control Wheel do not involve physical harm. I had denied that my relationship qualified as domestic violence simply because physical altercations were somewhat infrequent. However, the tactics described on this diagram happened daily. According to this tool, bodily harm is simply the last resort when all other tactics fail to get an abusive person what he wants. Since most domestic violence does not include physical harm, DV advocates have recently adopted the phrase *"coercive control"* to better describe the pattern of behaviors seen in these relationships.[16] Coercive control is about abusers establishing patterns of complete domination over their victims using tactics that intimidate, isolate, and control. In biblical terms, we would call it oppression. Basically, the motivation is far more revealing than the behavior. In his book, *The Heart of Domestic Abuse*, pastor and biblical counselor Chris Moles states that abusive behavior "is driven by a heart of pride and self-worship."[17] Actual domestic abuse is not merely a reactive pattern of behavior but one that is intentionally self-serving. In fact, a look at the behaviors listed on the Power and Control Wheel shows just how self-seeking abusive conduct really is.

COERCION AND THREATS

At the top of the Power and Control Wheel, we see that abusers use coercion and threats to maintain control. In the years I have worked with victims, nearly all of them have confirmed that these behaviors were used regularly in their homes. Some abusers threatened to abandon their families and leave them destitute, some threatened suicide to make sure they got their way, some threatened physical harm, and others just threatened to humiliate their wives somehow. In several cases, I've seen abusers go out

---

[14] See footnote 5 in chapter 8 for more on the Power and Control Wheel.

[15] https://www.cdc.gov/violenceprevention/pdf/nisvs_report2010-a.pdf, p. 39. Accessed July 28, 2023.

[16] Coercive control was first described by British forensic social worker and researcher, Evan Stark, in his book *Coercive Control: The Entrapment of Women in Personal Life*, (New York, NY, Oxford Press, 2007),

[17] Moles, Chris, *The Heart of Domestic Abuse: Gospel Solutions for Men Who Use Control and Violence in the Home* (Bemidji, MN, Focus Publishing, 2015), 43.

of their way to make their wives look incompetent. After years of living with control and manipulation, my friend Jill became seriously depressed and ended up being prescribed anti-depressants. Her husband, Jim, made sure to let the pastors at church know how concerned he was about his wife's erratic behavior, her "inability" to parent properly, and her dependence on medication. Of course, the church had no idea of what really went on behind closed doors, and Jill knew better than to try to tell them. At the same time, Jim made sure she knew if she decided to leave the marriage, he would have no trouble having her declared incompetent and getting full custody of the children. For Jill, this threat was far more potent than bodily injury ever could have been. Jim's threats were highly effective in promoting his selfish interests.

USING THE CHILDREN

Abusive people will aim their threats directly at whatever their victim values most, so that means threats involving children are incredibly common in these situations. In fact, many women stay in horrible circumstances for far too long because they know if they leave, their spouses may harm the children. Such was the case with my friend Amy. She had endured occasional physical violence and relentless threats from the beginning of her marriage. Her husband kept a gun beside their bed and let her know that if she ever tried to leave him, he would use it on her. He even held it to her head on a few occasions. She knew she needed to leave but was concerned about her children if she did because he told her that even if she left, he would "still have the children." She was never sure what he meant by that, but knew it wasn't good. Finally, there came a day when she felt if she didn't get out, she would not live to parent her children at all, and mustered up the courage to take them and leave. Shortly after their separation, Amy had to go to court to try and get legal custody of the kids. She told the judge her concerns about the children being with their father, but he granted regular, unsupervised visitation to her husband anyway. Amy wanted to believe her husband wouldn't make good on those vague threats, and also wanted to believe the court had made the right decision. However, within a short amount of time, her three-year-old son came home and reported that he was regularly being locked in a closet, and she also learned that his sister was being sexually abused. Amy was finally able to stop the unsupervised visitation, but she knew then that the threats against her children were not idle.

Unfortunately, Amy's story is not an exception when it comes to domestic violence. In my own experience, I have seen abusers intentionally hurt their children multiple times to punish their spouses. They often use the courts to wage war against their exes by seeking full custody or making false claims of child abuse or parental alienation by the mother. Sadly, judges and court officials are widely uninformed on the dynamics of domestic abuse and coercive control, so these attempts are often met with success. In other cases, it is not unusual for abusive fathers to attempt to turn the children against their mothers. Basically, abusers will do whatever they deem necessary to maintain control, regardless of how it impacts those they are supposed to care for and love. Their victims understand that their threats are not empty or idle.

I have watched so many women struggle, frozen in fear because of these types of threats, but most who decided to leave believe they made the right decision—even Amy. She thinks things would have been far worse had she stayed. Living in fear of a man will never lead to the life God intends for you. However, not everyone can leave. Some women choose to stay in destructive marriages simply for the sake of their children or other valid reasons. When it comes to domestic abuse, there is no one-size-fits-all solution. Working with a DV-trained advocate or counselor can help you determine the best course of action for moving forward and help you get educated on available resources. Whatever you decide to do, I pray that God, rather than fear, will be your guide.[18]

Intimidation

Besides using the children to hurt their wives and partners, abusers make regular use of intimidation techniques to instill fear and attain unfettered power in their families. Intimidation can range from a harsh look to extreme physical violence. Most abusive people have conditioned their victims to know when they are about to snap. As a result, a single angry glance can cause victims and their children to completely freeze up or change their course of action. If a nasty look or threat of retaliation doesn't get the desired result, the abuser may resort to more violent tactics like throwing and smashing things, destroying property, or even abusing the household pets. A lady at the shelter told me her abuser killed the family dog in front of her and the kids. The message behind that sort of violence is to let their victims know that if they don't conform to their abusers' demands, they could be next.

Intimidation is a highly effective tool for perpetrators of domestic violence, and there seem to be infinite ways for abusers to instill fear in their partners. A woman once told me that her husband once filled her car with poisonous snakes just to make sure she didn't go anywhere. While intimidation tactics can start out subtly, they usually increase in intensity over time. Common behaviors often seen in the progression of violence include blocking the exit from a room, denying access to prescription medicine, screaming, raising a fist, restraining her, jerking, shoving, and so on. If these methods do not work, then punching, kicking, and other methods of inflicting more serious physical harm may follow. An interesting thing to note here is that even when hitting occurs, many abusers, in efforts to keep the abuse hidden, maintain enough control over themselves to make sure they hurt their victims in a way that doesn't leave obvious bruises. It is important to note that some oppressive men are far more subtle and would never resort to physical force. This type of abuser is often more destructive as he may use spiritual intimidation, which includes the twisting of Scripture, to instill fear in his wife. I have known so many godly Christian women who thought God was always angry with them because they couldn't constantly please their husbands. Intimidation for them included threats of divorce, exclusion from the church, or even eternal punishment in hell.

Emotional Abuse

Women who live with domestic violence often tell me they prefer hitting to the emotional torment their abusers put them through. The Power and Control Wheel describes it as emotional abuse, and while some may disagree with the terminology, there is definitely an emotionally destructive element to these relationships. "Emotional abuse systematically degrades, diminishes, and can eventually destroy the

---

[18] I appreciate Leslie Vernick's discussion on leaving well or staying well in her book *The Emotionally Destructive Marriage*. There are many valid reasons women choose to stay with abusive husband, often related to financial issues or fears related to their abusers having unsupervised access to their children. Ultimately, good helpers do not tell victims what to do, instead them provide them with information and encouragement to make their own decisions. People helpers must try to support victims of abuse in whatever decision they make about staying or leaving, although it is always important to assess safety concerns and make recommendations that encourage them to escape danger.

personhood of the abused."[19] Tactics include name-calling, putting her down, humiliation, and making her feel bad about herself. However, it can be far more subtle. Several years ago, I watched a friend in a store ask her husband if she could buy a $3 item. Her husband's response was to question her judgment in front of everyone present. He implied she would be foolish to want to buy something of such poor quality and then inferred she probably wouldn't even use it. As he subtly criticized her for her stupidity, he looked over at us and chuckled. Clearly, he enjoyed taunting her and saw her as inferior. Her face turned red as she tried to mumble answers to his questions until she finally put the item back to avoid further humiliation. It seems silly that something so small could ignite such harm, but that's the nature of emotional abuse. Molehills become mountains on a regular basis when you live with an abuser.

When we live with emotional abuse, we often begin to think we're crazy. Abusive partners are masters at creating confusion and use tactics like gaslighting[20] to keep us confused. The Power and Control Wheel calls this tactic "crazy making" as it can lead victims to question their very sanity. Abusers also use guilt to control their partners. They often present themselves as victims and infer that their wives' minor choices have victimized them even more. For example, when "Judy" spent $5 on a cup of coffee, her husband seemed panicked about their finances. He scolded her for being frivolous and made her feel awful about that cup of coffee. A week later, when she signed into online banking, she saw that he had recently spent over $100 on video games. When it comes to emotional abuse, there is always a double standard. He can do no wrong, but nearly everything she does is called into question. Her decisions are often ridiculed to the point she begins to question her worth. Many of the survivors I meet struggle with severe depression and anxiety after years of living with partners who treat them as worthless.

One woman at the shelter told me she would sometimes purposely do something to get her husband to hit her just because she knew that once the abuse was over, there would be a break in the verbal assaults for a while. Victims are made to feel like they are constantly wrong, incompetent, and worthless. No matter the issue is, and no matter who is right or wrong, everything gets turned around and the victim gets blamed for everything. The sad thing is abusers are often skilled enough to convince counselors and pastors that their wives really are to blame for most of the problems in the marriage. They go to great lengths to portray themselves as morally superior and intellectually more reasonable than their victims. By the time they get to counseling, many victims are so traumatized and insecure about themselves that they do, in fact, seem unstable.

ISOLATION

Many abusers love to isolate their victims from people and situations that might provide them with support. I have had women tell me that after getting married, they eventually lost every single friend. My friend Kathy was rarely allowed to see her family, even on holidays. On several occasions, her

---

[19] Vernick, Leslie, *The Emotionally Destructive Marriage* (Colorado Springs, Waterbrook Press, 2013), Kindle Version Location 256.

[20] Gaslighting is a form of manipulation that causes a victim to question the validity of her perception of reality or memories. An abusive person may change his story and insist that he never said what she heard. The term is based on the 1944 movie, Gaslight, in which a husband tries to drive his wife insane by changing her perception of reality.

husband reached out to her friends and family and told them it was her decision to cut off the relationships. He led them to believe she was mentally unstable, and he was doing his best to help her. All the while, he was the one controlling her contact with others. She was only allowed to go to church (with him) and to the grocery store—as long as she wasn't gone too long and came home with a receipt to prove her whereabouts.

Controlling people use isolation to make sure their victims have nowhere to turn when things get tough. Most of them live in fear of losing control, so they go to great lengths to maintain it. Linda's husband, Dave, bought a seventeen-acre farm twenty minutes from the nearest town, and he had the only car in the family. He was retired, so Linda had him as her constant companion. Although he didn't physically harm her, Dave controlled what she ate, what she read, and even her opinions. She was not allowed to disagree with him in any way. When I met her, they had been married for over thirty years, and up until just before she came to the shelter, he had never laid a hand on her. Despite not allowing Linda to have friends, Dave had several, but when he invited his friend Carl out to visit, Carl brought his wife, Lucy, along. This was the first friend Linda had been allowed in years, and she was grateful. One day, when the men were out hunting, Lucy told Linda that she needed to stand up to Dave's bullying and let him know that she had a right to her own opinion. A few days later, Linda told Dave she wanted something different for dinner, and Dave went ballistic. He beat her with a skillet so badly that she nearly died, and he ended up in prison. For all the years they had been married, isolation had achieved its goal. When she was completely isolated, Linda was too afraid to refuse any of Dave's demands, but as soon as she found some external support, she found the courage to challenge him. Unfortunately, the price of freedom was steep for Linda, but in the end, she was able to escape his control.

MINIMIZING, DENYING, AND BLAMING

Grace had been married to Charlie for over ten years and was a stay-at-home mom. Although she took extreme measures to please Charlie, he criticized her constantly. The house was never clean enough, the kids were never good enough, and meals never seemed to meet his approval. One day, Grace decided to cook two meals in an attempt to find something he would like. That night, he came home late, went straight upstairs, and ignored both meals. Soon after, Grace discovered Charlie was seeing another woman, and he'd had dinner with her that evening. When she confronted him, Charlie turned the whole situation back on Grace. First of all, he explained, he had done nothing wrong, and she was being ridiculous. He criticized her for even bringing it up, and when she pressed him on the subject, he started blaming her for his actions. Maybe if she had been more attentive to his needs or managed to do something right occasionally, he wouldn't have needed to find outside companionship. Basically, he told her she had no right to question his actions, and if she wanted to see things improve in the marriage, she needed to try harder.

One day, Grace caught Charlie slapping their nine-year-old son, but he acted like it was no big deal. When she expressed her concern that it was contributing to their son's anger issues, he turned it back on Grace. "Of course, he's angry! He has to live with you!" No matter what she said or did to confront the wrongs against her children and herself, Charlie either denied wrongdoing, minimized it, or blamed someone else. He never accepted responsibility for his actions.

Minimization, denial, and blame are probably the most common traits we see in abusive people. Denial is the standard response to challenges about their behavior, but if that doesn't work, minimization and blame come next. Towards the end of our marriage, I was feeling particularly desperate, and after a few explosive events, I insisted Doug go to marital counseling with me. When the counselor asked us why we were there, Doug knew he couldn't deny what he had done, so he completely minimized it, which included making excuses for his behavior. Along with the excuses, there was usually some sort of indication that I was to blame. Abusive people are masters at this age-old tactic that dates all the way back to Adam and Eve. In all our years together, I received a few apologies from Doug, but he never fully acknowledged what he had done. Looking back, I liken it to the difference between King Saul and King David when confronted by the prophet. Saul made excuses, minimized his sin, and even blamed the people (1 Samuel 15:21), but David admitted to the full weight of his sin and repented (2 Samuel 12:13). I fell for Doug's false repentance many times because I missed the Scriptural model of true repentance.

Economic Abuse

Jan's husband, Buddy, put her on a very strict allowance, and it usually fell far short of meeting the basic needs o their family of six. When she went to the grocery store, Jan had to bring back her receipt so Buddy could analyze every item she bought. He ridiculed half of her purchases and called them wasteful. On the other hand, she had to make sure she bought him special (and somewhat expensive) snacks that nobody else was allowed to touch. When extra expenses popped up, such as prescription co-pays or extracurricular fees for the kids, Jan didn't have enough money to cover them. She had two little ones in diapers and one on formula, but the budget barely allowed for these items. If she ran out of money, Buddy ridiculed her for being frivolous. Eventually, Jan decided it might help to take on a part-time job in the evenings to help out, but he refused to let her work. Although he constantly claimed to be broke, he often bought high-dollar items for the kids and himself. The older kids were given the latest smartphones, and he bought a boat, but Jan was still using an old flip phone her sister had given her several years back.

Buddy made sure Jan did not have access to his income or bank information. She only had access to the joint account he'd set up for her allowance. At tax time, he simply had her sign their tax returns without looking at them, but one day, she caught a glimpse at his annual income and found that, despite his claims of being broke, he was earning well over six figures. She barely survived on what he gave her, but he wasn't struggling at all. He simply enjoyed wielding power over her.

Economic abuse can take many forms. It can look like Buddy and Jan's situation, or it can be the other way around. The husband may not work at all and may force the wife to be the primary breadwinner while taking control of all the money she makes. I have seen many variations of this sort of abuse over the years. In one of our early support groups, a pastor's wife reported that she worked for her husband's church as the office administrator. Her take-home pay was about $700 a week, but her husband gave her an allowance of $40 a week. Outwardly, she looked spoiled. He bought her expensive clothes—that he picked out— and a luxury car, as well as many other perks. However, she never had access to more than $40 cash on a bank card that he controlled. The bottom line with economic abuse is that the abuser has control over how the family income is spent, and he uses that control to promote selfish interests.

Using Male Privilege

When Jan finally gathered enough courage to ask the church for help, Buddy discredited everything she said. Since she had struggled with postpartum depression, he used that to convince the church she was completely unstable. Buddy was considered a leader in the church, and his outstanding service gave people little reason to doubt him. On the other hand, Jan usually seemed somewhat frazzled. She was in a Bible study I taught a few years prior. At the time, Buddy approached me to say he hoped I could help her with her issues. He acted like she was very troubled but didn't give me details. He seemed like such a good guy that even I fell for his portrayal of her.

When she approached me in tears and asked to meet a few years later, we set up a meeting. I'm ashamed to say that at the time, I doubted her more than him. Eventually, as we met, I began to recognize the abusive patterns, and I approached our pastor to say I felt the situation was potentially dangerous. He responded that I was only hearing one side of the story, and he believed Jan was "making up lies to destroy her husband." When I asked why she would do such a thing, he referred me to years of joint counseling sessions in which Buddy was able to get her to admit she was wrong for accusing him. Buddy had also shown him a video of Jan "freaking out" and yelling. Of course, nothing on the videos showed what led up to that, but his efforts to discredit her were hugely successful. The consensus among church leaders was that he was a great guy with a very troubled wife. The worst part was that he used his role as head of the house to keep Jan subdued. At home, he reminded her that she was to submit to him and did not involve her in any family decisions. He basically dictated how things would be. In counseling sessions, he often complained that Jan was not submissive. In addition to exercising male privilege, Buddy used spiritual abuse as he twisted the concept of marital submission to force his selfish agenda. As with all the tactics abusers use, the ultimate goal is self-seeking.

In Evangelical circles, using male privilege often intersects with spiritual abuse. The way some churches teach passages on headship and submission can cause great harm. A woman once told me that her husband's treatment of her worsened dramatically after he got saved and sat under the teaching of a church that treated submission like blind obedience. Steven Tracy of Mending the Soul Ministries has written extensively on the link between Evangelical teachings and domestic abuse. In a 2007 article, he cited a study that suggested that "conservative Protestant men who are irregular church attendees are the most likely to batter their wives."[21] The same study showed that the same demographic of men who attend church regularly are less likely to be abusive, but in my experience, it depends on the church. Many wonderful conservative evangelical churches teach men sacrificial Christlike love for their wives, while others focus on authority over. Jesus' kingdom was never meant to be one of lording it over (see Matthew 20:25-28), yet abusive men are masters at twisting Scripture to justify oppression.

---

[21] Tracy, Steven R., "Patriarchy and Domestic Violence: Challenging Common Misconceptions," *Journal of the Evangelical Theological Society, JETS 50:3* (Sep 2007).

Chapter 12

Managing Your Emotions

> Trust Him at all times, O people; Pour out your
> heart before Him; God is a refuge for us.
> *~ Psalm 62:8 (NASB)*

Coming through the trauma of abuse can leave us overwhelmed with emotion, or over time, many of us shut down or become numb to escape the pain. In fact, the ladies in our support groups say they know they are starting to heal when they begin to feel again. There was a time when all I could do in my spare time was lie around and watch old movies. Anything else required too much energy because I was so emotionally drained. Sometimes, it is just easier to check out mentally than to feel. I have met many women who used drugs or alcohol to escape painful memories and emotions, but in the end, it made matters worse. The good news is that we serve a God who heals the brokenhearted and binds up their wounds (Psalms 147:3). About four years ago, I stumbled on a key to healing that I wasn't fully able to articulate in the first edition of this book. I knew that posting Scripture verses and repeating them over and over had helped me heal, but I did not understand how it worked until I learned about the brain science behind trauma. As it turns out, meditation is a powerful tool for healing traumatized minds and bodies.

Research in recent years has shown that trauma is held in the autonomic parts of our brains, mainly in the amygdala, which controls our automatic fight or flight response.[22] These subconscious parts of our brains do not communicate very well with the conscious parts. When I was coming out of abuse, I remember having involuntary panic attacks that were completely illogical. Physically, I knew I was safe, but inside, I felt this awful sense of impending doom, as if I was reliving the abuse. I eventually

---

[22] For a thoughtful review on secular books that have taught us to think carefully about trauma see Ed Welch, *Trauma and the Body an Introduction to Three Books*, JBC 33:2 (2019): 61–83. For research on the impacts of trauma see Lisa M. Shin, P. D. (2005, March 1). "A functional magnetic resonance imaging study of amygdala and medial prefrontal cortex responses to overtly presented fearful faces in posttraumatic stress disorder." Archives of General Psychiatry. Retrieved March 18, 2023, from https://jamanetwork.com/journals/jamapsychiatry/fullarticle/208374.

recognized that trauma had generated a constant negative discourse in my mind, and the only way I knew to counter it was by desperately seeking God. I spent hours in His Word, listening to and singing worship music, and even using my God-centered imagination as I spoke His truth to myself. True meditation involves the entire brain, not just our logic centers. Brain scientists have discovered that movement, singing, and other whole-brain activities help reach traumatized parts of our brains with truth.[23]

Finding healing means facing the truth about what has happened to us, putting our hurts in His hands, and applying His solutions. God-centered meditation is a wonderful way to get the truth to our subconscious minds. In this chapter, we'll take a look at how that works with the major emotions we experience with abuse—anger, sadness, fear, and shame. You'll probably notice that there is much overlap between these emotions and the solutions for healing.

ANGER

In my years of counseling victims of domestic violence, I have met some pretty angry people, and in many cases, their stories have angered me as well. Domestic violence can be unimaginably cruel, and it is difficult to hear the accounts without feeling upset about the injustice of it all. Quite often, victims are not only injured by their spouses, but they also find very little support when they reach out for help. The judicial system frequently favors perpetrators, who tend to have greater financial resources and often seem more composed in court. Even churches can make matters worse for victims when they don't understand the dynamics of abuse, or they harshly interpret Scriptures on marital roles. For victims, insult is added to injury on a regular basis.

Living with abuse gives us plenty of reason to be angry, but sometimes our anger becomes destructive. In recent years, I have seen this dynamic playing out in public forums on social media. There has been such a backlash against victim blaming that many advocates now become outraged at those who encourage victims of abuse to take responsibility for their own healing process. In an effort to right the wrongs of the past, victims are told they don't need to take responsibility for their broken responses to what happened to them. Let me clarify before I get in trouble. When a woman is coming out of abuse, the last thing she needs is to have her mistakes and sins pointed out, particularly in a way that indicates she was somehow responsible for the abuse. Survivors generally live with a great deal of shame, and we need to avoid adding to it. That is not how Jesus dealt with broken people. To the woman at the well, He offered living water and relationship rather than chastisement and confrontation. He reserved that type of treatment for arrogant religious leaders. "A bruised reed He will not break, and a dimly burning wick He will not extinguish; He will faithfully bring forth justice."[24] I believe that bringing forth justice includes showing extra grace to the oppressed while challenging oppressors. I also think that anger is a necessary part of our healing journey that shows we are finally admitting the truth about what happened to us.

Becoming upset over injustice is not only understandable, but it is also common. Ephesians 4:26–27 seems to imply that anger is common, but warns, "In your anger do not sin; do not let the sun go down while you are still angry, and do not give the devil a foothold." The problem isn't becoming angry as

---

[23] For details on meditation and other whole brain approaches to healing PTS, see Lesson 4 in *The CTP Workbook*.

[24] Isaiah 42:3, NASB.

much as failing to deal with it quickly. When we stay angry and allow it to control us, we are headed for trouble. It seems that unresolved anger opens our lives to Satan's destructive schemes (Ephesians 4:26–27). There was a time when I became so angry that I began to suffer physical symptoms. Even worse, I found myself snapping at my children for the littlest things. Rather than being able to offer them the love and support they needed to get through the devastating events they were experiencing, I found myself so consumed with anger that I had nothing left to give. The problem with allowing anger to take over is that you can't simply contain it to one area of your life. It is like a poison that damages every relationship, including the most important one of all—your relationship with God. During this period, I felt as if my prayers were hitting the ceiling. Although I continued to reach out to God, resentment controlled me rather than His Spirit, which left me isolated from my Helper. I needed to learn how to handle my anger biblically.

DIVINE VS. HUMAN ANGER

Scripture clearly tells us there are things that anger God, and we are created in His image as emotional beings. God's wrath is provoked by sin, and He particularly hates violence. In Genesis, God told Noah, "I am going to put an end to all people, for the earth is filled with violence because of them" (6:13). It was enough to cause God to want to destroy His own creation, so it is certainly understandable when we get upset about it. Even the second part of Malachi 2:16, which says, "God hates divorce,"[25] indicates that He particularly hates it when a husband deals violently and unfaithfully with his spouse. The Bible is filled with passages proclaiming our Creator's hatred of injustice and unfaithfulness. As His children, we should naturally hate the evil He hates. Our problem is that we usually carry it a little too far. Rather than turning the situation over to God and leaving justice in His hands, we try to control it.

In reality, human anger often reveals a lack of trust in God. We may be questioning why He has allowed bad things to happen in our lives and if He really cares. In our minds, we profess that He is good, but in our hearts, we doubt it. We know His Word commands us to forgive, but we believe forgiving is like giving a stamp of approval to the abuse. Thoughts like this unconsciously charge God with injustice. When we see our offenders "getting away" with sin, we want to take matters into our own hands because it seems as if God is sitting back doing nothing. I know that's how I felt, and I became so miserable that I thought life was not worth living. Over time, God graciously intervened, but it was not an overnight event. It was a process which required me to take some specific steps.

FACE THE TRUTH

People who live with abuse live with lies, and I was certainly no exception. I told myself that my husband couldn't help it when he blew up and that he was simply a product of the environment he had grown up in. I tried to hide our violent episodes from everyone to the point that I almost seemed to hide them from myself. For over two decades, I went to great lengths to avoid the truth until one day, I could avoid it no

---

[25] Note that this well-known phrase from Malachi 2:16 does not accurately reflect the original text. I used to constantly quote "God hates divorce" to myself., but I never understood the true meaning. The good news is that the text shows God's heart for women who were being mistreated. The following link compares various translations and shows how difficult it can be to interpret some ancient texts— https://lifesavingdivorce.com/malachi/.

longer and found myself angrier than I had ever been. I was worn down by months of constant offenses. Doug had been calling and threatening me fifteen to twenty times a day. I was afraid not to answer because I feared he would come to wherever I was and make good on the threats if he didn't get me on the phone. Normally, I would just hold the phone away from my ear and let him rant because I learned that saying anything just made matters worse. During one call, I heard the screaming stop and put my ear up to the phone just in time to hear him threaten suicide. He slammed down the phone, and that was that. He had made similar threats in the past but had never followed through, and he usually started harassing me again within hours. However, this time I heard nothing for two whole days and soon became concerned about him. I drove past his house both days and noticed that his car had not moved.

On the third day, I decided to take my key to our former home and go check on him. I was petrified to go in but was so worried about him that I did it anyway. He was not downstairs, so I tiptoed upstairs and saw him lying deathly still on his bed. He looked extra pale, so I went up and nudged him. As soon as I did, he woke up cursing at me, and I ran out as quickly as possible. Within a few hours I got a call from the county sheriff's department saying that Doug had come in and charged me with criminal trespassing. They had a warrant for my arrest, and the sheriff urged me to turn myself in. I was released on my own recognizance, but I was furious! How dare he have me charged as a criminal when my only motivation was concern for his well-being? Foolishly, I decided to call and let him know just how awful his action had been; the conversation only left me more upset. I told him he was the one who needed to be arrested for violence against me, but he said he had only hit me one time in the entire history of our relationship. He essentially denied being abusive, and I couldn't believe his nerve!

My response was pure rage. By this point, I was learning to turn my strong emotions over to God, so I started writing in my journal, telling Him about all the horrendous things Doug had done over the years. As I was banging out complaints on my computer keyboard, my friend Karen happened to call to check on me. I told her about my earlier conversation with Doug and the already lengthy list of offenses I was compiling. Much to my surprise, Karen said, "Don't forget the time he tore up the house because he was mad at the cat." I was confused because I didn't remember that incident at all. I only began to remember once she reminded me how she and her husband had provided housing for me after it had happened. The odd thing was that it had occurred only twelve months earlier! I was amazed I could forget it, but I believe I had gone to such great lengths to hide it that I had almost convinced myself it didn't happen. As victims of abuse, it is easy to bury these memories because they reveal the truth that someone we loved intentionally chose to hurt us. Forgetting helps us maintain the status quo without shutting down.

ENTRUST IT TO HIM

After admitting the truth, we must put the offenses in God's hands. A great deal of healing happened in me the day I finally faced the truth and conceded just how horrible things had been. Let me clarify—I do not think I was healed simply because I finally told myself the truth. That was only part of it. I found healing because I poured out my hurts to God and committed my heart to Him. The truth was too overwhelming for me to handle on my own, but I knew I was safe with Him. Psalms 62:8 encourages us to pour out our hearts to God, and that is what I did on that day. When you face constant injustice, it will often require you to surrender your anger again and again, but it will guard your soul. Commit the offenses you have suffered to Him. It is the only way to avoid carrying them yourself, and He is far better equipped to handle them. Each night, when you lay your head on your pillow, drop those heavy burdens at His feet and trust Him to fight your battles.

CHOOSE TO FORGIVE

Over the years, I've met women who have casually told me they had no problem forgiving their abusive spouses, but they could barely talk about what had happened. Some who did open up were still making excuses or denying the severity of the abuse. That is burying anger, not dealing with it. For many of us, forgiving our abusers can be the toughest battle we face in the recovery process, but it is a necessary step in overcoming the anger that comes from abuse. Although it may seem that facing the truth about the abuse I had experienced would've made it harder to forgive, it actually helped because I realized it was too big for me to handle alone. I knew I could not face the pain without God's help. I also knew His Word commanded me to forgive, but I needed a lot of help working through it.

At the height of my anger, our ladies' Bible study decided to work through Kay Arthur's *Lord, Heal My Hurts*. When I picked up the book, I noticed a chapter in the table of contents entitled "How Can I Forgive?" It was the very question I had been asking myself, and this wonderful Bible study helped me figure it out. When I was able to forgive, it was as if a thousand-pound weight had been taken off my shoulders. There were a few common misconceptions I had to overcome to truly forgive, and I've seen many other survivors struggle with them as well.

As a child, I was taught to forgive and forget. When my siblings and I asked for forgiveness, we were taught to respond with, "That's ok. I forgive you." Then we were expected to hug and make up. Essentially, that formed my view of how the process should look, but it was a flawed perspective because it caused me to believe that forgiveness would always lead to reconciliation. I also thought forgiving meant I simply had to minimize or dismiss the offenses as though they had never happened. Thankfully, I was wrong on both counts. Biblical forgiveness is placing the offender in God's hands and leaving justice to Him. It is letting go of our own need for vengeance, but it is not dismissing the hurt as though it wasn't that bad or as if it had never happened.

Romans 12:17–21 gives us instructions on dealing with those who harm us. It teaches us not to repay evil with evil and not to take revenge but to leave room for God's wrath. We must trust that He will handle the situation in His time and with perfect justice. Also, we need to refuse to stoop to our abusers' level by taking revenge. Usually, when we refuse to let go of our anger and desire for retaliation, it is because we don't believe that His way of dealing with it is better than ours. Peace comes from recognizing and believing that He always has our best interest at heart and is working all things together for our good (Romans 8:28–29). Regardless of how things may look in the present, there will come a day when your abuser will have to bow before Him, perhaps in great fear and trembling, and confess that He is Lord (Philippians 2:10–11). I realize it can be a struggle, but choosing to believe He is good and trusting Him to make all things right in due season is tremendously freeing.

RESOLVE TO BELIEVE HIM

Letting go of anger and believing God is a choice and not a simple process. For me, it was hard work. It meant learning how to choose His truth over my feelings and trusting that He cared deeply for me— even when it didn't feel that way. One day, a phrase from Isaiah 50:7 spoke to me. This prophecy about Jesus predicted He would set His face "like flint" to accomplish the Father's plan. Something about His determination in this verse resonated with me because I knew my outcome would be tied to my decision to believe Him. I resolved to believe, no matter what happened or how I felt. I pray that as you read this, you will decide to do the same. To overcome anger and its damaging consequences in your life, you must determine to do it God's way rather than your own.

THE PROCESS

Dealing with anger His way requires taking several steps. It means being honest with yourself and no longer minimizing or making excuses for the abuse. To truly heal, it is important to face and give the full weight of the burden to God. Commit your anger to God quickly, and do not let it fester. There may be times when this seems impossible, but as you learn to pour your complaints out to Him, you will find a peace that surpasses human comprehension as you let Him fight your battles. Sure, there may be actions you'll need to take to protect yourself and your children, but you won't have to try and control things or force your version of justice anymore. Choose to forgive your abuser, recognizing that it will set you free and leave justice in God's hands. Seek to correct any thinking that is contrary to God's truth and trust that He will redeem your sorrows. Remember that He is for you, and even though He will not violate the free will of your abuser, He is sovereign, and He wants to use your trials for good. Finally, seek Scriptures that provide instructions on wisely dealing with anger and choose to apply them. Please see Scripture Database at the end of this book for a list of verses.

Sadness & Grief

There is nothing sadder than feeling despised and rejected by the one person you have chosen to love and honor above all others. Many times, over the years, I struggled with suicidal thoughts because Doug's opinion of me was so low. Like many young women, I dreamed of living happily ever after with a man who adored me. Instead, I felt worthless and hopeless. Nothing I said or did could stop the criticism and contempt he regularly directed at me, and it was devastating. I had made him and our marriage the center of my universe, so having to walk away from both left me shattered. Sorrow overwhelmed me until I was able to learn to surrender it to Him. Grief is to be expected in these situations, but we have a choice about how we will grieve. We can either become self-focused and filled with self-pity, or we can lament in His arms.

GRIEVE WELL

There is nothing wrong with grieving. Jesus wept at the tomb of His friend Lazarus, and God is not so cruel that He expects us to just deal with it and move on. He longs to relieve your burdens, dear friend, and to carry your griefs and sorrows (Isaiah 53:4). Knowing that you do not have to carry the burden alone and that you can bring your heavy burdens to Him is so important. The picture of God as a comforter in Zephaniah 3:17 was particularly precious to me. "He will quiet you with His love, He will rejoice over you with singing." I often curled up into a ball and imagined myself lying on His lap as I poured my hurts out to Him. I knew in my spirit that He was rejoicing because I was bringing my burden to Him. I still treasure those times of grieving in His arms because He was so faithful, and I came to know Him on a deeper level than I ever had before. The process of healing from sadness and grief is much the same as it is for anger. We must learn to trust His goodness.

BELIEVE HIS WORD

Praise God for His Word because as I sought Him in those pages, I found that the Perfect One loves and cherishes me unconditionally. I realized I had allowed a flawed man to determine my worth, so I was filled with shame, but his opinion of me was based on lies. (We'll talk more about this in Chapter 14). Discovering God's heart toward me was extremely healing.[26] As it turned out for me, unresolved anger turned inward and manifested as depression, but I've also seen it the other way around. Some people mask their sadness by lashing out in anger. The two are interrelated, so the cure is the same either way. Pour your heart out and roll the burden onto Him. Choose to be controlled by the truth revealed in Scripture rather than by your feelings. This doesn't mean the sadness will automatically disappear, but as you move closer to Him, you will find healing. Grief comes in waves. Just when you think you're recovering, another wave (a memory or another trigger) comes and knocks you over. But just as we can get past the breakers by moving forward in the ocean, we can move past grief by seeking out and moving toward our loving Redeemer.

FEAR

Camille worked very hard to keep her husband, Jack, happy. She tried to make sure dinner was on the table, and the house was clean before he got home each day. However, every now and then, her day wouldn't go as planned. Some days, one of the kids would make a mess just before Jack walked in the door, or she might accidentally burn part of the meal. When things like that happened, Camille would begin to panic inside, and sometimes, the panic would begin to spill out in the form of angry demands at the kids. Didn't they know their dad would freak out if he came home to things so out of order? Even if they had lost their respect for Jack, why couldn't they at least care enough about her to help make things run smoothly around the house?

Perhaps the children hadn't figured out the rules yet, though, because sometimes Jack came in happy from his day at work, and even when things weren't according to his specifications, he was cheerful and joked around. But other times, even the slightest infraction against his wishes (or nothing at all) would send him into a rage. All Camille knew to do was to try to control every detail within her power and hope for the best. She bought Jack's required he grocery brands and other things he approved for the kids and her. In the beginning of their relationship, he had accompanied her on all shopping trips until she had become clear about his wishes. It was fine for her to buy small personal items for herself as long as she stayed within the prescribed budget, but even then, she only bought things she thought Jack would like. For instance, she knew if her clothes weren't baggy enough, it would, at the very least, result in a tortuous interrogation by Jack about the men she might be trying to impress. If he didn't like her answers, he could easily become violent.

It's no wonder that Camille struggled with fear continuously. By this point in their marriage, Jack had fully conditioned her to live in the fear of him, rather than the fear of the Lord. It certainly would not have been wise for her to suddenly start telling him no—at least not without a good safety plan in place. If you find yourself in a similar situation, a trained advocate or local DV shelter can help you with

---

[26] Understanding God's goodness is often difficult for abuse survivors, but it is one of the most powerful keys to healing. To learn more, see Chapter 13 and Lesson 1 "Knowing God" in this book.

safety planning but remember that moving forward victoriously involves so much more than escaping. It requires learning a whole new way of thinking and of fearing.

A WORSHIP PROBLEM

The Bible talks about both good and bad types of fear. For most of my life, I struggled with the worst sort of all—fear of man. It started long before I met Doug; he was simply able to recognize it, cultivate it, and use it as a weapon to gain complete domination over me. Therein lay the problem—someone other than my Lord had lordship of my life. I was unconsciously yielding my autonomy to him. It wasn't willful idolatry, nevertheless, allowing fear to control me and lead me into bondage.[27] Proverbs 29:25 proved to be a theme in my life before and after abuse. "Fear of man will prove to be a snare, but whoever trusts in the Lord is kept safe." Living in constant fear of my husband was surely a trap. I was so worried about his reactions that I centered my life on preventing his wrath. The trouble was I couldn't do it! There was always something beyond my control that would set him off. I believe that whatever we fear controls us, so he unconsciously became my lord. I'm sure that's one of the reasons God repeatedly commanded His people to fear Him, so He had charge of their lives instead of something, or someone else.

I used to shake my head when I read the history of the Israelites in the Old Testament. How could they have seen God's miraculous provision so many times and still turn to idols? It made no sense to me until after I got out of the abuse, and God convicted me that my husband and my marriage had become idols. God had been so faithful to me over the years, yet I was so full of fear that I did everything in my power to control circumstances and even people in an effort to make sure my worst fears didn't come to fruition. The bottom line was that I feared people and circumstances more than God. I feared my husband's temper, and I feared being divorced. For years, I did what I now call "the dance of fear." I tried to avoid his anger and the ending of our marriage, and I believed my efforts gave me some power over my circumstances.

Fear both controls us and compels us to try to control. All my efforts amounted to attempts to control my husband's reactions. It took nearly losing everything for me to see I had only been fooling myself to think I had any power over such things. In this world, circumstances can change suddenly and dramatically for any of us at any time, and none of us have the ultimate charge over our lives. Yet that doesn't keep us from trying to run the show. Those who have lived with abuse tend to be the worst when it comes to trying to micromanage things. I suppose the same thing must have been true of the idolatrous Israelites. Of course, they didn't want to sacrifice their children to false gods like Moloch, but apparently, the fear of consequences for not doing it was worse than the prospect of doing it. When I look back at my life, I realize that fear of my husband caused me to put my children in a terribly destructive environment for far too long, but I believed I was holding it together. The reality was the exact opposite.

The first step to overcoming this vicious cycle of fear and attempted control is to replace the unhealthy fears with a proper fear of the Lord. It took me a long time to learn what that meant. For one thing, I wasn't quite sure what it looked like. I certainly didn't fear God the way I feared my husband.

---

[27] See more on the concept of idolatry, and how it has been misused against victims, in Lesson 15. While idolatry language has been twisted to condemn victims, in my case, the notion was freeing.

I knew God was love and that I didn't have to fear constant punishment with Him, but I must admit, I did struggle with thoughts that He could never be pleased with me. The interesting thing is that I cared a whole lot more about pleasing my husband than pleasing Him. Do you see the problem? Misplaced fear leads to misplaced reverence. To move forward, we must learn to put God on the throne of our lives rather than a man. To fear the Lord simply means honoring Him above all and yielding ourselves to Him rather than giving into fear of man. For many of us, one of the first steps is overcoming our misconceptions about Him.

PERFECT LOVE

First John 4:8 tells us that God is love, and then further down in verse 18, we are told that "perfect love casts out fear." When fear has been your constant companion for decades, it is difficult to imagine ever living without it, but this verse in 1 John gives us the key. Understanding and connecting to His perfect love will drive fear out. When children are afraid, it is normal for them to run to their parents. Even flawed, earthly parents will respond to their frightened children by holding them, and Scripture gives us a beautiful picture of our perfect God doing the same for us. Numerous verses mention God hiding us in the "shelter of his wing" (Psalms 91:4, 17:8, Deuteronomy 32:11, Ruth 2:12). Jesus also used this word picture in Matthew 23:37 when he lamented over the Holy City. "Jerusalem, Jerusalem, you who kill the prophets and stone those sent to you, how often I have longed to gather your children together, as a hen gathers her chicks under her wings, and you were not willing." Have you ever seen a mother hen gather her chicks under her wings? They run to her for protection and are completely hidden once they get under those wings. God longs for you to run to Him, but you must be willing. This requires making a choice to seek Him rather than your old ways of doing things. It requires believing His promises and running to the One who loves you most. When you know how great His love is, nothing can devastate you because you realize that you are in His care regardless of the outcome. He is bigger than anything that causes you distress.

If you still find it difficult to believe His love for you, I encourage you to look up passages on fear, anxiety, and God's love from the Scripture Database in the back of the book. Write out some that speak to you and meditate on them repetitively. Ask Him to help you find rest from anxiety in His loving arms and thank Him. There is power in praising Him because you are choosing to make Him greater than anything else vying for control of your life. It also helps to turn on worship music and sing along because you are choosing to focus on and exalt Him rather than your problems. Trauma can have a tremendous impact on our faith, but it is possible to rebuild it.[28]

HOLY FEAR

"Twas grace that taught my heart to fear and grace my fears relieved." I love that line from the song "Amazing Grace." It is an unbelievably powerful thing to exchange your unhealthy fear for the holy fear of God. Doing this means you will become concerned about honoring and revering your Lord first and foremost. It amounts to caring more about what He thinks than what anyone else thinks. This type

---

[28] I set forth a process on rebuilding faith in at a session entitled "Rebuilding Faith After Abuse & Trauma" at our CTPM 2022 women's retreat. You can access it at https://youtu.be/wDi6jHwZITk.

of godly fear will help relieve ungodly ones. Jesus said no one can serve two masters—just as you cannot serve your husband and God. When you truly put God on the throne of your heart, you will not be as easily manipulated by people. When you care more about pleasing Him, you will want your responses to any given situation to bring Him glory. Those who live in fear usually seek the path of least resistance, but taking His path means loving others enough to challenge their sin. Please remember that this must be done with safety in mind. It can be dangerous to challenge an abuser, so be sure to enlist the help of a trained advocate or counselor to figure out the safest and wisest way to proceed. Early in my marriage, I was able to stop the violence by taking a firm stand against it, but as my husband became more successful, I started to worry more about his reputation and what people might think. Caring more about pleasing God means you will seek His best in every situation, and being a slave to unholy fear is certainly not His best for your life. Neither is it the best for the one causing you to fear—it merely promotes their sin. Just remember, it is vitally important to follow God's timing and guidance. There is not a one-size-fits-all response to domestic abuse, so you do not need to feel pressured to do things a specific way. My hope is that you will be able to overcome living in fear and learn to experience His peace and leading, even during adversity.

MAKING A CHOICE

When you make God your true Lord and begin to care most about pleasing Him, you will find yourself becoming more secure than you've ever been. Please note that, especially in the beginning, you may not feel secure. It often takes our emotions time to catch up with the truths our minds are embracing. Still, when you choose God's truth over your feelings, things will begin to change because He is faithful to keep His promises. As you learn to take your thoughts captive and surrender them to Him (2 Corinthians 10:5), you will no longer be so easily devastated because you will know that the mighty God who created the universe holds you and promises never to leave or forsake you. What an awesome privilege! As His child, circumstances will no longer have the same power to cause you overwhelming panic because you will know that He is sheltering you beneath His wings. He has you, and is more than able to help you survive the fiercest storms of life. Jesus gave us a beautiful word picture revealing the importance of making Him Lord in Matthew 7:24–27.

> "Therefore, everyone who hears these words of mine and puts them into practice is like a wise man who built his house on the rock. The rain came down, the streams rose, and the winds blew and beat against that house; yet it did not fall, because it had its foundation on the rock. But everyone who hears these words of mine and does not put them into practice is like a foolish man who built his house on sand. The rain came down, the streams rose, and the winds blew and beat against that house, and it fell with a great crash."

Notice this parable indicates that storms will come to everyone. Having your life grounded in the truths of His Word will not exempt you from trouble. Scripture is clear that we will all face difficulties in life, but God is faithful and can use even our difficulties for good (See John 16:33, Psalms 37:19–25, Romans 8:28–29). We may not be able to avoid suffering in this life, but we do have a choice about how it will affect us. If we allow misdirected fear to rule us, the trials of life will devastate and overwhelm us. However, if we choose to base our lives on His truth, we will stand firm regardless of our circumstances. My prayer for you is that you will choose to believe His promises and stand firm on the solid Rock who is able to keep you secure.

Chapter 13

Knowing God

> "I consider everything a loss because of the surpassing
> worth of knowing Christ Jesus my Lord."
> ~ *Philippians 3:8*

When somebody you love oppresses you, it can begin to warp your view of God. Many times, my husband used Scripture to keep me under control. Even worse, I used it to convince myself that I had to submit to just about anything and that leaving the marriage was not an option. "God hates divorce" was my mantra, and I believed He would be angry or disappointed in me if I gave up on my marriage. When the violence became so deadly that I had no choice but to leave, I felt as though I'd let God down. I also felt He had let me down. I had done my best to live in obedience to Him, but He had not saved our marriage. It seemed horribly unfair. Deep down, I began to question His goodness. To move past my doubt and fear, I had to correct my faulty view of Him and realize He was not demanding that I stay in that deadly situation.

Identify with Christ

From the time things had started going dreadfully wrong in my marriage, I'd spent hours a day reading Scripture and praying. Although I questioned God, I continued to seek Him because people offered no answers, and I was utterly overwhelmed. The Bible studies I had done in the previous years served as an anchor for my afflicted soul. I knew I needed to choose to cling to His promises rather than to my feelings. So, as I read His Word, I looked for His heart and found it. As Jesus's sufferings had touched my heart in the dumpster, they also became a source of comfort as I pondered Scripture. "For we do not have a high priest who is unable to empathize with our weaknesses, but we have One Who has been tempted in every way, just as we are—yet He did not sin" (Hebrews 4:15). Scripture is filled with passages that point to Jesus's familiarity with pain and suffering. See Isaiah 50:6, 53:3, Psalm 22:14–18, Matthew 26:6–7, Luke 22:63–65, and Luke 24:20. He chose to suffer so He could know our pain and redeem us. As catastrophic as my circumstances were, they couldn't compare to what He had endured, and I thanked Him for His goodness toward me.

While I was grateful for Jesus, I still found myself struggling with the Father. My opinion of Him was different. Years ago, I heard a pastor say that we often form our image of God based on our earthly fathers, and I believe, it's largely true. Our view of God can be warped by those who abuse us. I have counseled numerous women whose fathers victimized them as children, and most find that relating to a Heavenly Father is extremely difficult. Women coming out of domestic violence also struggle with their view of God, and often see Him as stern and distant. When I ask them how they feel about Jesus and it's usually a different story. They can relate to Him because He was abused and rejected. It is helpful to remind these women of Jesus's words, "Anyone who has seen me has seen the Father" (John 14:9). Jesus perfectly reflected the Father's heart of love for us. It was crucial for me to recognize this truth and to challenge any faulty beliefs about His character.

For nearly two decades, I had been injured under the "authority" of my husband, and it damaged my trust of anyone in authority, including my Heavenly Father. Sadly, the way I interpreted some Bible passages further alienated me from Him. Rather than recognizing God's intention to protect women, my interpretation of some passages on marriage caused misgivings about His nature, and I realized I needed to change my views. Bible study proved to be very helpful when it came to doing this. As I pored over scripture, I found several verses that compared God to a loving mother and this mother's heart could relate to them. In Isaiah 49:15–16, God's response to His children who felt forsaken was, "Can a woman forget her nursing child, that she should have no compassion on the son of her womb? Even these may forget, yet I will not forget you. Behold, I have engraved you on the palms of My hands."

In Zephaniah 3:17, we get a picture of God singing over and holding His children, and in Isaiah 66:13, He promised to comfort His people as a mother comforts her children. Finally, Jesus used a motherly analogy when he lamented over Jerusalem in Matthew 23:37–39. His kindness and compassion were evident throughout the Gospels. He showed mercy when the religious leaders were hard and judgmental. The stories of the woman caught in adultery in John 7–8, and the woman at the well in John 4, are prime examples of Jesus's love and compassion for individuals who were harshly judged by those who claimed to represent the Father.

If we see Him as demanding and unjust, we will harbor anger toward Him and carry unnecessary shame. Even though I didn't verbalize it, this was a struggle for me. I had to recognize that the Father and Jesus are one (John 10:30), and it was wrong to see them so differently. The Father's heart was perfectly demonstrated in Jesus. It was the Father's loving plan that sent Him to suffer and die for us (John 3:16, Isaiah 53:10). As you identify with Christ's suffering and mercy, you must also identify with One who sent Him on your behalf. Relating to Him in suffering certainly helped change me.

Know His Love

Before suffering changed me, the things I valued were superficial. I constantly asked God to bless my kingdom and was always anxious to get what I wanted—even if it was just a ceasefire. The thought of divorce shattered me, so I did everything in my power to avoid it. The problem was that I had no control, and it devastated me beyond words. Like the disciples in the storm on the Sea of Galilee, I found myself asking, Lord, don't you care if I perish? (Mark 4:38). It is almost impossible to overcome doubt and fear if you don't understand that "He cares for you" (1 Peter 5:7). The day He met me in a disgusting dumpster, He gave me a glimpse of His amazing love and let me know He chose to suffer on my behalf. During the worst time of my life, I chose to cling to Him and to believe His loving promises toward me. It is helpful to meditate on Scriptures that reinforce His loving intentions toward you. The "Scripture Database" (Appendix F) at the end of this book contains a section of passages about His love. Again, I urge you to find and meditate on a few that speak to you, write them out, and repeat them often, out loud, until they sink into your heart.

Recognize His Sovereignty

God is able to hold you together because, ultimately, He—rather than your abuser—is in control. This truth was extremely beneficial to me as I was coming out of abuse. Although He has given people freedom to choose sin, nothing can thwart His purposes (Job 42:2). He is powerful enough to work out His good intentions, even when people act against His will. Believing He is sovereign is worthless if you do not believe He loves you and is for you. Our Lord is a Redeemer. He promises to work all things together for the good of His children (Romans 8:28), but our problem is that we often interpret good as simply a change in circumstances. Immediately after reminding Believers of God's promise to work things together for good, the Apostle Paul stated that God intends for those who come to know Him to be "conformed to the image of His son" (Romans 8:29).

I often say I would never have chosen the path of suffering that abuse brought me, but twenty-seven years after the fact, I can honestly say I am grateful for what it accomplished in my life. At the time, all I knew to do was to hold on to God. I knew He was my only hope, and even though I struggled through fear, doubt, and anger, He certainly has used it all for good. When I look back at that horrible period of my life, I always think of Philippians 3:8: "I consider everything a loss because of the surpassing worth of knowing Christ Jesus my Lord, for whose sake I have lost all things." In my suffering, I lost everything and found everything, all at the same time.

Chapter 14

Finding Your Worth in Him

> But you are a chosen race, a royal priesthood, a holy nation, a
> people for God's own possession, so that you may declare the goodness
> of Him who has called you out of darkness into His marvelous light.
> ~ *1 Peter 2:9*

Many of us identify ourselves according to our relationships—as a wife, mother, boss, or whatever positions we hold in life. For those of us who've suffered abuse, this can be a real problem because we view ourselves based on what has happened to us in the past rather than God's truth. To heal and move on, we must realize that we are not defined by what has happened to us! Every time I start teaching on this subject, the name of a dear friend comes to mind because she refused to let a tragic past become her identity.

Several years ago, I had just set up a display for Called to Peace Ministries at an event when a precious woman named Latonya Allen stopped by. She said, "We need to talk," and then proceeded to tell me her story. She explained that two years earlier, her estranged husband had murdered both of her parents, then beat her, shot her, and left her for dead. Her children, who had been hiding in a closet, were able to call 911. Although Latonya was still alive when medics arrived, the prognosis was grim, and the family was planning three funerals. Doctors told her family that if by some miracle she did live, she would have multiple complications and a diminished quality of life. She lay in a coma for a week, but then suddenly woke up. To hear her tell it, she woke up knowing that God had touched her and saved her for a reason. Even more amazing, she woke up filled with gratitude.

As she was telling her story, I was so amazed by her sweet spirit. She didn't seem traumatized, bitter, or fearful, but truly grateful. In the years since we've met, I have watched this dear woman share her story and use her past as a catalyst for change. She's honest about her struggles but knows He is redeeming all she and her children have suffered. When I see Latonya, I am overwhelmed with God's goodness because I see how He is holding her up, and I see that all things are possible with Him. My dear friend knows that she is precious in His sight, and that knowledge has brought an amazing amount of healing to her life.

Not understanding your value to God can keep you from moving past the abuse you've endured. It's essential to learn to see yourself as He sees you. If we allow our self-image to become tied up in wrong things, we can end up either exceedingly prideful—like many abusers—or feeling worthless, like most survivors. Both extremes focus on self rather than God. Some symptoms of not knowing your identity as His child include insecurity, judgmental attitudes, pride, defensiveness—when someone disagrees with your ideas, you see it as a rejection of you, hardness, distrust/self-protection, disrespect, and jealousy. Not understanding who you are in Him can also manifest as a competitive spirit, perfectionism, rebellion, pretense, controlling of others, and escapism/addictive behaviors. Neither of the extremes—pride or feelings of worthlessness—accurately reflect who we are in Christ. We have no reason for arrogance, and no business acting like we are worthless; He thought we were worth giving up His life.

Because of what Jesus did for us on the cross, we become new creations (Ephesians 2:8-9, 2 Corinthians 5:17), and our response should be gratitude rather than pride or shame. The human race was created faultless in His sight. We were made to have fellowship and intimacy with God, but when sin entered the world, that fellowship was broken. Thankfully, He loved us enough to pursue us, even after we rejected Him. Jesus came to earth to restore our broken relationship with God. He became sin on our behalf so we could become "the righteousness of God" (2 Corinthians 5:21, 8:9). Interestingly, Jesus taught us that denying ourselves was one of the keys to finding abundant life. Some misinterpret that to mean we must degrade ourselves. However, I believe this simply means that as we move our focus from self to God, we will find the joy and freedom He intends for us (Matthew 16:24-25). Self-image problems are also worship problems. Whatever consumes the bulk of our thoughts unconsciously gains lordship of our lives. If we are meditating on other than Him, we will may easily find ourselves controlled by fear and filled with either pride or shame.

As we embrace our true identity as beloved children of the King, we will find ourselves filled with gratitude rather than feelings of worthlessness. Listed below, you will find just a few truths from Scripture to help you better understand your worth in Him. I suggest you take some time this week to look them up and journal your reaction in prayers to the One who treasures you most.

- You are fully known and loved. – Psalm 139, Luke 12:4-7
- You are reconciled, holy, and beyond reproach in Him. – Colossians 1:21-22
- You are blessed with every spiritual blessing (look them up and list them) – Ephesians 1:3-14
- God is for you, and you are more than a conqueror. – Romans 8:31-39
- You've been chosen by the King, even though you had nothing. It is solely by His grace. – 1 Corinthians 1:26-30

Knowing Your Worth Affects Relationships

Until you know the truth about your worth in Him, you may easily find yourself experiencing abuse in future relationships. I often tell people that getting a victim out of an abusive relationship is very much like getting someone out of a cult. I have seen the struggle firsthand and have also lived it. Looking back on the journal I wrote during the years I was living with abuse, it is clear that my thinking had become warped as if I had been programmed (perhaps even brainwashed) to accept behavior I would never have accepted in the beginning of our relationship. I was conditioned to believe that I was supposed to put up with it. This is the deceitful nature of abuse. Ladies in our support groups tell me that over time, they also came to tolerate more and more cruelty from their partners, and in the end, they found it nearly impossible to leave men who had repeatedly harmed them. Not only was it difficult to leave, but many also found themselves longing to be back with their abusers. Circumstances had to become so damaging that staying was no longer an option, but even then, they found themselves consumed with grief over the loss of their relationships. It seems to defy all logic that something so toxic could be so appealing but abuse nearly always leaves us trauma-bonded to our abusers.[29]

When I was finally able to break free, I determined I would learn all that I could about abuse so I could avoid it in the future. God was faithful to correct my warped thinking with His truth, but in the beginning, I longed to be in a relationship with someone. I felt like I desperately needed to be in a relationship. Fortunately, my fear of being hurt and my rigid thinking about divorce and remarriage kept me from putting myself out there, but this hasn't been the case for many of the ladies I've worked with over the years. In fact, many of them have been quick to jump into new relationships, and soon found themselves facing abuse again. In fact, this became the theme of a local support group I led a few years back. Two of the ladies told of how they had been snagged by abusers a second time around. One said, "There's comfort in what you're used to. It just felt normal to me."

I think the abuse felt normal because these dear ladies had never overcome the brainwashing that occurred with their first abusers. If domestic violence is anything, it is mentally deceptive. It involves mind games that systematically destroy our confidence and sense of self-worth. It conditions us to tolerate the intolerable and to doubt our own instincts. Overcoming this doesn't happen quickly, but it's not impossible. In my case, Scripture had to be the standard. I had to learn to identify my faulty thinking and replace it with His truth—truths like I am loved and highly valued by God (Psalms 149:4, Zechariah 2:8, Zephaniah. 3:17), that fear of man is a snare (Proverbs 29:25), and that He calls me to peace (1 Corinthians 7:15). Even then, it was hard to break old habits. When I met my second husband, I immediately found myself walking in fear of his reactions when I had no reason to fear. Very quickly, pleasing him became more important than pleasing God, and it didn't take long for trouble to come. I had been so accustomed to living for the approval of people that I found it easier to lie than tell the truth to avoid disapproval. After this harmful dynamic nearly destroyed my second marriage, I let our crisis become a catalyst for change in me. God taught me a huge lesson in that whole ordeal. When I learned to fear Him more than my husband, things began to turn around.

If we get into a new relationship and find ourselves stressing about how to please a man, we are already off to a bad start. It is unhealthy to live for a man's approval and to feel like that is the path to fulfillment in this life. I've often said that abusive relationships can feel addictive because we feel as though we can't survive without our partners. Sadly, that gives them complete control over our lives. The only One worthy of such esteem is God, and He is not a control freak. He also loves us exactly as we are. We don't have to jump through hoops to win His approval. He desires the best for us, rather than harm (Jeremiah 29:11). He is completely trustworthy and able to shield us from harm when we choose to walk in truth. And guess what? He does not condemn you for making the same mistake twice, or even three or four times. Jesus went out of His way to meet a shamed woman at a well in

---

[29] See footnote 11 on trauma bonding in Chapter 9.

Samaria. She had been married five times and was living with a man who was not her husband. Yet, He pursued her and offered living water to satisfy her longing soul (John 4), just as He is pursuing you and wants to satisfy your deepest longings. Abusers set us up to believe we need them to exist. They condition us to long for them to find meaning in this life, but they are like broken cisterns that can't hold water (Jeremiah 2:13). You'll never be satisfied. God invites you to come and drink freely from His water of life and promises that you'll never thirst again (Revelation 22:17).

CHAPTER 15

No Longer a Victim

>When Jesus saw him lying there and learned that
>he had been in this condition for a long time,
>He asked him, "Do you want to get well?"
>~ *John 5:6*

By the time I realized I would not be able to reconcile with my husband, I had lived with abuse for nearly two-thirds of my life, and finally breaking free was the hardest thing I've ever done. In the final years of that relationship, I lost nearly all my worldly possessions. I faced severe financial loss, angry children, and continued threats on my life. I had nightmares and found myself freaking out about little things that had nothing to do with me. Essentially, I had all the signs of PTSD. When I heard people around me complain about everyday struggles, I wanted to laugh in their faces and say, "Are you kidding me? That's nothing!" I wanted everyone to know that I had been wronged, and I wanted somebody to come make it right. The odd thing is the more I complained, the less people wanted to listen. They seemed to alienate themselves from me, which made my situation even more miserable. I could have stayed in that pattern forever, but as I cried out to God, I began to realize that I would never be an overcomer until I stopped seeing myself as a victim. I realized that people did not know how to handle the severity of my losses. I am sure it made them uncomfortable—perhaps even guilty—that they had been blessed with easier lives. I realized I needed to stop making my unfortunate past my identity, so I made the decision to pour my complaints out to God rather than to people. I decided to believe His promises to me rather than my feelings. Although that decision did not immediately change my circumstances, it did make all the difference in the world in me. Today, I am a victor rather than a victim because I chose to believe Him.

In the years since I transitioned from victim to victor, I have had many opportunities to work with other victims. I have seen some apply themselves to the truths of God's Word and blossom before my very eyes. In those cases, it has been like watching butterflies emerge from their cocoons. From all outward appearances, their situations seemed hopeless, but God has performed miracles for those who have learned to trust Him. Trust like this involves a decision to believe God rather than to rely on emotions and past experiences. I have never seen God disappoint those who have chosen to trust Him. The outcome has always been beautiful.

On the other hand, there has been an unfortunate backlash against the victim blaming and shaming that has been so prevalent in our culture. Many Christian victims' advocates have emerged on social media, offering forums and resources for those who have experienced abuse and oppression. Their tone is angry, and while they are skilled at validating the experiences of survivors, their solutions fall far short of leading them to healing. Survivors are told they don't have to forgive their abusers,[30] that they don't need to look at their own faults, and that they never need to apologize for anything. Because they have been victimized, they have the right to be perpetually angry, and to lash out with a vengeance. How I hate seeing women getting caught up in this sort of thinking! It is reactive and counterproductive. It not only prevents victims from healing, but it also damages the influence of effective advocates, as all advocates are assumed to operate the same way. I pray that as time goes on, we will see a decrease in this type of combative advocacy because of how it harms victims.

Working with women who fail to move past their victimhood is heartbreaking. Many women I have tried to help have simply refused to let go of their identity as victims. Post-Traumatic-Stress (PTS) can result in this sort of thinking, so that must be addressed with trauma-informed intervention. However, even after the trauma has been addressed, there are individuals who will not let go of their victim status.[31] This attitude reminds me of the man Jesus healed at the pool in Bethesda in John 5. Even though he stationed himself by the pool where the angel stirred the water to be healed, he basically told Jesus it was impossible because somebody always beat him to the water. He was full of bitterness and excuses. When Jesus healed him despite his negativity, he showed no joy, nor did he stop to thank Jesus. Instead, when the religious leaders rebuked him for carrying his pallet, he blamed Him. Jesus knew his heart and came to him later with a warning, "See, you are well again. Stop sinning or something worse may happen to you" (5:14). But he simply went out and reported Jesus to the leaders. He had been set free, but he certainly didn't seem to embrace that freedom. That's the problem with so many victims; they fail to see and appreciate God's provision in their lives. Instead, they choose to stay angry and make excuses for hanging on to their anger. They essentially cut themselves off from God's blessings and blame everyone around them (even God) for their negative circumstances.

I love to contrast the story of the man at the pool with the healing of the man born blind in John 9. When Jesus healed the blind man, his life was changed immediately. He became a Believer and was willing to profess his faith in the face of harsh opposition. As far as outward circumstances go, he probably fared worse than the man healed at the pool. Yet, he was filled with joy over what Jesus had done for him. Like King David (who spent years running from abuse), he chose to praise God in the presence of his enemies rather than cling to bitterness.

The truth is that bad things happen in this fallen world. Many of us end up as victims at some point, and it grieves God's heart. We suffer unjustly and it isn't fair, but God knows exactly how that feels

---

[30] Please note that a proper understanding of forgiveness does not subject victims to continued abuse. See Chapter 12, Managing Your Emotions in Lesson 13 in *The CTP Workbook*, Understanding Forgiveness in this book.

[31] There is a difference between being unwilling and unable. For many women trauma is deep and takes years to heal. I am not referring to these individuals, but to those who refuse to take steps to heal.

(Hebrews 4:15). Our God is a redeemer, though, and nothing is wasted when we know Him. He can turn our mourning into dancing (Psalms 30:11) and use tribulation to mold us into the image of His son (Romans 8:29). But amid our troubles, we must choose to trust Him. We must choose to let go of the bitterness that poisons every relationship in our lives and keeps us in bondage (Hebrews 12:15). The problem is that some victims are not willing to make this choice. Instead, they hold tenaciously to their right to be miserable and angry, and unwittingly finish the job their enemies began. I pray that if you are reading this and you feel stuck as a victim, you will see that Jesus offers a better way.

Resolve to Move Forward

If you're reading this book, I assume that you, or someone you know and love, has experienced abuse. Some people never recover from the trauma of oppression and abuse, so you may be wondering if it really is possible to move from victim to victor. First of all, God's Word assures us that all things are possible with God and that nothing is impossible to Him (Mark 9:23, Luke 1:37). It also promises us that He can bring redemption, triumph, and beauty out of ashes (Romans 8:28, 2 Corinthians 2:14, Isaiah 61:3). The question is, will you choose to believe what He says? It all boils down to a choice. I can attest to the fact that it is not easy, but if you persevere and resolve to believe His truth over feelings, circumstances, or whatever else tries to discourage you, you will overcome.

This requires learning to claim God's promises over your life. Choose to renew your mind with truth from His Word, refuse every deceptive thought (2 Corinthians 10:5), and determine to dwell on good things (Philippians. 4:6-8). I often have counselees set a timer to check and record their thoughts throughout the day. Next, I have them examine their thoughts and beliefs in the light of Scripture. Does it line up with truth? His Word is full of promises to those who are afflicted: "We are hard pressed on every side, but not crushed; perplexed, but not in despair; persecuted, but not abandoned; struck down, but not destroyed" (2 Corinthians 4:8–9). I held tightly to passages like this. I also camped out in Psalms for a few years and found great comfort in them—particularly 27, 34, 46, 55, and 56. I had to continually remind myself that God is for me. When the person you love most has been against you for so long, sometimes it's hard to believe that anyone can be on your side. That is why you must persistently choose to counter negative thoughts with the truth about who He is. You won't get it right every time but don't give up. As I was coming out of the abuse, I came up with my own personal Scripture database to remind myself of His beautiful promises and made cryptic notes beside these passages to remind myself of the truths I wanted to remember (see Appendix F). I encourage you to take these promises, write them out, and recite them out loud often to remind yourself often. Also, ask God to enable you by His Spirit. You are not in this alone. His Spirit will empower you as you continually choose His path over your doubts.

For many of us, doubting God is the biggest hurdle to overcome, but for others, it may be issues we've tackled in other chapters, such as unforgiveness, anger, fear, or even idolatry. Some of us may crave the attention or sympathy we get when people discover what we've experienced. After all, living through domestic violence can be every bit as traumatic as going to war. In my case, the inability of the church to help me deepened my sense of desperation. Over the years, I have often seen churches believe abusers and dismiss the victims' claims. Some have even gone so far as to bring victims up on church discipline for leaving the violence or for being "unsubmissive." There's no doubt that many victims are re-victimized again and again, from their churches to the courts—justice often seems illusive, and genuine support is challenging to find. I've seen women move from wealthy to impoverished and on government assistance. This lack of resources can add to the bitterness of being abused and betrayed by the one who was supposed to love and protect them. All in all, moving from victim to victor is extremely difficult! However, with God all things are possible.

We serve a God who specializes in redemption. This means He can take the worst of human suffering and use it for good. The ultimate example of this is seen in Jesus. He willingly came into the world and suffered to reconcile us to God. He was despised, rejected, and abused beyond recognition, yet God had a good plan. I love to read Isaiah 53, which describes Jesus's earthly suffering, to abuse victims because I want them to know that God truly understands their suffering. Hebrews 12:2 tells us that Jesus endured the shame and misery of the cross because of the "joy set before him." He knew the Father's plan was to use it to reconcile a lost world to Himself, and He knew it would allow Him to fully relate to those who suffer. Before I go any further, let me just say that I am not saying you should stay and suffer abuse! Please do whatever it takes to get yourself, and your children, out of harm's way! What I am saying is that recognizing God's desire to take and redeem your pain is the first step in moving from victim to victor.

Consider the story of Joseph found in chapters 37–50 of Genesis. When his wrongful suffering was over, God used him to save a whole nation, and the same brothers who had betrayed him. Although he had the power to destroy them, he chose mercy instead. Genesis 50:20 is one of my favorite Bible passages. It records Joseph's response to his brothers when they stood before seeking forgiveness. While many people would savor the opportunity to get even, Joseph pointed to God's sovereign and good purposes. He told them, "As for you, you meant evil against me, but God meant it for good in order to bring about this present result, to preserve many people alive" (NASB). Do you believe God could ever use your suffering for good? I can tell you, without doubt, that if I had not suffered abuse, I wouldn't have written this book, and I have had many tell me that my story has given them hope to overcome their abuse. I can also tell you that my experiences drove me into my Savior's arms and deepened my relationship with Him beyond anything I would have ever imagined. When we remain stuck in our victimhood, we are self-consumed, but God wants us to use our pain to help others. "Praise be to the God and Father of our Lord Jesus Christ, the Father of compassion and the God of all comfort, who comforts us in all our troubles, so that we can comfort those in any trouble with the comfort we ourselves receive from God" (2 Corinthians 1:3–4). It's not easy, but God has given you all the resources you need to overcome. You have the very same Spirit who raised Christ from the dead dwelling in you (Romans 8:11)! You also have His Word, which is alive and active to perform the spiritual surgery needed for change (Hebrews 4:12). You have a choice. You can allow our Lord to use your suffering for good, or you can let your past define you. Oh, dear friend, how I pray that you will know God's love and good intentions towards you, and that you choose to walk His path to transition from victim to victor!

THE CALLED TO PEACE WORKBOOK

Workbook Table of Contents

CALLED TO PEACE WORKBOOK

WORKBOOK INTRODUCTION — 76

- LESSON 1 Knowing God — 78
- LESSON 2 Finding Your Worth in God — 87
- LESSON 3 The Most Powerful Instruments of Healing — 95
- LESSON 4 The Path to Healing, Facing the Truth — 108
- LESSON 5 Healing From Trauma — 119
- LESSON 6 Managing Your Emotions — 131
- LESSON 7 Overcoming Fear — 140
- LESSON 8 Dealing With Anger — 149
- LESSON 9 Managing Sadness and Grief — 155
- LESSON 10 Overcoming Shame, Guilt, and Regret — 164
- LESSON 11 The Power of Disengagement — 175
- LESSON 12 Learning to Set Healthy Boundaries — 183
- LESSON 13 Understanding Forgiveness — 191
- LESSON 14 Worship Him — 199
- LESSON 15 Finding Beauty in Suffering — 207

AFTERWORD — 214

SUPPLEMENTAL LESSONS

- Is it Sexual Abuse? — 221
- Loving Your Enemy — 224
- The Importance of Community in the Healing Process — 226
- Characteristics & Tactics of Coercively Controlling People — 228

APPENDICES

- APPENDIX A: Finding Peace After Abuse Recovery Groups — 231
- APPENDIX B: Power & Control Wheel — 233
- APPENDIX C: Healthy Relationships Begin With Healthy People — 234
- APPENDIX D: Developing a Safety Plan — 235
- APPENDIX E: Checklist of Abusive Behaviors — 236
- APPENDIX F: Scripture Database — 237
- APPENDIX G: Additional Resources — 241

ACKNOWLEDGMENTS — 245

ABOUT THE AUTHOR — 246

WORKBOOK INTRODUCTION

This workbook is a companion to *Called to Peace: A Survivor's Guide to Finding Peace After Domestic Abuse* (*CTP*). It can be done individually, with a counselor, or in groups. If you are participating in a group, please see Appendix A at the back of this workbook for further instructions. My prayer is that this study will help you find God's path to healing. While reading a book on healing can be helpful, *true healing is a process that requires participation*. If you've read *CTP*, you should have learned that my healing came as I spent time meditating on Scripture and then choosing to believe what I read and discovered there instead of the lies I had come to believe. In other words, healing was the result of a decision to seek Him and a commitment to act on the truths I was learning.

The healing path God led me on has proven to be effective for hundreds of women I have met over the years; however, healing is a process that will be unique to each survivor. The process and timing will be as individual as we are. Even though the process generally includes the same steps to healing, how those steps are internalized can look very different from one individual to another. While meditation on the Word is powerful, it may take time for someone who has experienced spiritual abuse to be able to re-engage with Scripture. There are many ways to engage with healing truth, including counseling, coaching, prayer ministry, creative arts, small groups, journaling, support groups, breathing/grounding exercises, and other methods that help get the truth to the traumatized parts of our brains.

If you are feeling stuck and easily triggered, there are other things you can do to begin the healing process. Skip ahead to Lesson 5, "Healing from Trauma," for practical tips to help you start moving forward. As you are able to find stability, I pray you will be able to find the time to complete the entire study. In fact, it is a good idea to go through the truths in this workbook more than once. Each lesson here could take up a semester-long class, and there are stages to the healing process, so repeating the lessons will be most effective. Before you start, I recommend you get a journal to write out your observations as you interact with the material presented.

The process of healing will require you to do the following:

- Identify and reject lies!
- Plug into God's Truth through His Word and His Spirit
- Know His love and goodness
- Know your worth
- Understand the Impacts of Trauma
- Surrender your hurt and anger to God—learn to manage your emotions
- Choose to forgive
- Change your thinking
- Worship Him
- Resist mistreatment
- Learn healthy relational patterns

Work on each lesson for at least five days a week if possible. Even if you finish the lesson material in fewer than five days, continue to journal. You may notice overlap and repetition in the Scripture passages from lesson to lesson, but that is because the truths they present are crucial to healing. Look up the passages and ask God to show you how they apply to your situation (meditate on them and internalize them). If you see a verse more than once, trying to commit it to memory. Take time to journal what you are learning.[32] This can be very powerful, especially when your focus is on deepening your relationship with God. I often tell people how I wrote my very own version of Psalms when I was coming out of abuse. There was so much emotion inside me that I even began to write poetry for the first time in my life. They weren't just any poems though, they were prayers. Often, I found myself writing out promises from His Word and reminders of His faithfulness. I am sure that the majority of my healing came as I connected to God through this process of meditation on His truth. My view of Him had become so warped that this time was vitally necessary as He met me in my anguish and showed me His true nature. He became everything I needed, even when everything and everyone else failed. There is something very beautiful in connecting with our God in suffering. My prayer is that this workbook will help you connect to the healing power of His love and that you will truly be able to say that He made beauty out of the ashes that were once your life.

---

[32] It's worth noting that some people are not fond of writing or journaling. If this is true for you, understand that you can make brief notes. It doesn't have to be anything special. Just be sure to cover it in prayer. If journaling absolutely isn't your thing, other modalities such as art, music and dance can be helpful in the healing process. This is especially true if you add prayer and meditation to your activities. It is important to express your heart and feelings to God while trying to identify and counter lies you have come to believe.

LESSON 1

KNOWING GOD

*For now, we see in a mirror dimly, but then face to face;
now I know in part, but then I will know fully just
as I also have been fully known.*
~ *1 Corinthians 13:12*

Over the years, as we have hosted support groups through Called to Peace Ministries, some of our group leaders began suggesting I change the order of the lessons. Their rationale made sense. While I started the workbook by focusing on the necessary step of recognizing the truth about the abuse we've endured, it turns out that facing such unpleasant truth right up front is not the best way to invite folks into a discussion on healing. The group leaders suggested that I start with the chapter "The Most Powerful Instruments of Healing" on Scripture and the Holy Spirit. However, as I began working on the revisions, I began to think about all the women I have worked with over the years who have had the Bible used as a weapon against them. Many find themselves very triggered by it. As I was pondering what to do about that, I had a conversation with a volunteer of the ministry who expressed the same concern about the "Instruments" chapter being first. She suggested making the "Knowing God" chapter first, which really resonated with me. My experience in ministry over the past twenty-seven years has shown me that abuse warps our view of God, and when that happens, we are cut off from our greatest source of healing. When I led in-person support groups, I often introduced the "Knowing God" chapter as the most crucial part of the healing process. When we truly connect with His character and goodness, He becomes an anchor for our souls and illuminates the way for us to move forward.

The feedback we've received from group participants over the years has shown me that not knowing God's goodness is one of the biggest impediments to moving forward. When somebody you love oppresses you, it can begin to distort your view of God. Many times, my husband used Scripture to keep me under control. Even worse, I also used it to convince myself that I had to submit to just about anything, and that leaving the marriage was not an option. I believed that God would be angry or disappointed in me if I gave up on my marriage. When the violence became so deadly that I had no choice but to leave, I felt as though I had let God down, but I also felt He had let me down. I had done my best to live in obedience to Him, but He had not saved our marriage. It seemed horribly unfair. Deep down, I began to question His goodness. I never would have expressed it out loud, but inside, I was filled with questions about His nature. To move past these doubts and fears, I had to find a way to correct my concept of Him.

If we see God as demanding and unjust, we will harbor anger toward Him and carry unnecessary shame within ourselves. How important is knowing God? It's crucial! If we don't know Him, we won't trust Him—which means we are inclined to be controlled by something else. We might be ruled by our emotions, circumstances, fear, other people, or even our own desire for control. If we don't know His true nature, we won't understand His redemptive purposes in all life's circumstances. We may find ourselves overwhelmed and panicking when things catch us by surprise. We're all blind until we allow God to remove the scales from our eyes. None of us see Him as clearly as we should. If we did, nothing on this earth could shake us.

God is able to hold you together because ultimately, He is in control, not your abuser. This truth was extremely comforting to me as I was coming out of abuse. Although He has given humanity freedom to choose sin, nothing can thwart His purposes (Job 42:2). He is powerful enough to work out His good intentions, even when people act against His will. Believing He is sovereign is worthless if you do not believe He loves you and is for you. Our Lord is a Redeemer. He promises to work all things together for the good of His children (Romans 8:28), but our problem is that we often interpret "good" as simply a change in circumstances.

Even though I didn't verbalize it, believing He was there during the abuse was a struggle for me. Like the disciples in the storm on the Sea of Galilee, I found myself asking, "Lord, don't you care if I perish?" (Mark 4:38). Understanding that "He cares for you" (1 Pet. 5:7) is such an essential step in the healing process. The day He met me in a disgusting dumpster (see chapter 7 in *CTP*), He gave me a glimpse of His amazing love. He let me know that He chose to suffer on my behalf and restored my hope.

During the worst time of my life, I made a choice to cling to Him and to believe His loving promises to me, even though I still had doubts. It is especially beneficial to meditate on Scriptures that reinforce His loving intentions toward you. The Scripture Database at the end of this workbook contains a section of passages about His love. I urge you to find a few that speak to you, write them out, imagine them, and repeat them often, out loud, until they sink into your heart. For those triggered by Scripture, trying to find at least one truth from His Word that speaks to you and meditating on it repeatedly is a good way to get started. In my own life, God's goodness had been eclipsed by years of oppression, and I desperately needed to become reacquainted with His true character. As I sought Him, Bible passages in which He compared Himself to a mother became particularly healing to me. "Can a mother forget the baby at her breast and have no compassion on the child she has borne? Though she may forget, I will not forget you" (Isaiah 49:15—also see Hosea 11:3-4, and Matthew 23:37-39). As a mother, I knew how strongly I felt about my own children, and these verses helped me see how much greater my Lord's tender love was for me. You may find other verses or phrases from hymns or worship songs, or even time spent in nature helpful in connecting with Him.

For those struggling to recognize His goodness, I have listed some important truths from Scripture below:

- You are inscribed on the palms of His hands. Nothing can separate you from His love, and though all others forsake you, He will not (1 John 4:7-8, 15-19, Isaiah 49:14-16, Zephaniah 3:16-17, Psalms 27:10, 34:18-19; Matthew 11:28-30, Romans 8:37-39, Hebrews 12:2, 13:5).
- He is our strength (Isaiah 40:27-31, John 15:5, 2 Corinthians 12:7-10).
- He is our justification and our life (Colossians 3:3-4, Philippians 1:21).
- He hates sin but loves us and took the punishment we deserve (Isaiah 53:4-6, Romans 5:8-10).
- He is just. He will right all wrongs in His time (Deuteronomy 10:17- 18, Psalms 89:14, 2 Thessalonians 1:6-8).
- He understands our weaknesses and doesn't condemn us for them (Romans 8:1, John 3:17, Hebrews 4: 15, 1 John 3:20).
- Jesus was the embodiment of the Father. He loved us enough to suffer and die and always showed grace to sinners (John 10:30, 14:4-9).
- He is Truth in a world filled with lies. He cannot lie (John 14:6, 8:32, Eph. 6:14a, Titus 1:2).
- He is in control (sovereign) and working things together for your good (Romans 8:28-29, Proverbs 19:21, Genesis 50:20).
- He does not see or do things as we do. Our view is often distorted. (Numbers 23:19; 1 Samuel 16:7).
- He is mighty, awesome, and holy (Revelation 1:13-19, Isaiah 6:1-7, Exodus 3:6).
- He is infinite/eternal (Psalm 90:2, Revelation 4:8, 1 Timothy 1:17).
- He never changes (Malachi 3:6; James 1:17).
- He is good! (Psalms 34:8 & 31:19, Isaiah 63:7, Titus 3:4-5).
- He's our deliverer and Savior (Psalms 1, 27:1 & 37:39-40, John 4:14).
- He is incomparable (Ps. 40:5; Romans 11:34).
- He is so much more than we can even comprehend, and His ways are higher than ours (Romans 11:33-36, Isaiah 55:8-11).
- He longs to have relationship with you! (Matthew 23:37, Isaiah 65:2, Revelation 3:20, John 3:16-17, John 14-17).
- Only He can provide the satisfaction we seek (Psalms 63:1-5 & 73:25-26, John 4:13-14).
- His heart is for you! (Psalm 56:8-11, Romans 8:31-39).

These are just a few of our God's amazing attributes. He is unlike any person on this earth, so please do not allow earthly relationships to define Him. If you are struggling to see His goodness, I challenge you to dive deeper and read more on these truths. Write out verses that speak to your heart, commit them to memory, and meditate on them. It takes time to overcome skewed thinking after abuse, but when we seek Him, we will find Him (Jeremiah 29:13). Knowing the truth of His character will transform your life!

Signs We Don't Know Him as We Should

- We're unloving. Anyone who does not love does not know God (1 John 4:7-8).
- We're filled with doubt and fear (Mark 4:37-41, "Lord, don't you care?").
- We're performance-driven rather than grace-driven (See Martha's example in Luke 10:40). She thought she needed to perform and missed His grace. Brother Lawrence suggested that many fail to advance in the Christian life because they become more focused on their actions than on a love relationship with Him.
- We're unstable, tossed by circumstances and emotions (James 1:5-8; Matthew 7:24-27).
- We live by our own standards. We're more interested in our desires than His (Judges 21:25, Proverbs 12:15).
- We grow weary and faint (Isaiah 40:27-31).
- We stumble if we fail to walk in his light (John 1:4).
- We're prideful. "But if anyone thinks that he knows anything, he doesn't yet know as he ought to know. But if anyone loves God, the same is known by him" (1 Corinthians 8:2-3).
- We're legalists and focus on minor issues (Matthew 23:23-24). We live to please people rather than God (Galatians 1:10).
- We're judgmental. Read Luke 7:44-47 and contrast the Pharisees to the sinful woman.
- We are unforgiving. Knowing His great mercy helps us forgive— Matthew 18:23-32.

Notice that most of these traits define abusive people, but they can also define us when we fail to find the healing our God offers. It was certainly true for me, but when suffering led me to desperately seek Him, everything changed. My hope for you, as you work through this study, is that you will come to know Him as He truly is. I pray that if your view of God has been distorted by abuse and trauma, you will run to Him, rather than away from Him. Ask Him to show you His true nature and be diligent to find it. I am confident that as you do, you will find healing for your soul, and your life will be entirely transformed by His amazing love (2 Corinthians 3:16-17, Romans 12:2).

> *"Everything in your spiritual life depends on the sort of God you worship. Because the character of the worshiper will always be molded by the character of what he worships: If it is a cruel and revengeful God, the worshiper will be the same, but if a loving, tender, forgiving, unselfish God, the worshiper will be transformed slowly, wonderfully, into his likeness."* [33]

---

[33] Smith, Hannah Whitall, *The Unselfishness of God* (New York, The Fleming H. Revell Company, 1903) 14-15.

LESSON 1 EXERCISES

1. Read Chapter 13 in *Called to Peace*. Can you relate to the misconceptions about God mentioned there? If so, list the ways you related.

2. Do you question His love when circumstances are bad? Describe how you have done this.

3. Read 2 Kings 5:1-14 (Naaman's story). Can you relate to Naaman's experience and your expectations of God? Have you ever been upset when He didn't move in the way you wanted or expected? Write it out.

4. How accurate is your view of God? Is it based on truth from His Word or your own experiences, feelings, or traditions? Describe how you truly feel about God. Do you trust Him fully, or are you afraid to surrender all to Him? Be honest! He can take it and understands.

5. Read Luke 10:38-40. Do you think Martha's view of God was distorted? What did she think Jesus expected from her? What do you think God requires of you?

6. Read Hebrews 4:14-16. How confident do you feel in approaching God? Do you hold back—stopping to analyze your true feelings, needs, or desires—before presenting them to Him? If so, discuss some of the reasons below.

7. Read Titus 1:2 and Hebrews 6:18. We were raised by imperfect parents in a sinful world. So, until we come to the Lord, even our best relationships have been, and will be, marked by pain and disappointment. No wonder God repeatedly reminds us that He is not like us! Do you think your view of God is based more on natural human experience or truth? Ask Him to show you what you need to see and write it out.

> "For My thoughts are not your thoughts, neither are your ways My ways," declares the Lord. "As the heavens are higher than the earth, so are My ways higher than your ways and My thoughts than your thoughts. As the rain and the snow come down from heaven, and do not return to it without watering the earth and making it bud and flourish, so that it yields seed for the sower and bread for the eater, so is my word that goes out from My mouth: It will not return to Me empty, but will accomplish what I desire and achieve the purpose for which I sent it" (Isaiah 55:8-11).

"Because God wanted to make the unchanging nature of His purpose very clear to the heirs of what was promised, He confirmed it with an oath. God did this so that, by two unchangeable things in which it is impossible for God to lie, we who have fled to take hold of the hope set before us may be greatly encouraged. We have this hope as an anchor for the soul, firm and secure" (Hebrews 6:17-19a).

8. We must make a conscious choice to replace our faulty views of God with truth. The Bible says that God is love. Read the description below of love found in 1 Corinthians 13: 4-8a. Are there any characteristics listed here that you have not believed to be true of God? If so, write out a prayer asking Him to show you the truth.

"Love is patient, love is kind. It does not envy, it does not boast, it is not proud. It does not dishonor others, it is not self-seeking, it is not easily angered, it keeps no record of wrongs. Love does not delight in evil but rejoices with the truth. It always protects, always trusts, always hopes, always perseveres. Love never fails" (I Corinthians 13:4-8).

9. Read Psalm 63:1-6. Meditate on the truth that His "lovingkindness is better than life." As you look to Him, trust Him to give you a new perspective that will enable you to soar above the storms of this life, and to know the fullness of joy that is found only in His presence. Write out your prayer here.

Notes

LESSON 2

FINDING YOUR WORTH IN GOD

> But God chose you to be his people. You are royal priests.
> You are a holy nation. You are God's special treasure.
> You are all these things so that you can give Him praise.
> God brought you out of darkness into His wonderful light.
> ~ *1 Peter 2:9, NIRV*

Years ago, I was teaching a group of young mothers a lesson on domestic abuse when one of the participants raised her hand to ask about the most serious effects of abuse on victims. Without hesitation, my response was that "abuse warps our view of God and of ourselves." I had never put the two in the same sentence before, but as soon as I did, I recognized that these two impacts should be the overarching themes of intervention with victims. In other words, those who are victimized first need to correct their view of God and then their view of themselves—in light of who He is—in order to heal. I believe the two emphases are the opposite sides of the same coin. As our Creator, God has the unique right to define us. Neither our abusers nor anyone else should have that right, and to understand our significance, we must first understand who He is. Therefore, it is only fitting that this lesson comes directly after "Knowing God."

Many of us identify ourselves according to our relationships in life. For those of us who've suffered abuse, this can be a real problem because we view ourselves based on what has happened to us in the past rather than on God's truth. This can be amplified for those who experienced abuse as children. Shame overshadows their identity. They often see themselves as mistakes who can do nothing right. So many women we work with come to us beaten down and confused about their purpose and worth. The trauma of abuse attacks us at the core. Besides being subjected to constant criticism or disapproval, many of the women we work with report that their spouses were unfaithful or addicted to pornography. Betrayal of this sort usually intensifies feelings of insignificance. Abusive people are usually impossible to please and make us feel as though we can't do anything right. It is difficult to live with someone who constantly berates you without beginning to wonder if their disparaging comments are valid.

Living under the heavy burden of constant condemnation changes how we view ourselves. It is as if our abusers try to remake us into their own image. We often begin to act like them and adopt their false standards –which are usually much harsher than God's. Basically, we must learn to ask ourselves by whose standard we are living. "You assess yourself either in your own eyes, in the eyes of other people, or in God's eyes."[34] Our goal should be to please Him, but when we set up rigid, graceless standards we are basically saying that Jesus' work on the cross was not sufficient to cover our sins and flaws. To heal and move forward, recognizing that your value is not determined by what has happened to you, or by what someone else thinks of you, is essential! God treasures you and has made you worthy through His Son. It is crucial that you challenge any thinking that contradicts that fact. Not understanding your value to God can keep you from moving past the abuse you've endured. It's so important to learn to see yourself as He sees you.

Sometimes, trauma can make this especially difficult because of the way it impacts our brains. Overwhelming feelings of shame can be a lingering effect of trauma, and since trauma is held in a part of the brain that does not respond to logic, simply telling ourselves we are worthy is usually unsuccessful. Journaling your struggles and identifying the lies you believe about yourself, and God can be very helpful. Once you have done that, find truths from His Word that counter those lies. Repeat them out loud, meditate on them, and pray them back to Him. Connecting with God is a powerful way to overcome feelings of worthlessness.

Jesus clearly valued and cared for people who were marginalized. He specifically went out of His way to show care for women who were disregarded and maligned by society and religious leaders, such as the woman at the well (John 4:4- 26), the woman with the flow of blood (Mark 5:25-34), and the immoral woman who washed His feet with her tears (Luke 7:37-48). Yet, while He showed great care, He did not use particularly affirming words to help these women recognize their worth. Instead, He directed them to the God who cared for them. It is interesting that Jesus taught his disciples that denying themselves was a key to finding abundant life. Some people misinterpret that to mean we must degrade ourselves. However, I believe this simply means that as we move our focus from self to God, we will find the joy and freedom He intends for us (Matthew 16:24-25). A healthy sense of self is based on a relationship with the One who loves us most. It can't be conjured up by simply focusing on loving ourselves or saying positive things to boost our self-esteem. While many promote positive self-affirmations, I've never found them to be helpful. Besides running the risk of promoting a self-absorbed, self-seeking mindset, those who don't know their worth don't believe they have enough significance or authority to declare such things to themselves. This is where Scripture meditation can be so powerful. If Almighty God tells us we are significant to Him, who are we to debate what He has proclaimed? As we understand His love and care for us, we can begin to grasp who He has created us to be.

Self-image problems can also be worship problems because whatever consumes the bulk of our thoughts—which is meditation—usurps God's rightful place in our lives. If we continually focus on ourselves, we will be controlled by fear and filled with either pride or shame. He has given us a glorious identity, and when we embrace that truth, we will be filled with gratitude rather than feelings of worthlessness. Below are some truths from Scripture to help you better understand your worth in and through, Him. Please take the time to look up each one and allow the Lord to speak directly to your heart. Write out one or two verses that apply to your faulty beliefs and pray/repeat them throughout the day.

---

[34] Powlison, David. *Good and Angry: Redeeming Anger, Irritation, Complaining, and Bitterness* (pp. 212-213). New Growth Press. Kindle Edition.

THE TRUTH ABOUT WHO YOU ARE

- You are made in His image (Genesis 1:26-27).
- You are His child (John. 1:12).
- You are fully known and loved (Psalm 139, Luke. 12:4-7).
- You are reconciled, holy, and beyond reproach in Him (Colossians 1:21-22).
- You are a saint and blessed with every spiritual blessing (Ephesians 1:1-14). Look up the spiritual blessings from these verses and write each of them down.
- You are free from condemnation (Romans 8:1-2).
- God is for you; you are more than a conqueror (Romans 8:31-39).
- You have been chosen by the King. It is by His grace alone (1 Corinthians 1:26-30).
- You are His workmanship—His masterpiece (Ephesians 2:10).
- You have a vital life-giving relationship with Jesus. He chose you and calls you friend (John 15:5-17). While reading this verse, note that you must choose to abide in Him to see fruit from this relationship.
- You are His dwelling place on earth (1 Corinthians 3:16).
- You have been given a spirit of power, love, and a sound mind (2 Timothy 1:7).
- You can approach God boldly, and He will hear you (Ephesians 3:12, Hebrews 4:16).
- God invites you to drink freely from His water of life and promises you'll never thirst again (Revelation 22:17).

LESSON 2 EXERCISES

1. Read Chapter 14 in the *Called to Peace* book and write below any truths you want to apply to your life.

2. I often tell people that trying to get a victim out of an abusive relationship is very much like getting someone out of a cult. Do you agree? Can you see how your view of yourself has changed because of the abuse? If so, write it out below, and then try to apply a truth from the lesson above or from Scripture to counter these false beliefs.

3. Years of living with constant abuse often warps our way of thinking, and we may become programmed (or brainwashed) to accept behavior that we never would have accepted in the beginning of our relationships. This is not God's plan. Look up Philippians 4:6-8. God calls us to live in peace. How might the words from this passage be applied to your current situation?

4. If we find ourselves stressing about how to please a person, we are already off to a bad start. Scripture tells us that it is impossible to live to please people and to please God at the same time (Galatians 1:10). Feeling like we need approval from someone to have fulfillment in this life will always leave us feeling as though we've failed. You can never find the satisfaction your soul desires in a person—they are like broken cisterns that can't hold water (Jeremiah 2:13). Write out a prayer and explore how trying to please a person has affected you and your relationship with God.

5. Abusive people condition us to feel as though we can't survive without them. Sadly, that gives them complete control over our lives, and God is the only One worthy of such esteem. Thankfully, He is not a control freak. He loves us exactly as we are. We don't have to jump through hoops to win His approval. Read the following passages and write out what God is speaking to your heart about your value in His eyes.

"So, from now on we regard no one from a worldly point of view. Though we once regarded Christ in this way, we do so no longer. Therefore, if anyone is in Christ, the new creation has come: The old has gone, the new is here! All this is from God, Who reconciled us to Himself through Christ and gave us the ministry of reconciliation: that God was reconciling the world to Himself in Christ, not counting people's sins against them... God made Him who had no sin to be sin for us, so that in Him we might become the righteousness of God..." (2 Corinthians 5:16-19, 21).

When I consider Your heavens, the work of Your fingers, the moon and the stars, which You have set in place, what is mankind that You are mindful of them, human beings that You care for them? You have made them a little lower than the angels and crowned them with glory and honor. You made them rulers over the works of Your hands; You put everything under their feet..." (Psalm 8:3-6). He created you with value and purpose!

"For we do not have a high priest who is unable to empathize with our weaknesses, but we have one who has been tempted in every way, just as we are—yet He did not sin. Let us then approach God's throne of grace with confidence, so that we may receive mercy and find grace to help us in our time of need" (Hebrews 4:14-16).

6. Domestic violence is mentally deceptive. It involves mind games that systematically destroy our confidence and sense of worth. It conditions us to tolerate the intolerable and to doubt our own instincts. Overcoming this does not happen quickly, but it is not impossible. You must learn to identify faulty thinking and replace it with the truth that you are loved and highly valued by God; you are the "apple of His eye" (Zechariah 2:8).

Write out any thoughts that come to mind that you know are not from God. Ask God to reveal your faulty beliefs and ask Him to help you replace despondency with His hope, truth, and life.

7. Read Zephaniah 3:17 and Psalm 149:4. These verses describe how much God loves you. He delights in you and rejoices over you with singing. What is your response to this? Do you believe it? Why or why not? Take time to write a prayer to God asking Him to speak to your heart right where you are. Ask Him to reveal His love toward you and to fill your heart, soul, and mind so that His truth speaks louder than any other voice.

When we truly know God, we can better understand our worth.
Meditating on these truths can be a powerful way to internalize His freeing truth.

Because God Is... ▶ I Am/I Have...

♥ GOD IS LOVE

◆ Everyone who loves has been born of God and knows God. Whoever does not love does not know God, because God is love. This is how God showed his love among us: he sent his one and only Son into the world that we might live through him... (1 John 4:7a-9).

I AM LOVED ♥

◆ For I am convinced that neither death nor life, neither angels nor demons, neither the present nor the future, nor any powers, neither height no depth, nor anything else in all creation, will be able to separate us from the love of God in Christ Jesus our Lord (Romans 8:38-39).

GOD IS UNCHANGING

◆ Every good and perfect gift is from above, coming down from the Father of the heavenly lights, who does not change like shifting shadows (James 1:17).

I AM SECURE

◆ No one can snatch me out of his hands.
◆ I am free from condemnation...
◆ I have a solid foundation in him...
(John 10:28, Romans 8:1, Psalm 40:2, Luke 6:48).

GOD IS FAITHFUL

◆ And God is faithful; he will not let you be tempted beyond what you can bear. But when you are tempted, he will also provide a way out so that you can endure it (1 Corinthians 10:13). ◆ Let us hold unswervingly to the hope that we profess... he who promised is faithful (Hebrews 10:23).
◆ If we are faithless, he remains faithful...
(2 Timothy 2:13).

I AM BLESSED

◆ All praise to God, the Father of our Lord Jesus Christ, who has blessed us with every spiritual blessing in the heavenly realms because we are united with Christ (Ephesians 1:3). ◆ The LORD is good; blessed is the one who takes refuge in him (Psalm 34:8). ◆ But even if you should suffer for the sake of righteousness, you are blessed (1 Peter 3:14).

GOD IS CONTROL

◆ And we know that in all things God works for the good of those who love him, who have been called according to his purpose (Romans 8:28). ◆ Are not two sparrows sold for a penny? Yet not one of them will fall to the ground apart from the will of your Father. And even the very hairs of your head are numbered. So do not be afraid; you are worth more than many sparrows (Matthew 10:29-31). ◆ I know that you can do all things; no purpose of yours can be thwarted (Job 42:2).

I HAVE HOPE

◆ For I know the plans I have for you, declares the LORD, plans to prosper you and not to harm you, plans to give you hope and a future (Jeremiah 29:11). ◆ We who have fled to take hold of the hope set before us may be greatly encouraged. We have this hope as an anchor for the soul, firm and secure (Hebrews 6:18b-19a).
◆ You intended to harm me, but God intended it for good... (Genesis 50:2a). ◆ God is in the midst of her, she will not be moved..."
(Psalm 46:5a).

GOD IS COMPASSIONATE

◆ The LORD is compassionate and gracious, slow to anger, abounding in love... he does not treat us as our sins deserve or repay according to our iniquities (Psalm 103:8, 10). ◆ But when the kindness and love of God our Savior appeared, he saved us, not because of righteous things we had done, but because of his mercy (Titus 3:4-5).

I AM FORGIVEN & BLAMELESS

◆ Therefore, there is now no condemnation for those who are in Christ Jesus... (Romans 8:1).
◆ God made him who had no sin to be sin for us, so that in him we might become the righteousness of God (2 Corinthians 5:21).
◆ The Lord redeems the soul of His servants, and none of those who take refuge in him will be condemned (Psalm 34:22).

LESSON 3

THE MOST POWERFUL INSTRUMENTS OF HEALING: THE WORD & THE HOLY SPIRIT

> His divine power has granted to us everything pertaining to life
> and godliness, through the true knowledge of Him who
> called us by His own glory and excellence.
> ~ 2 Peter 1:3

A COMMON PROBLEM

A few years back, I spoke for an online event, and as the host introduced me as the author of *Called to Peace*, she indicated to her audience that my book would not be helpful to everyone listening because of all the Scripture in it. Perhaps I was unaware of the extent of spiritual abuse and twisting of Scripture some women experience because in the years since the books were published, I have found myself dumbfounded that even passages written to encourage the oppressed and downtrodden have been misused to oppress and control. I know that in my own story there were Bible verses I quoted to myself in an oppressive way; however, Scripture still played a vital role in my healing process. It is living, active, and powerful! It is God's gift to His children—an invitation into a life-giving relationship with Him. Yet, it can also be, and has been, misused horribly. The Bible contains abundant examples of power-hungry men twisting Scripture to their advantage, most notably seen with the religious leaders in their dealings with Jesus and the apostles. There's even a passage about twisting Scripture.

> "And count the patience of our Lord as salvation, just as our beloved brother Paul also wrote to you according to the wisdom given him, as he does in all his letters when he speaks in them of these matters. There are some things in them that are hard to understand, which the ignorant and unstable twist to their own destruction, as they do the other Scriptures" (2 Peter 3:15-16).

So many women who have come through our ministry have experienced extreme harm by religious leaders and husbands who distorted passages of the Bible to keep them under control. Most of these women sincerely wanted to please God, so nothing could have been more effective to motivate compliance. Instead of the Word being a healing balm to their souls, it simply deepened their pain and reinforced the lies they had come to believe. It has been hard for me to comprehend how so many powerful passages have been distorted to heap condemnation on broken and shame-filled souls. This offense is particularly heartbreaking because it cuts victims off from the One who is their greatest source of healing. Rather than seeing His love, compassion, mercy, and redemption, victims of twisted Scripture most often see Him as angry, cruel, and demanding. After witnessing this phenomenon a multitude of times, I realized I wanted to update my workbook to help those who have been harmed by this sort of thinking.

For some of us, a mere lack of knowledge about how to study and discern the Word for ourselves resulted in distorted interpretations of Scripture. For others, popular teachings in the church have led to erroneous beliefs about God and the Bible. I certainly struggled in these areas. However, what I have seen in recent years goes far beyond mere misinterpretation; it is an intentional twisting of God's life-giving truth to gain power and control over individuals. Even as I write this update, several prominent religious leaders are in the news because they have been exposed for perpetrating abuse within their ministries. In nearly every case, victims reported that Scripture, or spiritual language, was used to manipulate. It is the worst of offenses, and those who engage in it will surely face His wrath (Ezekiel 34:4, 10; Matthew 18:6, 23:23-25).

It usually takes a great deal of time for those who have experienced this sort of oppression to break free. In my own case, only a small number of Scriptures were used against me, but there were still verses of Scripture that elicited a physical reaction in my body several years after I got out of the abuse. I felt nauseous and weak when I heard them. When I recognized that I had come to loathe those passages, I cried out to God, "Lord, this is your living and active Word, and there are parts I literally cannot stomach. Please help me!" Soon afterwards, I began to prayerfully study the verses that bothered me so much and came to see just how warped my interpretation of them had become. It took another year or so for me to research and embrace the true meaning of those passages, but in the meantime, meditating on passages that confirmed God's true nature had begun healing work in my life. Sadly, those who have experienced extreme spiritual abuse through twisted Scripture are sometimes too traumatized to even open a Bible.

If this has been your experience, I pray you will find other ways to begin to connect with God and to love His written message to you.[35] I've had women tell me they had to start with simple things like time spent in nature pouring their hearts out to God or choosing to meditate on one truth about His character—perhaps a Scriptural truth paraphrased. Since trauma impacts us emotionally, spiritually, and physically, and since it impacts areas of our brains that aren't affected by reasoning, it is helpful to participate in activities that engage the entire brain. Music, meditation, movement paired with prayer, and breathing exercises to calm the nervous system can be immensely helpful. Lesson 5, "Healing from Trauma," contains many practices and suggestions to help you move past being overcome by debilitating triggers.

---

[35] You can download and read a free report "How to Enjoy the Bible Again (when you're ready) after Spiritual Abuse" on Rebecca Davis's website www.heresthejoy.com.

RECONNECTING WITH SCRIPTURE

Scripture is often and easily twisted by arrogant and malicious people to promote selfish interests, but that does not change the fact that this amazing book holds the most powerful keys to healing after abuse. We simply can't afford to underestimate its power, and our goal should be to overcome what the enemy has done to alienate us from it. This process will take longer for some than others, but I pray you will be willing to hang in there and do the work of untwisting passages that have been used against you[36] because when our view of Scripture is warped, our view of God is too. John 1:1 tells us that Jesus is the Word. Just like the words on the pages of our Bibles, He is God's message of grace and redemption to us. He is nothing like He has been portrayed to you by those who abused you, and how I pray that nothing will hinder you from receiving the healing balm contained in His Word! Be honest with God about your struggle and ask Him to help you. He wants you to be free, and He has not left you alone to figure it out on your own.

THE HOLY SPIRIT

> In the same way, the Spirit helps us in our weakness.
> We do not know what we ought to pray for, but the Spirit
> Himself intercedes for us through wordless groans.
> ~ *Romans 8:26*

When we receive Jesus as our Savior, we receive His Holy Spirit. He comes to dwell inside us and empowers us to live the life of faith, even in the face of adversity. When we know the Word, His Spirit brings it to our minds to encourage, comfort, and help us just when we need it. The Spirit-filled life is not about following a set of rules; instead, it's about pursuing the Lover of our souls and allowing Him to change us into His likeness—where anxiety is replaced by peace, depression by joy, bitterness by kindness, and so forth. Our hearts become filled with His love that fulfills the law (Romans 5:5, 13:8-10; Galatians 5:14). The Bible urges us to walk in the Spirit and indicates that there will be fruit in our lives as we yield ourselves to Him. When we follow His lead, our lives will be characterized by joy, peace, patience, kindness, goodness, faithfulness, gentleness, and self-control (Galatians 5:22-23). We cannot live the life of faith on our own, but as we draw near to the Spirit, He illuminates Scripture to us and helps dismantle the lies we have come to believe about Him and ourselves (1 Corinthians 2:9-14, 1 John 2:24). His Spirit lets our hearts know we are beloved children (Romans 8:16), and miraculously, because we have the Spirit, we have the mind of Christ to recognize truth (1 Corinthians 2:16).

Problems arise when individuals interpret Scripture in their flesh, apart from the Spirit. Those whose minds are set on the flesh—many who can quote Scripture fluently— do not have His mind or His heart. He is the One who guides us in all truth (John 16:13), but a life devoid of the Spirit is characterized by the deeds of the flesh, including selfish ambition, fits of rage, hatred, and more (Galatians 5:19-21)—the very fruit we see in those who oppress. People who use Scripture to oppress are working against the Spirit Who offers life and peace, rather than bondage (Romans 8:6). Oppressors

---

[36] Rebecca Davis has a series of books called *Untwisting Scripture* that you can check out, and I recorded a 2-part series, "When Scriptures Are Used to Oppress," with Chris Moles and Darby Strickland dealing with specific passages used against victims of domestic abuse available on YouTube and Vimeo.

see God's life-giving Word as a means of selfish gain and focus on legalistic directives to control and condemn others. So, while the Word of God is living, active, and powerful to transform lives, without the ministry of the Holy Spirit, it can become an instrument of oppression.

There are those within our churches who seem to deny the power of the Holy Spirit in the lives of Believers. Their view of God is so limited they miss the many benefits He has for His children. He offers us intimate fellowship, and that includes two-way communication with Him. Jesus said His children know His voice (John 10:27) and that when we call on Him, He will "answer [us] and tell [us] great and unsearchable things [we] do not know"(Jeremiah 33:3). Yes, the Bible is the ultimate authority when it comes to discerning truth, and most of the time, He will speak through His Word and quicken it to our minds as we meditate. He will never say anything to contradict the truth of Scripture, but I believe as we take time to dwell on His promises and His goodness, He will speak to our hearts. What would He say to you about that awful situation you're facing? How does He see you? I believe if you get quiet and meditate on His Word, you will find He has a beautiful message for you. We should never underestimate the power of the Holy Spirit in our lives— the very Spirit who raised Jesus from the dead dwells in us. Not only is He more than able to restore our broken hearts and minds (Psalms 34:18-19), but He truly wants to (John 3:17, Jeremiah 29:11, Romans 12:2)!

THE WORD

> For the word of God is living and powerful, and sharper
> than any two-edged sword, piercing even to the division of soul
> and spirit, and of joints and marrow, and is a discerner of
> the thoughts and intents of the heart.
> ~ *Hebrews 4:12*

Most women I've worked with over the years have come out of abuse struggling with a small number of Bible verses or passages. For them, there were still passages that brought peace and comfort. If you are in that category, I urge you to start by meditating on passages about knowing God and His true character. Doing that has made all the difference for so many, including myself. I posted Scripture passages all over the walls of my house, ran to them, and prayed them aloud many times over. I imagined myself being held by God as I meditated on those passages. Sometimes, I rocked on my bed as I poured my heart out to Him, and often sang reassuring hymns and worship songs. The bottom line is that I was doing battle. I knew that without making a conscious effort to dispute the negative, false narrative that was constantly running through my head, I would never overcome the anxiety, depression, and hopelessness that plagued me. I had to choose a different narrative based on His truth. In the process, I stumbled onto a form of meditation that helped get the truth to those unconscious, traumatized parts of my brain. We will talk more about this process later, but for now, please keep in mind that God's Word, *illuminated by His Spirit*, is powerful to heal!

CHALLENGING COMMON DISTORTIONS OF SCRIPTURE

Many women I have met over the years have told me that they were not allowed to question the teaching of their church leaders and husbands. They were told that because women were so easily deceived, they needed men to help interpret the Bible for them. Interestingly, when they refer to Eve being deceived, they fail to mention that Adam was not deceived but willingly disobeyed God when he ate the fruit in the Garden. Romans 5:12 tells us that sin entered the world through Adam, so it doesn't appear that Scripture paints him as more virtuous than Eve, even though many suggest it does. People who teach that women are too naïve or easily deceived to interpret the Word for themselves simply ignore a body of Scriptural evidence to the contrary. His Spirit indwells women, and His gifts and calling apply to them as well as to men. Below, I have listed a few passages of Scripture on the role of women in God's kingdom. If the Bible has been used to hold you back from walking in the fullness of life he offers based on your gender—I encourage you to consider these passages and beyond.[37]

- **Acts 1:14, 2:4,17** — at Pentecost, both men and women received the Spirit, fulfilling Joel 2:28-29.
- **Acts 21:9** — Philip's daughters operated in the spiritual gift of prophecy.
- **Acts 18:26** — both Priscilla and Aquila explained the way of God more adequately to Apollos.
- **1 Corinthians 11:5** — Paul refers to women praying or prophesying in the assembly when discussing the cultural practice of head coverings.
- **Galatians 3:28** — In Christ, we are equal in God's eyes, regardless of ethnicity, social status, or gender.
- **1 Peter 3:7** — Husbands are to show honor to their wives as fellow heirs of the grace of God.
- **Romans 16:1** — Paul sent Phoebe as his ambassador to the Romans. She carried his letter to them, and he commended her as a servant of a church near Corinth. The Greek word for servant, *diákonos*, can also be translated deacon.
- **Judges 12** — Deborah led Israel.
- **Exodus 15:20** — Miriam was described as a prophet and served alongside Moses and Aaron.
- **2 Kings 22:14-20** — Huldah was described as a prophetess who brought an important word to the king of Judah.
- **John 4:4-42, 20:11-18** — Women were the first to be commissioned by Jesus to spread good news about His identity as Messiah and His resurrection.

As done above, it is always important to determine your beliefs in light of all Scripture, not just a few passages that may have been used against you. It is also a good idea to study Bible passages that trigger you. In fact, when I was in seminary, I chose to study passages that had caused me anxiety after coming out of abuse. As it turns out, to my detriment, I had entirely misinterpreted every one of those passages. For example, I had interpreted marital submission as meaning blind obedience, but the word for submit does not mean obedience at all. Rather, it is a voluntary yielding that cannot be forced, and as my friend Chris Moles often says, "When submission is forced, it ceases to be submission and becomes subjugation."

Perhaps church leaders, or your spouse, have told you that questioning their teaching is rebellious and unscriptural. However, Scripture itself encourages us to be good students of the Word and to check the validity of what we're being taught. Acts 17:11 tells us that "the Berean Jews were of more noble character than those in Thessalonica, for they received the message with great eagerness and examined the Scriptures every day to see if what Paul said was true." Basically, the Bible tells us that being alert

---

[37] To study more about Scripture has to say about women, I recommend *Worthy: Celebrating the Value of Women* by Elyse Fitzpatrick and Eric Schumacher, and *Jesus and Women: In the First Century and Now* by Kristi McLelland.

to potential deception is commendable. Both Jesus and Paul declared that wolves would come into the church with the sole purpose of taking advantage of the sheep and warned us to be on guard (Matthew 7:15, Acts 20:29-31, 2 Timothy 3:6).

WHY STUDY THE BIBLE?

God's Word is supernatural, otherwise it would have no power! It is also reliable and inerrant in its original form.[38] Jesus declared it was to be our source for living (Matthew 5:17, John 17:17, John 5:39-40). The Bible was compiled over a period of 1,500 years by over forty authors yet has a common theme. There are hundreds of prophecies in the Bible. Many of them are very specific and have been undeniably fulfilled. There is no other book like it in the world. No other religion has a book filled with prophecies that have been fulfilled, one right after the other. There are no significant deviations from the original texts because of the meticulous process Jewish scribes used when copying them. No other literary work has so many copies in existence. For example, there are nearly 5,700 ancient copies of the New Testament, but only six of Plato's work, yet nobody questions the famous philosopher's works. How much more then can we trust the accuracy of the Bible?[39]

The Bible is God's instruction manual for life to His people. It provides the wisdom we need to live victoriously in a fallen world. If we fail to live by His Word, we will reap the consequences— see Proverbs 1:20-33, 4:20-22, and Psalm 119:118. We must measure everything we hear, then believe and live according to His Word as our standard for living. If we do not acknowledge the authority of God's Word, it will have no power in our lives. This is why His Holy Spirit is so vital! He is our Comforter, our Helper, our Advocate, our Teacher, our Encourager, and our Counselor. He is the One who makes Scripture come alive for us and guides us in the truth (John 16:13). When we know the Word, He will bring it to our minds to encourage, comfort, and help us just when we need it. His words have the power to deliver, even when we've gotten ourselves into bondage— see Psalm 107:1-20. God's Word is essential to your walk as a Christian. You are not likely to grow or fulfill your calling as a Christian without it.

Only a few years into my first marriage, my mind had already become so warped by abuse that, often, when I picked up a Bible, I felt condemnation and judgment. In my early years as a Christian, I had recognized His gracious character, even in the most challenging passages of Scripture, but suddenly I was questioning His goodness. I have met hundreds of women who have reported having the same struggle, and the dilemma for most of us coming out of abuse is to figure out how to overcome our problems with Scripture. Amazingly, God brought two powerful Bible studies into my life at just

---

[38] There have been a small number of errors in some *translations* over the centuries, which is one reason you will want to study passages that have triggered you. However, when scholars look at the early manuscripts, dispersed a throughout the Middle East, Europe, and Africa (after the first century A.D.) it is evident that the entirety of the original manuscripts have been passed down to us. Bible scholars continue to work on better translating complex passages that have been misinterpreted in the past. For example, the passage I quoted to myself repeatedly, "God hates divorce" (Malachi 2:16) has been interpreted numerous ways over the centuries. The following link compares various translations and shows how difficult it can be to interpret some ancient texts— https://lifesavingdivorce.com/malachi/.

[39] Adapted from *Living by the Book* by Howard & William Hendricks., Moody Press, 2007.

the right time. The first was *Lord, Where Are You When Bad Things Happen?*, and the other was *Lord, Heal My Hurts*, both by Kay Arthur.[40] Not only did these books teach me to how to rightly examine Scripture for myself, but they also directly addressed my struggles. I am still in awe of how He used those studies in my life. Reading them and watching the corresponding videos that went along with the lessons reconnected me to His amazing love and goodness. They also helped me recognize just how lax my approach to Scripture had been. I saw that it had not been the foundation of my life. My life was entirely transformed after I committed myself to the instruction of His Word. Oh, how I pray that you will make a similar commitment and begin a life-changing relationship with His freeing truth!

HOW TO READ AND STUDY THE BIBLE

If you have never studied Scripture before, you might want to start with an organized study. The Kay Arthur studies I did years ago were so powerful to speak to the tribulations I faced, and there are so many good studies available today. If you've been told you have less value because you are a woman, it might be good to start with either Kristi McLelland's book, *Jesus and Women: In the First Century and Now,* or *Worthy: Celebrating the Value of Women* by Elyse Fitzpatrick and Eric Schumacher. Both books have corresponding Bible Studies that can be accessed online.[41] Many other excellent, easily accessible Bible study tools are available to help you understand the history and culture of the Biblical texts. Without this understanding, it is easy to misread the true meaning of the authors. I particularly like Tara Leigh Cobble's *Bible Recap*, which is available in book form, but the content is accessible for free in 365 brief videos on YouTube. The Bible Project has an animated series that covers many books of the Bible, which is also available on YouTube. I find both resources helpful with passages that are more obscure and difficult to understand, and they do an excellent job of pointing everything back to God's good character.

Once you feel proficient in reading Scripture on your own, there are numerous ways to approach it. In the first edition of my book, I referred to Howard Hendricks' book, *Living by the Book,* as a comprehensive guide to Bible study. I also mentioned a more devotional method, that I love to use, described in Wayne Cordeiro's book, *The Divine Mentor*. Both books refer to the three primary aspects of Bible study: observation, interpretation, and application, but I find Codeiro's S.O.A.P. approach easier to remember and put into practice, especially on days when time is short. The letters in the acronym stand for 1) Scripture, 2) observation, 3) application, and 4) prayer. The process is to 1) choose a *Scripture* passage to read for the day—it can be long or short, depending on your timeframe, and ask the Holy Spirit to highlight a single verse or thought from that passage. You will want to write out that verse or passage, and 2) write down your *observations* about the passage. 3) As you observe, ask God to show you how it *applies* to your life right now, and write it down. 4) Finally, you will want to wrap up your time with a *prayer* based on what God showed you during this exercise. I wrote a blogpost about how this approach revolutionized my quiet times several years ago that you may want to check out for an example of how the SOAP method looks.[42]

---

[40] You can find these and all of Kay's studies at https://shop.precept.org.

[41] Learn more about these studies at https://elysefitzpatrick.com and https://www.lifeway.com/en/product-family/jesus-and-women-bible-study.

[42] Access this blogpost at https://www.calledtopeace.org/revolutionizing-my-quiet-times/.

TIPS FOR READING SCRIPTURE

1. Pray before you read. We need His Holy Spirit to illuminate Scripture to us. Ask Him to help you understand and love His Word.
2. Read it as if for the first time. Sometimes, it helps to read an unfamiliar version.
3. Read it as a love letter. Look for His character and focus on developing a relationship with Him.
4. Read it thoughtfully, prayerfully, meditatively, and imaginatively. Imagine yourself in the passage or insert your name into truths spoken to God's children.
5. If you find it difficult to understand the Bible, find a version that is easier to read, such as the New International Version (NIV) or the New Living Translation (NLT). Once you get familiar with it, you can move to more literal translations.
6. Be aware that if condemnation creeps in, it is not from God. He may convict us of our sin, but He does not condemn us (John 3:17, Romans 8:1, John 8:11, 1 John 3:20).
7. Recognize that there are many nonessentials of the faith that are debated by solid, Bible-honoring Believers. You can study Scripture for yourself and decide what you believe on these tertiary issues which include subjects like: modes of baptism, gifts of the Spirit, divorce and remarriage, and more. Early church fathers devised a motto regarding this concept: "In essentials, unity; in non-essentials, liberty; in all things, charity." Basically, this statement means that genuine Believers can come to different conclusions on issues that are not central to the faith and still love each other. It seems a far cry from what we see in social media these days, but I believe we should honor other Christians' right to believe differently than us unless their beliefs are hurting others. For example, I have noticed several domestic violence advocates on social media blaming all complementarian theology for the abuse of women. However, there is a broad spectrum of beliefs among those who call themselves complementarians. While there is a far end of that spectrum that is extremely patriarchal and does greatly harm women, that is not the case for all who hold to this doctrine. We can still honor people who sincerely study Scripture and come down on opposite sides of the issues—without doing harm— as brothers and sisters in Christ. When we live with abuse, we are told how to think and believe, but our God gives us freedom to disagree and still respect one another. Being able to do this is a sign of Christian maturity. Both healthy people and healthy churches allow space for people to disagree over nonessential issues of faith.
8. Avoid approaching Scripture to justify or prove your own agenda (eisegesis). This is exactly what people who twist Scripture do! Instead, when you study the Bible, you should prayerfully ask the Holy Spirit to help you understand the text's true meaning as intended by the original authors.
9. Recognize that not all Scripture is written to you, but it is for you. It is crucial to understand the context and the audience for whom the texts were written.
10. Recognize that much of Scripture is describing culture, sin, etc. That does not mean it is promoting or prescribing these things. For example, issues like polygamy, concubines, and slavery were never commanded by God, but He did give guidelines for the protection of those who found themselves in those situations.
11. Finding resources to help you understand literary genres and devices like hyperbole, personification, and metaphors will help you better interpret confusing passages. The Bible Project covers literary style and issues in several of its videos.

SORTING OUT DIFFICULT PASSAGES

There's no doubt about it; some parts of Scripture can be hard to read and difficult to comprehend. For example, how are we to understand God's character when He commanded the Israelites to wipe out entire populations after entering the Promised Land? That was a question I used to ask myself when I read the Old Testament, that is before I began to encounter women who had experienced severe ritual abuse and trafficking— the same type of ritual abuse the Canaanites practiced. As I began to hear their stories that involved horrific evil, including the torture, abuse, and trafficking of small children, I began to cry out to God. I told Him that I understood the flood much better than the cross because if I were in His place, I would have wiped out every cruel person who had delighted in hurting the dear women who shared their stories with me. At that moment, I truly understood how God would want to put an end to such detestable practices and bring those suffering children to Himself in heaven. This is just one example where Scripture needs to be researched and understood in context. Anytime we have a problem with Bible passages, it is a good idea to do some research to figure out what is truly happening.

Another thing that you will notice in Scripture is that there are always exceptions to the rules. Even before the cross, God showed kindness and grace to individuals who turned to Him. An early example of this was seen when the Canaanite prostitute Rahab became a part of the Jewish nation after she turned to God and married an Israelite, in an act that defied God's command that Jews should not marry Canaanites (Deuteronomy 7:3). In Deuteronomy 23:3 God prohibited Moabites from entering the assembly of the Lord (because they had mistreated Israel), but within a few generations, the Moabite Ruth, was not only welcomed into the nation as convert, but she would also be included in the lineage of King David and Jesus, as were Rahab, Tamar, and Bathsheba (Matthew 1:3-6), all women with scandalous pasts. In most genealogies, women were not mentioned, yet Scripture made a point to include all these women in the lineage of Jesus. Isn't it amazing that the God Who created the universe did not choose to come to earth through a picture-perfect family but one characterized by brokenness and flaws? I believe He did it to show us how deeply He cares for us and our struggles here on earth. I pray that as you interact with His Word, you will truly begin to connect with His amazing love and goodness towards you.

SUMMARY

Through Him, we have the power to overcome and heal from abuse. I often tell people that God brought me through a supernatural healing process. As we meditate on His Word, His Spirit will be faithful to soothe our aching souls and speak peace to our hearts. The Bible is like an owner's manual for us. Of course, the One who created us knows us best, and His Word holds the answers for all of life's struggles. As you surrender to Him and seek Him, I believe He will speak to your heart through Scripture. His Spirit will bring passages to mind, and His truth will surely set you free over time as you identify and reject the lies that have kept you in bondage.

LESSON 3 EXERCISES

1. Has Scripture been weaponized and used against you, or have you misinterpreted passages of the Bible in a way that results in distress when you read or hear those passages? If the answer to either of these questions is yes, please write a summary of the most troubling passages below.

2. Looking at the passages above, write out how your understanding of those passages has impacted your life. Identifying specific lies you have come to believe should be included here.

3. How influential have God's divine resources (His Word and His Spirit) been in your life so far? Can you think of times when He used them to speak to you? Write out one or two times below. If not, write out a prayer asking God to show you how to connect to them.

4. Are you committed to allowing His Word to change you? Look at the following passages and write out your reaction/prayer below:
   - Psalm 107:20 — He sent His word and healed them and delivered them from their destructions (NKJV).

   - Psalm 119: 28 — My soul is weary with sorrow; strengthen me according to Your word.

   - Psalm 119:107 — I have suffered much, preserve my life, LORD, according to Your word.

5. Read the following passages and record your thoughts. Jot down ways the Holy Spirit functions in our lives. Has He operated in your life in the ways described here? If so, write about a time when He did. If not, write down prayers asking Him to begin directing you in these ways.
   - Psalm 16:7 — I will praise the LORD, who counsels me; even at night my heart instructs me.

- John 14:16-18— And I will ask the Father, and He will give you another Advocate, who will never leave you. He is the Holy Spirit who leads into all truth. The world cannot receive Him because it isn't looking for Him and doesn't recognize him. But you know him, because He lives with you now and later will be in you. No, I will not abandon you as orphans—I will come to you (NLT).

- Romans 8:12-16— For you did not receive the spirit of bondage again to fear, but you received the Spirit of adoption by whom we cry out, "Abba, Father." The Spirit Himself bears witness with our spirit that we are children of God (NKJV).

6. How much authority does Scripture have in your life? Is it just another book, a book of wisdom—or the standard by which you live your life? The answer to this question will determine how effective Scripture will be in your healing process.

7. Have you put more hope in human counselors and solutions than in Him? Describe below where you find yourself putting your hope. If it isn't God, commit yourself to finding His path to healing instead.

NOTES

LESSON 4

THE PATH TO HEALING, FACING THE TRUTH

> Heal me, LORD, and I will be healed; save me and
> I will be saved, for you are the one I praise.
> ~ *Jeremiah 17:14*

When I was growing up in the 1960's and 1970's, psychology implied that traumas like abuse wounded people for life. Those who experienced intense suffering in this life could only hope to find some way to cope with the pain and misery that would always be with them. The focus of much of the counseling in those days could be reduced to one question, "How do you feel about that?" In the *CTP* book, I mentioned that my dad invited me to his work with children and teens who, in those days, were labeled "emotionally disturbed." The summer after I ran away, he brought me with him to a weeklong therapeutic camp that included daily group therapy. My assessment of these sessions? The goal seemed to be emotional vomiting. Everyone in the group talked about their hurt feelings, mostly because of how other people in the group had offended them. There was also some talk about hurts from the past, but the result was a lot of venting without any solutions ever offered. After interactions with each of the children over the course of that week, it seemed to me that group therapy was producing kids who, while very emotionally aware, were self-centered and easily offended. If only I had recognized that therapeutic approach contradicted Scripture, perhaps it would have saved me trouble in years to come. "A fool vents all his feelings, but a wise man holds them back" (Proverbs 29:11—NKJV). This is not to say we should stuff our feelings, but that we should be wise about how we share them.

Regardless of my negative impressions of therapy earlier in life, when marriage problems surfaced less than a decade later, I still thought psychology held the answers to our problems.[43] At the time, I

---

[43] It is interesting that, in the 21st century, neuroscience and psychological research are proving Scripture's claims that God created us with the capacity to heal, and that correcting lies we have come to believe and meditating on truth are powerful means to healing. However, there are still psychological practices that do not line up with Biblical principles. Practices that keep us self-focused and trauma-focused for too long, can leave us worse off. This is not to say we don't express our feelings, but learning to do it wisely is so important. To find genuine healing, it is wise to choose counselors and therapists who are committed to counseling models that line up with the truth of Scripture. In recent years, I have appreciated the work of the Christian Trauma Healing Network (https://

thought that the Bible was the answer for spiritual matters only. Hoping to find some relief from the pain I was experiencing, I sought help from mental health professionals, but based on what I knew about psychology at the time, true healing was unattainable. The best we could hope for was to find a way to cope. I thought the abuse my children and I had endured meant we would be damaged for life. One day, when my ex had done something particularly hurtful to the children, I cried out, "Lord, they're going to be scarred for life!" Suddenly, I sensed the gentle voice of my Savior asking me, "Can't I use their scars for good?" He reminded me of some terrible situations He had used to work good in my life and reminded me of the ultimate good that came from the ultimate evil at the cross. Our God is a Redeemer! That means He can take the worst of human suffering and turn it into something beautiful (Isaiah 61:3, Romans 8:28).

Maybe, like me, you've thought what you've suffered means life will always be a struggle and that you will never be able to experience lasting joy or find relief from the lingering pain you carry. But I'm here to tell you that doesn't have to be the case. Our God is a Healer. Nothing is impossible with Him. The only requirement is that you make a choice to believe and apply His healing truths to your life. It's not an overnight process, but as you learn to identify yourself according to what He says about you, rather than what your past experiences or what a flawed person has told you, you find a depth of relationship with Him that will change everything. The One who made you is more than able to heal you. He treasures you, and you can trust Him with your heart. I love that Jesus began His earthly ministry with this passage from Isaiah:

> The Spirit of the Sovereign Lord is on Me, because the Lord has anointed Me to proclaim good news to the poor. He has sent Me to *bind up the brokenhearted*, to *proclaim freedom for the captives* and *release from darkness for the prisoners*, to proclaim the year of the Lord's favor and the day of vengeance of our God, to comfort all who mourn, and provide for those who grieve in Zion - *to bestow on them a crown of beauty instead of ashes, the oil of joy instead of mourning, and a garment of praise instead of a spirit of despair.* — Isaiah 61:1-3 (Emphasis added).

After closing the scroll, He told those listening that His purpose on earth was to fulfill this passage. If your heart is broken, bring it to Him. If you're filled with despair or mourning, come to the One who longs to heal and set you free. You will not be disappointed as you commit yourself to Him. Healing starts with a choice. Many turn to shallow substitutes for comfort (alcohol, new relationships, or other cravings), but only He can bring true satisfaction. I pray that as we take this journey together, you will choose His path to healing. Step one of that path is to recognize and face the truth about what has happened to you.

---

christiantraumahealingnetwork.org), an organization that offers certification, webinars, and support to counselors and clinicians who desire to effectively respond to trauma and abuse. In addition, the Association of Biblical Counselors, (https://christiancounseling. com) provides biblically solid, trauma-informed training to its members, including an advanced certification for counselors who want to work with domestic abuse cases. I believe that either of these organizations can help you find someone who can provide biblically solid, trauma-trained counseling.

TELLING YOURSELF THE TRUTH

I've been working with victims and survivors of domestic abuse for nearly three decades, and one of the most interesting dynamics of working with this population is that many, if not most, of the women I have worked with have failed to identify themselves as abused. The first key to healing from abuse is identifying and rejecting the lies others have told us, as well as the ones we have told ourselves. When it comes to abuse, we must recognize the unpleasant truth before we can embrace the beautiful truths that will ultimately set us free. This often means admitting that what you experienced was truly abuse and that someone you love made a choice to hurt you. As mentioned in the *CTP* book, laying eyes on a Power and Control Wheel[44] was precisely what I needed to finally admit that hard truth to myself. In the exercises at the end of this lesson, I will ask you to identify and journal any of the abusive behaviors identified there. Some tactics are blatant, but others are subtler. Women who live with domestic abuse, also known as coercive control, often tell me they prefer the physical hitting to the emotional torture their abusers put them through. The Power and Control Wheel labels this as emotional abuse, and while some may not agree with the terminology, there is truly an emotionally destructive element to these relationships. "Emotional abuse systematically degrades, diminishes, and can eventually destroy the personhood of the abused."[45] Tactics abusers use include putting her down, making her feel bad about herself, name-calling, mind games, making her think she's crazy, humiliating her, and making her feel guilty.

Several years ago, I watched a woman in a store ask her husband if she could purchase a three-dollar item. Rather than saying yes or no, her husband began to put her down in front of everyone present. He asked her how she could be so foolish as to want to buy something that cheap and indicated that she probably wouldn't even use it. As he criticized her for her "stupidity," he looked over at the group I was standing with and chuckled. It was clear that he enjoyed taunting his wife and that he saw her as inferior. Her face turned red as she tried to mumble out answers to his questions, and finally she put the item back to avoid further humiliation. It seems silly that something so small could ignite such fury, but that's the nature of domestic abuse. Molehills become mountains on a regular basis when you live with an abuser. Victims are made to feel that they are constantly wrong, incompetent, and worthless. No matter what the issue, and no matter who is right or wrong, everything gets turned around and the victim gets blamed for everything.

---

[44] See Appendix B. The Power and Control Wheel is a tool developed by the Duluth Model, based on interviews with over 200 victims of DV, describes typical traits of abusive behavior, which I have found present in every case of abuse I've seen (3000+ as of 2024). Much to my surprise, most of these tactics do not involve physical violence. To learn more, visit https://www.theduluthmodel.org/wheels/. While some in our circles deny the value of this tool and see it as unbiblical based on the worldview of those who collected the information, I believe it is important to honor the experiences of the victims who participated in the study as well as those who have benefitted from it over the last 4 decades. We can honor valid observations without endorsing every aspect of the program that made them.

[45] Vernick, Leslie, *The Emotionally Destructive Marriage* (Colorado Springs, Waterbrook Press, 2013), Kindle Version Location 256.

When we live with abuse, we tend to make excuses for our abusers— basically we lie to ourselves. We don't want to believe they are choosing to hurt us, so we blame their broken pasts, drugs, and alcohol, or perhaps mental illness. Yet studies have shown that for the majority of abusive people, it is a choice. I used to think my ex was completely out of control when he started breaking things around the house, but later, in a domestic violence program, the speaker asked, "If he is really out of control, why does he only break your stuff in his fits of rage?" It was true; he had never destroyed his own stuff! The speaker said, "The reason isn't that he is out of control. The whole point of his anger is to maintain control over you."

What a painful eye-opener that was. Making excuses for him had simply kept me feeling sorry for him and rendered me unable to move forward. I thought he loved me, but his actions were nearly always the opposite of God's description of love in 1 Corinthians 13:4-7. Sure, there were times when he was kind, and those times kept me fooled. I thought the benevolent person I enjoyed from time to time was the real man, but over time, I learned that even his kindness was aimed at controlling me. Admitting the truth was crucial for me to break free from patterns that had kept me in bondage for so long. Have you been making excuses for your husband or partner? Perhaps it's time to admit the truth.

Domestic abuse is all about power and control. It is characterized by a pattern of behaviors that are intended to gain and maintain power and control over an intimate partner. It can be emotional, physical, sexual, economic, or psychological, and can include any behaviors that intimidate, manipulate, humiliate, isolate, frighten, terrorize, coerce, threaten, blame, hurt, injure, or wound someone. If you constantly find yourself "walking on eggshells" to avoid upsetting your partner, you are likely in an abusive relationship. When one person in the relationship clearly has more power than the other and consistently uses it to promote selfish interests, that's a clear sign that the problem is far more than just a marital problem.

We believe one reason domestic abuse is often mishandled and misunderstood is that it is often so covert. Most of the time, there is no physical injury at all. To identify whether a relationship is abusive, we need to look for an overall pattern of coercive control. Even if you are only experiencing one of the tactics on the Power and Control Wheel on a regular basis, it can be considered domestic abuse. A severe loss of freedom in any area recorded on the wheel qualifies as coercive control. Do you feel free to express yourself? Do you feel as if the relationship is one-sided and only your spouse benefits from it? Do you often feel afraid of upsetting him? Abuse can be very subtle, but the bottom line is that it diminishes who you are and gives extreme power to your partner.

There are a multitude of ways abusive people gain this kind of control in their relationships. They keep their partners confused and on the defensive. Victims may blame themselves for the mistreatment they endure, and abusers often claim that they are the true victims. It's not uncommon for an abusive husband to purposely agitate his wife to the point of blowing up and reacting. When she does, he records her reaction and plays it back later as proof of her violent ways. Many abuse survivors I've met over the years have asked me how they know they're not abusive too.[46] The answer is in the power dynamic. Who wields most of the power in the relationship, and who is living in fear? Using the Power

---

[46] Another obvious answer to this question is that most abusers never wonder if they're abusive. They are far more likely to see themselves as victims and blame others rather than examining themselves.

and Control Wheel to identify patterns of controlling behaviors can quickly help you distinguish between perpetrator and victim. If you find yourself confused about these dynamics, it would also be a great idea to do further reading on the subject.[47]

---

[47] For a more thorough handling of domestic abuse and coercive control, I recommend the following books: *Is it Abuse?* by Darby Strickland, *The Emotionally Destructive Marriage* by Leslie Vernick, and Chapter 11 in *Called to Peace*. You can also take a warning signs quiz at www.calledtopeace.org to help determine abusive patterns in relationships.

LESSON 4 EXERCISES

1. Facing the truth is crucial to healing after abuse, and that includes first facing the ugly truth about what has happened to you. Don't worry, you don't have to hang on to that burden long, but you do need to get it out and give it to God—tell Him what has happened and how it's impacted you. If you don't, it will hinder the healing process. This week, I urge you to get your journal out and pour out the truths you are discovering. Entrust your broken heart to God and believe He will bring the healing that you long for.

   Find at least two comforting passages of Scripture from the Scripture Database (Appendix F) that speak to your struggles and write them down below. As you write them, read them out loud. Continue to read them out loud at least twice a day.

2. Check out The Power and Control Wheel (Appendix B). Do any of the behaviors there seem familiar to you? If so, take the time to write out incidences that fit the categories listed. You might need to take several days to complete this. You may also want to return and add to each of the following bullet points as memories surface. As you make your list, pour out your complaints and your hurting heart to God (Psalm 142:2) in your journal. (Note: If you find this process too painful, just do what you can, even if it is merely writing out a prayer to God asking for His healing.)

- Emotional Abuse

- Intimidation

- Minimizing, Denying, Blaming

- Coercion and Threats

- Using Isolation

- Economic Abuse

- Using Male Privilege

- Using the Children

3. Read 1 Corinthians 13:4-7. How do the words in this passage compare to what you've experienced in your destructive relationship? Take the time to write out your experience.

4. Understanding that we have a God who cared for us enough to come to earth and enter our suffering can be very powerful. Read Isaiah chapter 53, which describes Jesus's suffering in detail. Does it encourage you to know that He understands what you've experienced? Although He will never violate your abuser's free will, He has promised never to leave or forsake you, and He knows what it feels like to be abused and betrayed by those He loves. Write out your thoughts about what Jesus experienced on your behalf.

5. Scripture tells us He understands our weaknesses because He has experienced the same trials and temptations. Read Hebrews 4:15-16. Have you seen Him as distant in your struggles? If so, how does this verse counter your feelings?

6. Now that you've identified the hurts you've experienced and accepted the painful truth about your relationship, it's time to look at God's encouraging truth. Read Romans 8:18, 28-29, and 31-39. Write down whatever stood out to you from these passages. Then, write down your commitment to trust Him to work all things together for your good.

Sometimes in group, we joke that there must be a school for abusers because in comparing stories, the ladies can't help but notice that all their abusers used many of the same tactics.

Illustration by Shari Ellis: Used by permission.

Notes

LESSON 5

HEALING FROM TRAUMA

> Fear and trembling have beset me; horror has overwhelmed me.
> I said, "Oh, that I had the wings of a dove! I would fly away and be at rest.
> ~Psalm 55:5-6

Many of us define trauma as something that happens to us, but it is more about what happens inside of us as the result of highly distressing circumstances that may be perceived as life-threatening.[48] Some people have a much lower threshold to traumatization, particularly children, but it is also very common for victims of coercive control to experience all the signs of post-traumatic stress. People diagnosed with PTSD seem to get in stuck a constant state of hyperarousal. Their brains default to a physiological state that scientists have termed the fight or flight response, in which any perception of threat activates the sympathetic nervous system and triggers an acute stress response that prepares the body to fight or flee. In addition to fight or flight, we see responses such as freezing—becoming paralyzed by fear, fawning—doing our best to placate our abusers, and fainting—shutting down. Even after I escaped the danger of my abusive marriage, my body continued to experience aftershocks. I often woke up in a panic from nightmares that usually involved my husband coming at me with a gun or knife. I was constantly on guard, felt numb, and lacked motivation to complete daily tasks. Basically, I found no pleasure in life and often found myself fixating on the wrongs and injustices I had suffered. I didn't realize it at the time, but my symptoms were consistent with PTSD (post-traumatic stress disorder). After working with survivors for over twenty years, I have found that most of them and their children experience the same thing. Signs of PTSD include, but are not limited to:

- Hypervigilance. Your brain is on high alert and you're constantly on guard. You feel jumpy or easily startled, even in the absence of legitimate danger.
- Intrusions. This may include flashbacks or panic attacks. When something reminds you of past traumatic experiences, you feel anxious. The feelings can seem as real as when the actual experiences happened.

---

[48] Levine, Peter A, PH.D., *Healing Trauma*, (Boulder, CO, 2008) Sounds True, Inc., p. 7.

- Recurring nightmares. You experience dreams about the trauma or about something similar happening again and again.
- Feelings of numbness. You are unable to feel pleasure in things that used to please you.
- Feeling emotionally cut off from others.
- Sleep disturbances and an inability to concentrate.
- Feeling irritable, angry outbursts, and overreacting to things.
- Feelings of guilt, regret, and shame that you couldn't stop what happened to you and your children. You often replay events in your mind and berate yourself for failing to do something to prevent it.
- Avoidance. You go to great lengths to avoid anything that triggers memories of traumatic events you experienced.
- Shame. You feel ashamed and defective at the core. You see yourself as unlovable and unworthy.
- Absolutism. Trauma survivors tend to think in absolute terms. "Examples include thoughts such as, 'The world is completely unsafe, No one can be trusted, and All men are dangerous.'"[49] Overcoming this sort of thinking will be an important part of your healing process.
- Health issues. Extreme stress can wreak havoc on the immune system. Many women I've worked with over the years have experienced a multitude of maladies that cleared up after they got out of abuse. Some of the typical symptoms found in survivors of coercive control include:
    - Autoimmune issues
    - Endocrine problems such as thyroid malfunction
    - High blood pressure
    - Chronic pain and fibromyalgia
    - Migraine headaches
    - Asthma
    - Depression and anxiety
    - Digestive problems (spastic colon)
    - Reproductive issues and miscarriage

Studies indicate that around 80 percent of those who have experienced domestic abuse suffer from post-traumatic stress.[50] Although people have always suffered the impacts of traumatic events, PTSD did not become an official diagnosis until 1980. Before that, terms were coined to describe what we now know to be its symptoms. It was widely seen among combat veterans and given labels like "shell shock" and "combat fatigue."[51] These conditions were directly correlated to a history of exposure to traumatic

---

[49] Broom, Beth Trauma (2023), "Healing for Abuse Survivors" in Chris Moles (Ed.), *Caring for Families Caught in Domestic Abuse* (p.93), New Growth Press.

[50] Kubany, Edward S., Mari A. McCaig and Janet Laconsay, *Healing the Trauma of Domestic Violence: A Workbook for Women* (Oakland, New Harninger Publications, 2004) 15.

[51] Osei-Boamah, Emmanual, MD; Pilkins, Brunhilde J.; Gambert, Steven R., MD, "Post-Traumatic Stress Disorder: A Historical Perspective of an Evolving Diagnosis," in *Consultant 360*, Volume 21 - Number 6 - June 201. Accessed July 5, 2024 at 3https://tinyurl.com/mr2w3wkd.

events that put the soldiers in fear of death or severe injury or left them feeling helpless to change the outcome of those incidents. In recent years, researchers have discovered that victims of various types of abuse experience the same symptoms as combat veterans, and symptoms can occur in the absence of an overtly traumatic event. Living with intense, prolonged stress from oppression stemming from behaviors described on the Power and Control Wheel can leave victims of domestic abuse traumatized, and it seems that when harm is done by someone who is supposed to love and care for you the impacts are intensified.[52]

By its very nature, domestic abuse is characterized by a repeated pattern of destructive behavior. Over time, continual attacks using tactics like coercion and threats, mind games, leveraging the children, financial abuse, name-calling, isolation, and twisting Scripture to maintain control takes its toll. Eventually, the victims' thought processes completely change, and they find it hard to remember what they were like before the abuse began. In recent years, the term Complex-PTSD (C-PTSD) was devised to describe the impacts of this prolonged type of traumatic stress. In addition to the common signs of PTSD, victims of C-PTSD may also struggle with the following: emotional regulation, distorted perceptions of themselves and their abusers, dissociation, impaired relational skills, feelings of hopelessness, and even loss of their basic beliefs about the meaning of life, including their faith in God.[53] I have observed these added impacts of long-term trauma on victims of abuse hundreds of times over, especially when it comes to matters of faith.

Nearly all the survivors I have worked with over the years have experienced a crisis of faith at some point, especially when they reached out to Christian friends, counselors, and pastors for help, only to be told they needed to work harder on saving their marriages. The advice most received was exactly what they had already been doing, yet well-meaning advisors were convinced they were somehow at fault and not doing it well enough. This sort of response leaves victims feeling blamed, guilty, and hopeless. Many believe that if other Christians condemn them, God must too. If this has happened to you, dear friend, I pray that the information in these pages will encourage you to hope again.

God does not condemn you for seeking freedom from oppression. In fact, He hates oppression and injustice (Jeremiah 22:3, Isaiah 58:9-10, Psalm 12:5, 35:10, 82:3-4). The Bible is filled with stories of God's children running from those who intended to harm them. A few examples include David, who escaped being harmed by King Saul (1 Samuel 16-31), Elijah, who ran from Queen Jezebel (1 Kings 19:2), and Paul who fled the Jewish leaders (Acts 9:23-30). Proverbs 27:12 tells us "the prudent see danger and take refuge…" Even though people may, God does not diminish the mistreatment you have endured. He graciously used 1 Corinthians 7:15 to let me know He was calling me to peace. The day He quickened that verse to me, I knew it meant I could remove myself from the bondage and torture I was enduring. Even if you are unable to leave, I want you to know that God is calling you to peace. It may look different in your situation, but no matter what, God is for you (Psalm 56:9, Romans 8:31).

---

[52] Platt, Melissa, Jocelyn Barton, and Jennifer J. Freyd (2009), "A Betrayal Trauma Perspective on Domestic Violence" in Stark, Evan Stark and Eve S. Buzawa (Eds.), *Violence Against Women in Families and Relationships: Victimization and the Community Response*, (pp.190-198), Bloomsbury Publishing USA.

[53] Herman, Judith, *Trauma and Recovery: The Aftermath of Violence—from Domestic Abuse to Political Terror* (New York, Basic Books, 1997) 121-122.

A CHANGE IN TERMINOLOGY

Now that we've looked at the history and research on PTSD, I want to share a change in terminology. In his book, *I Have PTSD: Reorienting After Trauma*, Curtis Solomon suggested that we remove "disorder" from our descriptions of post-traumatic stress, and I love his rationale below. Therefore, I am adopting the acronym PTS to describe post-traumatic stress throughout the remainder of this workbook.

> "I prefer to call [trauma] responses post-traumatic stress (PTS) rather than post-traumatic stress disorder. Why? First, adding the word "disorder" to post-traumatic stress can communicate that you, the sufferer, are disordered—that you are somehow weaker or lesser than others. Many people who are diagnosed with PTSD feel like something is inherently wrong with them. They worry they are weak, freakish, broken, or abnormal. One important truth I want you to take away… is that your experience of these symptoms is not an abnormal response to everyday life. It is a common response to extreme suffering."[54]

PRACTICES TO PROMOTE HEALING

Healing from PTS takes time, but it is not impossible in most cases. One thing is for sure, the process must be intentional. It will not go away on its own. Below are some helpful steps that should prove helpful in your healing process.

1. *Remove yourself from the source of the trauma or work on your ability to not react to it* (Proverbs 16:32, 22:24, 27;12, 29:11, and James 1:19—these verses are included at the end of this lesson). If you are still living in an abusive situation, it will be much more challenging to heal because you will be exposed to constant triggers. However, as mentioned in *CTP*, there can be valid reasons for staying. If you choose to stay it is wise to try to create space that supports healing. Limiting situations that make you more susceptible to abuse can be helpful, and it is important that you create a safety plan whether you choose to stay or leave.[55] Those who remain will want to attempt to create physical, emotional, psychological, and spiritual boundaries that may include not riding in the car together, not sharing a bedroom, not having physical intimacy, separating finances, and other suggestions listed on the Safety Plan in the back of the book. Leslie Vernick has many excellent resources for those who want to attempt to stay well in destructive marriages.[56]

2. *Identify lies you've come to believe because of abuse and fill your mind with truths that counter them* (2 Corinthians 10:5, Philippians 4:6-8, Romans 12:2). This includes making excuses for the abuse and all forms of negative self-talk, including, "I should/could have…", or critical

---

[54] Solomon, Curtis. I Have PTSD: Reorienting after Trauma (p. 27). New Growth Press. Kindle Edition.
[55] See Appendix D, Creating a Safety Plan.
[56] Leslie's book, *The Emotionally Destructive Marriage* offers great information on staying well in a destructive marriage. Visit her website, leslievernick.com for additional resources.

thoughts that suggest you are less than who God says you are. Find and proclaim Scriptural truths that refute the lies. It's a good idea to write out and read helpful passages aloud when you find yourself overcome by overwhelming thoughts and emotions. Pray and meditate on these truths often. (Lesson 2).

3. *Deal with regret and guilt (2 Corinthians 7:10b). Studies show that guilt is a major factor in stalling healing from PTS.* Remember that God is both sovereign and good. He wants to use *all* of your story for good, even your mistakes. Grieve your losses well and commit your life to His loving care (Lesson 9). Please note that abusers often use guilt to maintain control over us, and it takes a while to correct the faulty beliefs behind such guilt. When you are first breaking free from abuse, the following guideline is extremely helpful; "If a decision will lead to either guilt or resentment, go with guilt!" Abusive people almost always use guilt as a tool to manipulate, so most likely you're feeling guilt even when you've done nothing wrong. It is helpful to remember you've been conditioned to feel guilty for saying no to your abuser's demands, even when giving in promotes his selfish (sinful) agenda. Bowing down to sin is neither loving him well nor honoring to God. (Lesson13).

4. *Recognize that God is in charge and greater than anyone or anything you've faced* (Jeremiah 32:27, Colossians 1:17, Job 42:2, Romans 8:28). One of the reasons PTS lingers in so many of us is that we feel powerless to change things. Recognizing that you are in His hands and that He has a good plan for you will counter feelings of helplessness. Worshipping, gratitude, and intentionally making Him bigger than your abuser is powerful (exalting Him). (Lesson 15).

5. *Practice intentional "escape and avoidance busting"* (Isaiah 41:10, Psalm 46:1-5, Deuteronomy 31:6). When we have PTS, we can find ourselves easily panicked by the tiniest reminders of the past. Something as simple as a smell can set off an internal fight or flight (adrenaline) response that defies all logic, but there is a way to overcome these triggers. If something harmless still triggers you (start with the little ones), you can intentionally expose yourself to it until your reaction is reversed.[57] You may want to enlist the help of someone you love and trust to help if you are uneasy about trying this alone. When practicing this method, it is important to recognize and counter any untrue thoughts that come up with the trauma. Nearly always, unhealed trauma is reinforced by lies. We must be intentional to combat not only the lies we've come to believe, but also the reactions of our bodies to triggers. I once heard a domestic violence/trauma expert say, "Every time you avoid a trigger, you're feeding your PTSD."[58] Ultimately, healing from the trauma you've experienced will require you to overcome, rather than defer to, your triggers.

6. *Utilize healing techniques that engage the entire brain.* A somatic fear response is a normal God-given response to danger, but people with PTS experience these symptoms in the absence of current danger when the smallest reminder of past trauma triggers their internal fight or flight response. Since panic stemming from trauma arises from the autonomic parts of our brain, it

---

[57] Kubany et al., *Healing the Trauma of Domestic Violence*, 84.

[58] You can find this interview on Called to Peace Ministries' YouTube channel under the title, "Healing from PTSD with Julie Owens."

seems clear that remedying it requires methods that transcend reason alone. For example, music and meditation activate the entire brain, making it easier for the truth to get through to traumatized areas. In recent years, techniques such as Eye Movement Desensitization and Reprocessing (EMDR), brain spotting, somatic experiencing, and many other somatic techniques have become very popular with trauma therapists.[59] Hundreds of survivors we have worked with have attested to the benefits of these methods.

7. *Meditate on Scripture.* I believe the Bible also offers us a way to reach the traumatized parts of our brains. It is filled with commands for us to meditate on Scripture, and studies show that meditation reaches parts of the brain that reason alone cannot.[60] I did not realize it at the time, but I believe this is how God brought healing into my life. "When I say I meditated, I don't mean I repeated or prayed a verse a few times. I posted helpful Bible verses all over the walls of my house, ran to them during panic attacks, prayed them out loud repeatedly, and asked God to implant His truth in my spirit. At times, I rocked on my bed as I sang to Him and imagined myself in passages of Scripture, like Zephaniah 3:17, that describes the Lord rejoicing and tenderly singing over His child. This meditation was a continual process that involved every facet of my being— physical, emotional, and spiritual. Over time, I truly learned to "cast down" negative imaginations (2 Corinthians 10:5, NKJV) by persistently replacing them with His truth. In the beginning, allowing my mind to go idle for any amount of time usually meant the troubling thoughts would return, so I added worship music to my routine and chose to meditate on God's goodness instead."[61]

Over the years, I have found that quoting Scripture alone does not have the same effect as interacting with the Word and ruminating on it. Isaiah 26:3 tells us that God will keep "in perfect peace whose mind is stayed on [Him] (ESV). The Hebrew word translated as "mind" here can be translated as "imagination," and I believe we must engage our imaginations in this process. Most trauma survivors have overactive imaginations filled with distressing images, and replacing those images with truth from His Word is an effective and necessary part of Biblical meditation.

8. *Practice relaxation and grounding techniques.* There are a multitude of activities that can help reduce trauma responses in your body, including grounding exercises that can help soothe trauma responses.[62] Activities like art therapy, massage, and movement can also help. In recent years, numerous apps and YouTube channels have been created to help with relaxation that pair nature scenes and sounds with soft music. I particularly love a YouTube channel

---

[59] While EMDR is has been controversial among some in the biblical counseling movement, it simply involves bilateral stimulation (typically eye movements) to help awaken the autonomic parts of the brain, where trauma is held, to help desensitize the body's response to trauma. In recent years, the Biblical Counseling Coalition made a statement on EMDR rejecting the claims of some that the practice is sinful, which was posted on the organization's blog December 16, 2021 at www.biblicalcounselingcoalition.org.

[60] Van der Kolk, Bessel, *The Body Keeps the Score*, (New York, Penguin Books, 2014) 63-64.

[61] This article I wrote for the Biblical Counseling Coalition for counselors outlines a process of biblical meditation for trauma-related panic— visit https://tinyurl.com/574tw2bz.

[62] Visit https://tinyurl.com/349y7r4w for a sample of some methods you can try.

called Soakstream that will quietly read Bible passages to you. You can even choose to listen to those read by a female voice if you are triggered by male voices reading Scripture. Listening to music and meditating on the Word are potent ways to promote healing.

Finally, one of the easiest and most helpful things you can do to calm yourself when triggered is to take a deep breath and slowly release it. Slow breathing exercises have been shown to help calm the nervous system and lower our heart rate.[63] I recommend you learn and practice at least one exercise regularly so that when a trigger happens you will be ready to do it naturally.[64] Did you know that the name of God, YHWH, is associated with breath? When the letters, or characters, of His name are pronounced, they make the sound of a single breath, both inhaling and exhaling. Some Jewish rabbis say that with every breath we take, we are speaking God's name. When I do these breathing exercises, I imagine myself breathing in the fullness of His Spirit and exhaling all my cares to Him. Whatever breathing technique you decide to use, it will be beneficial to pair it with meditative prayer.

9. *Find support in community.* One of the ways abusers keep us from healing is by isolating us from people who might support us. Oddly enough, once we get out, we sometimes continue this trend by choice. However, Scripture talks a lot about the power of fellowship with others. Sadly, not everyone is worthy of your trust, so try to find churches, support groups, or people who understand domestic abuse and coercive control. There are healthy, loving people out there, but sometimes, you may need to make new connections to find them. Called to Peace Ministries offers local and online support groups that help get you started. Visit www.calledtopeace.org to learn more.

10. *Refuse mistreatment and speak truth in love.* To heal and stay healthy, we must learn how to challenge sin and refuse to allow further mistreatment. You will likely need to disengage or limit your contact with your abuser. This is true whether you choose to leave or stay. See point one above for more about this. (Lessons 10 & 11).

11. *Make God the center of your life.* Most of us who have lived with abuse have unconsciously allowed our abusers, or our marriages, to become the center of our lives. We allowed pleasing a person to become more important than pleasing Him. Unhealthy fear of man eclipsed our fear of the Lord. When He is truly the center of our life, we will not be as easily enticed to bow down someone else (Lessons 8 and 15).

---

[63] Zaccaro, A. *et al.* How breath-control can change your life: A systematic review on psycho-physiological correlates of slow breathing. *Front. Hum. Neurosci.* 12, 353.

[64] There are several deep breathing exercises that can be helpful, but I've noticed that what works for one person may not be as helpful to another, so I suggest you do a little research. The following article lists out several of the most popular techniques to help get you started. https://tinyurl.com/3npzuj2f.

SUMMARY

Healing from PTS is a multifaceted process that takes time and does not look the same from one survivor to another. Both Scripture and brain research tell us that healing is possible. To be restored, you will need to make some important choices, including facing the truth about what happened to you and identifying lies that are keeping you stuck. You will want to replace the negative running narrative in your mind with truth from God's Word using methods that get that truth to the autonomic parts of your brain. This will require patience and persistence, because it will take time. When I say this, I mean it typically takes years, rather than weeks or months. You will very likely experience setbacks, but don't give up, just keep repeating what has been helpful so far. A trauma-informed counselor/therapist, using biblically sound counseling practices, is ideal to help you find the path forward.[65] However, even the best therapist cannot be with you 24/7, and I believe moment-by-moment choices you make will either help or hinder your progress. As you intentionally choose to meditate on truths that counter the negative narrative in your mind, you will find restoration.

"You were taught, with regard to your former way of life, to put off your old self, which is being corrupted by its deceitful desires; to be made new in the attitude of your minds; and to put on the new self, created to be like God in true righteousness and holiness" (Ephesians 4:22-24). I believe that this Scriptural model of "putting off" and "putting on" can help you find the path to freedom. It is much easier to replace our old ways than to stop them. If you've ever tried to quit something cold turkey, you might have experienced this phenomenon—just the thought of stopping might have made you more focused on, and desirous of, what you were giving up. Finding a positive replacement for whatever you want to stop will be far more effective than pouring all your effort into stopping it. A few years after I got out of the abuse, the Holy Spirit convicted me that I was a complainer, and I determined I would stop it. However, that proved to be harder than I imagined. It wasn't until I began to thank and praise God each time I was tempted to complain that I was able to find victory over complaining. The idea of "putting on" reminds us of Ephesians 6:11, that commands us to "put on the full armor of God." This means we are not left to our own devices to overcome our struggles. Instead, we have a God who enters our hardships and empowers us to overcome by His Spirit. That, my friend, is a beautiful thing, and as I conclude this lesson, I am praying that as you draw near to Him, you will experience the supernatural power and presence of our great God to overcome your past. May He give you "a crown of beauty for ashes, the oil of joy instead of mourning, and a garment of praise instead of a spirit of despair" (Isaiah 61:3).

---

[65] When I refer to biblically sound counseling practices, I mean those that line up with Scripture principles, especially those that focus on correcting lies with truth in conjunction with whole brain methods. See Lesson 4 for more on unhelpful practices. The Association of Biblical Counselors, (https://christiancounseling.com) and The Christian Trauma Healing Network (https://christiantraumahealingnetwork.org) are two Christian organizations training counselors on the dynamics of abuse and trauma.

LESSON 5 EXERCISES

1. This week take the time to intentionally journal negative self-talk and beliefs. You might want to set an alarm several times a day and write down these thoughts. Is there a time of day when you particularly struggle with negative emotions? If so, be sure to set your alarm to include this time. Statements to be included often sound like this:

   - I should have never…
   - I can't believe I was so stupid!
   - I will never be able to move past this.
   - My children are doomed because of what they experienced. If God cared, why did He allow this to happen?
   - My situation is hopeless.
   - I'm not worthy of a better life. I can't do anything right.
   - The abuse was my fault.
   - Why didn't I do…so I didn't end up here?

   You get the idea. Remember that you will need stop beating yourself up over the past if you want to heal. This process should be repeated on a regular basis to assess whether your thinking lines up with God's truth.

2. After you have identified the negative thoughts, identify the lies behind them and write down a truth to counter each one. Refer to the Scripture Database in the back of this workbook to identify helpful passages to help. Write out a few helpful passages below.

3. This week try to repeat an appropriate passage when you catch yourself sliding back into negative thoughts. (Setting alarms to check your thoughts might be useful for this exercise). In addition to repeating Scriptures, be sure to meditate on them and pray them back to God. Imagine yourself in the passage and thank Him for His promises to you. Speak the truth out loud and constantly fill your mind with it. You might even want to incorporate an activity like tapping to help engage traumatized parts of the brain.[66] Write out below some things God has shown you as you have done these exercises.

4. Identify some helpful suggestions listed in the lesson. Choose two to intentionally practice this week and write out what happened below. Over time, try to add more techniques to your arsenal of resources.

5. Continue to journal and note how you are progressing in your healing journey. As you move through the remaining lessons in this workbook, please keep in mind the techniques you have learned here. If you still find yourself easily triggered, be sure incorporate healing strategies that will reach the traumatized areas of your brain. Write out your successes and struggles with this below.

---

[66] There are several videos online that teach simple tapping techniques for trauma. There is one called the butterfly hug that many of our clients have found helpful. These techniques merely awaken the subconscious/autonomic parts of our brains so that truth can be received.

6. Write out a prayer for your healing based on the results of the exercises you have done this week.

Notes

LESSON 6

MANAGING YOUR EMOTIONS
Taming Your Thought Life

For as a man thinks within himself, so is he...
~ Proverbs 23:7

After coming out of abuse, our emotions can often get the best of us. We may find ourselves overwhelmed by numerous feelings like sorrow, anger, and shame, or we may find ourselves too numb to feel anything at all. No matter which end of the emotional spectrum you are on, you should know that emotional regulation is a common struggle for abuse survivors. However, we can find victory over erratic emotions by altering the way we think because thoughts drive emotions.

Years ago, I was counseling a woman struggling with severe depression. She had a history of childhood sexual abuse, which explained her struggle. As we talked further, she reported that there were certain times of the day when her depression seemed to worsen. I was trying to discern if she knew what might have been triggering the sudden worsening of symptoms and asked if there were any specific thoughts in her head during the times she struggled most. Her immediate response was that she didn't really think that much during those times, so I challenged her to set an alarm to go off during those times the following week and record what she was thinking at the time. When we met again a few weeks later, she reported that the timer had helped her recognize that she had a constant negative narrative running in her head. That realization was the beginning of freedom for her as she eventually learned to counter the lies contained in those negative thoughts with the truth of Scripture.

After we receive Christ as our Savior, Satan's power over our souls is broken. Nothing can ever snatch us out of God's hands, but our enemy knows we have the freedom to choose our thoughts, so most of his attacks are aimed at our thought life. We must be on guard against deception, and it is easy to be deceived after we have experienced trauma. Often, our minds automatically default to dwelling on what has happened to us, and we tend to add a false narrative that explains what happened. Examples of this sort of thinking might sound like, "If I had been a better wife, he wouldn't have cheated," "I'll never heal from this," "God is punishing me for my sins," and more. I've told myself these lies, and most survivors have done the same. The problem with this type of reasoning is that our thoughts eventually sway our emotions. Allowing our minds to dwell on the trauma we've experienced can leave us overcome with emotions like fear, sadness, anger, and shame.

We are created in God's image with emotions like His. He designed us to have feelings; however, like everything else in creation, the Fall has skewed how they manifest in our lives. A good, healthy purpose for our emotions is to help us recognize what is happening in the world around us. They can alert us when something is wrong and enhance our experience when things are good. They are indicators of both good and bad and being aware of them is important to our well-being. However, problems occur when our emotions overwhelm us and start controlling our actions. To find victory over problematic emotions, we need to start by conquering our thought life, but first, let's look at some general truths about emotions.

POINTS TO CONSIDER

1. God is an emotional being (Genesis 6:5-6 — regret, Exodus 32:9-10 — anger, Isaiah 30:18 — compassion, John 11:35-36 — grief).
2. We are made in God's image, and emotions are neither good nor bad, but ours have been skewed by the Fall and can become unstable (Jeremiah 17:9, Genesis 4:6-7).
3. God cares about our emotions. In Scripture, He seems to command emotions as much as He commands actions (i.e., don't be anxious, don't let the sun go down on your anger, etc.).
4. It's not easy to control our emotions, especially after trauma. Without His help, it can seem impossible. Thankfully, He gives us His Spirit, so change becomes a supernatural process (Matthew 6:25-34, Nehemiah 8:9-12).
5. Strong emotion can reveal who or what has lordship over our hearts. Overwhelming emotions are like dashboard lights in a car. They reveal something wrong on the inside. Depression is a strong emotion. Many times, it is a response that says there is no hope and questions God's goodness. Trauma invades our minds, so we stop meditating on God, and our emotions get out of whack. There is transforming power in worship because it puts God in His place and us in ours. Proper emotions and affections arise out of hearts that love God with all their heart, soul, and strength.[67]

KEYS TO OVERCOMING OVERWHELMING EMOTIONS

1. *Understand it is common to experience strong emotions or numbness after abuse.* Your emotions are not wrong, but it is important to learn to express them in a healthy way.
2. *Although we can't always stop the overwhelming emotions, we should not allow them to control us or our decisions.* Sadly, strong emotions can work against us. Many of us are rightfully angry about what has happened to us, but the way we express it can cause people, including helpers, to see us as the problem. The problem is not having emotions but allowing them to take over. We must strive to use wisdom and yield to His Spirit instead (Galatians 5:16). It is normal to

---

[67] Taken from class notes from a counseling class on dealing with problematic emotions with Dr. Sam Williams at Southeastern Baptist Theological Seminary.

make mistakes as you are learning to do this but bring your mistakes to God— and/or a wise counselor— to process what happened as well as ways to do better in the next similar situation.

3. *Realize that His Spirit can enable you to live beyond skewed thoughts and emotions.* We do not have to do it in our own strength. (Colossians 3:1-17 — setting our hearts on His kingdom, 2 Timothy 1:7 — power over fear, John 14:26-2 — peace through the Spirit, Romans 12:1-2 — victory through renewed minds).

4. *Pour out your heart and emotions to God (Psalm 62:8, Lamentations 2:18-19) and perhaps a safe person.* Journaling to Him and meditating on His promises that counter false beliefs connected to the abuse is helpful. The meditation suggestions in Lesson 5 can bring peace and healing as you practice them.

5. *Recognize that God is in control, and He loves you.* Even when bad things happen, He promises to work them together for your good because you are His child (Romans 8:28-29). As you learn to trust God, your emotions will become more stable. Understanding His love and ability to redeem is so beneficial for your emotional well-being.

6. *When we choose to line our thinking up with His truth, our emotions will follow.* This is not a one-time event. It is a process that takes time, but as we take every thought captive by meditating on His truth, we will eventually find our emotions becoming less erratic.

7. *Remember, it's a choice! You must intentionally choose to change your thoughts (Philippians 4:6-9, 2 Corinthians 10:5).* It can be a struggle, but His Spirit dwelling in you will empower you in your weakness (2 Corinthians 12:9).

8. *Our desire for Him should be greater than our desire for anything else, including a change in circumstances.* This is not to say you should tolerate abuse! However, I have seen so much freedom come to those who put Him first. Those who seek His kingdom first can be assured He will take care of their every need (Matthew 6:25-34). Ask yourself what you desire most and remember that connecting with Him will help stabilize your emotions (Psalms 42:1-3 & 43). Psalms, in general, are very helpful when we are overwhelmed with emotion.

9. *Setting our minds on the Spirit brings life and peace.* One day, God highlighted Romans 8:6, to in the NASB to me, "For the mind set on the flesh is death, but the mind set on the Spirit is life and peace." Do you see that, friend? If you can succeed in setting your mind—or intentionally meditating—on Him that peace will be yours!

Ed Welch, author of *Depression: A Stubborn Darkness*, has a formula for the causes of depression. I believe this applies to all troublesome emotions.

1) Spiritual problems that remain unresolved and unaddressed will ferment.
2) Time/history of choices develops habitual patterns of responses. Many abuse survivors respond to new relationships with old habit patterns. Examples of these patterns would include ungodly anger, self-pity (victim mentality), bitterness, unforgiveness, clamming up, isolation/withdrawal, irresponsibility, procrastination, apathy, and fear. Just as we can develop bad response habits, we can develop good ones—even after trauma. We can determine to respond in a godly manner even amid horrible circumstances. If we choose to obey and follow Him, He will give us hope no matter what we are facing. Overcoming poor response habits will take time and support.

3) Biogenetic predispositions - the effects of the Fall on mankind. Here on earth, some of our emotions are processed through our bodies. We are not all spirit—our bodies do play a role. However, the physical issues do not cause us to sin. We still have a choice.

SCRIPTURE REFERENCES

- **Proverbs 22:24-25** — Do not make friends with a hot-tempered person, do not associate with one easily angered, or you may learn their ways and get yourself ensnared
- **Proverbs 27:12** — The prudent see danger and take refuge, but the simple keep going and pay the penalty.
- **Proverbs 16:32** — He who is slow to anger is better than the mighty, and he who rules his spirit, than he who captures a city (NASB).
- **Proverbs 29:11** — Fools give full vent to their rage, but the wise bring calm in the end.
- **James 1:19** — My dear brothers and sisters, take note of this: Everyone should be quick to listen, slow to speak and slow to become angry...
- **2 Corinthians 10:5** — We demolish arguments and every pretension that sets itself up against the knowledge of God, and we take captive every thought to make it obedient to Christ.
- **Philippians 4:8** — Finally, brothers and sisters, whatever is true, whatever is noble, whatever is right, whatever is pure, whatever is lovely, whatever is admirable—if anything is excellent or praiseworthy—think about such things.
- **Romans 12:2** — Do not conform to the pattern of this world but be transformed by the renewing of your mind. Then you will be able to test and approve what God's will is—His good, pleasing, and perfect will.
- **2 Corinthians 7:10b** — ... but worldly sorrow leads to regret.
- **Jeremiah 32:27** — I am the LORD, the God of all mankind. Is anything too hard for me?
- **Colossians 1:17** — He is before all things, and in Him all things hold together.
- **Job 42:2** — I know that You can do all things; no purpose of Yours can be thwarted.
- **Romans 8:28** — And we know that in all things God works for the good of those who love Him, who have been called according to His purpose.
- **Isaiah 41:10** — So do not fear, for I am with you; do not be dismayed, for I am your God. I will strengthen you and help you; I will uphold you with My righteous right hand.
- **Psalm 46:1-5** — God is our refuge and strength, an ever-present help in trouble. Therefore, we will not fear, though the earth give way and the mountains fall into the heart of the sea, though its waters roar and foam and the mountains quake with their surging. There is a river whose streams make glad the city of God, the holy place where the Most High dwells. God is within her; she will not fall; God will help her at break of day.
- **Deuteronomy 31:6** —Be strong and courageous. Do not be afraid or terrified because of them, for the LORD your God goes with you; He will never leave you nor forsake you.

LESSON 6 EXERCISES

1. Read Chapter 12 in *Called to Peace* and take notes on points that speak to your struggles with overwhelming emotions.

2. "For though we live in the world, we do not wage war as the world does. The weapons we fight with are not the weapons of the world. On the contrary, they have divine power to demolish strongholds. We demolish arguments and every pretension that sets itself up against the knowledge of God, and we take captive every thought to make it obedient to Christ" (2 Corinthians 10:3-5).

   How does this passage speak to struggles in your thought life? Are there recurring thoughts that need to be brought captive to the obedience of Jesus? Is the enemy using hurts from your past to keep you locked into unhealthy thought patterns? Does your way of thinking keep you from experiencing the abundant life Jesus promises you? Explain below.

3. Read Romans 12:1-2. Ask God to show you areas of your thought life that need to be renewed by Him (ex. doubts, fears, bitterness, temptations, etc.). List them here.

4. Read Ephesians 6:10-18. God provides us with weapons to win spiritual battles. What are those weapons? How do you use them? Remember that His strength is made perfect in your weakness (2 Corinthians 12:9).

5. First, Peter 5:7 urges us to "Cast all your anxiety on Him because He cares for you." This means you can entrust all your worries and fears to Him. What unsettling thoughts do you need to cast on Him? How will you resist those thoughts? Write out your plan.

6. Colossians 3:1-16 talks about setting our minds on Him and walking in His Spirit. God gives us specific instructions for overcoming the problems of this world, but we must choose to follow them. What does this passage say to you about your thought life?

7. Read the following passages and journal how they apply to what you are feeling and believing right now.
   - Isaiah 26:3 — You will keep him in perfect peace, whose mind is stayed on You, Because he trusts in You (NKJV).

   - Romans 8:6 — "For the mind set on the flesh is death, but the mind set on the Spirit is life and peace" (NASB).

8. Scripture is filled with stories of those who struggled with overwhelming emotions. Check out the following examples and see if you can relate. Journal any insights you get from your reading.
   - 1 Kings 18:17-19:19 — Elijah's victory at Mount Carmel followed by great fear and fleeing Jezebel

   - Jonah 4 — Jonah's anger at God when He saved Ninevah

   - Lamentations 3:19-26 — Hope in affliction after Judah's great destruction and captivity

   - 2 Kings 18:17-19:34 — Hezekiah's response to the threats and false charges of the Assyrians

Psalms 42:1-2. As the deer pants for streams of water, so my soul pants for you, my God. My soul thirsts for God, for the living God. When can I go and meet with God?

Notes

LESSON 7

OVERCOMING FEAR

> There is no fear in love. But perfect love drives out fear, because fear has to
> do with punishment. The one who fears is not made perfect in love.
> ~ *1 John 4:18*

For years, I was crippled by fear, because I did not fully comprehend the love, kindness, and sovereignty of God. I acted as if He wasn't paying attention, or like the disciples in the storm-tossed boat I thought he might not care that I was sinking (Mark 4:38). I did what I call "the dance of fear" trying to keep my husband happy so he wouldn't lash out. I basically feared and served him more faithfully than I did God. When I lived in fear, I lived with shame. Everything was hidden. I did not want people to know the truth about what went on behind closed doors in our home, so the children and I kept many secrets. I was ashamed that our family was so damaged and that I could not fix it. I did everything in my power to control circumstances, but my fears only increased as it became clear that all my solutions had failed. When the light finally came shining in to expose the awfulness behind the façade, our shame was exposed to the world. It was a terrible, but wonderful, place to be. At the time I did not see it as wonderful at all. I was devastated and overwhelmed. Only in retrospect could I see how freeing it was. It was terrible, because all my secrets were exposed, and I was betrayed by the person who had become my world. It was wonderful, because his reign in my life ended when I finally relinquished *everything* to God Who was and ever shall be enough!

Before I surrendered to God, my primary goal in life was to please my husband, and my primary desire was to have him respond with love and kindness, but it never happened. However, my true Lord had never stopped loving and caring for me. He had always been with me, and I didn't have to jump through hoops to win His approval. I had just been too blind to see it, as fear of man had gradually obscured His goodness from my sight. God says that His perfect love will rid us of fear (1 John 4:18), but abuse and trauma warp our view of Him so that we become unable to comprehend or receive it. The better we know Him, the less we will fear. To know Him is to know love, because He is love (1 John 4:8). As I found comfort in His love and care, my fears diminished.

Love is the defining characteristic of God, and the greatest expression of God's love for you is communicated in John 3:16. He loved you so much that He gave His one and only Son to redeem your soul! When you put your trust in Him, you not only receive eternal life but are adopted into His family. When children are afraid, it is normal for them to run to their parents. Even most flawed earthly parents will respond to their frightened children by holding them, and Scripture gives us a beautiful picture of our perfect God doing the same for us. There are numerous verses that mention God hiding us in the "shelter of His wing" even as a mother hen hides her chicks from harm (Psalms 91:4, 17:8, Matthew 23:37). He promises to be a very present help in trouble (Psalm 46:1), but He doesn't promise there won't be trouble. In every fearful event of life, we are faced with a choice. It is a choice that says, "even though the storms of life are raging, I know He is in control, and I will trust Him with my life. Even if He does not immediately rescue me when bad things happen, He still has my best interest at heart and will redeem my pain."

This does not mean we don't remove ourselves from danger or try to improve circumstances when we have the power to do so. There is a healthy, God-given fear that protects us when we are in danger. However, it means we do not desperately grasp to control things we cannot control. Fear and control are closely related, because *whatever we fear will gain control of us*. I believe that is why God commands us to fear Him so often in Scripture, and why the fear of the Lord is the beginning of wisdom (Proverbs 9:10). Unlike fear of our abusers, the fear of God is not associated with punishment (I John 4:18). It simply means we desire to honor Him more than anyone or anything else. Will you choose to honor Him by trusting His goodness and love towards you, or will you question His goodness and let fear rule you? Jesus told His disciples not to *let* their hearts be troubled or afraid, but to believe (John 14:1, 27). What a beautiful promise of peace! But that promise is connected to a command that we don't *allow* our hearts to be troubled. Obviously, we can't just turn off our emotions, but we can decide that when fear rolls in, we will proclaim His truth to ourselves. We can determine that His promises are true and that He always has loving intentions towards us. Meditation on truth will bring freedom from the bondage of fear as we resolve to declare it and refuse to be controlled by fear.

HARMFUL EXPRESSIONS OF FEAR

Fear, in and of itself, is not a sin. It is often a trauma response that may require trauma work, as described in Lesson 5, and there is no condemnation for struggling with fear. Still, if you want to heal and move forward, it will be important to overcome it. If we allow fear to take over our responses can become toxic to ourselves and others. We may not even realize how deeply it has affected us. Some of the ways it can manifest include:

- Worry — we rehearse our fear continually, so that it becomes our meditation. Allowing anxious thoughts to have precedence in our minds leads to anxiety.
- Lying — When we are afraid to face the truth the worst lies are the ones we tell ourselves, things like "He didn't mean it," He can't help himself," He loves me, but…" So often, the truth is so painful that we create a false narrative to counter it.
- Judgmental attitudes — people with a lot of insecurity become critical of others to validate themselves.
- Defensiveness.
- A general distrust of people.
- Self-protection.

- A competitive spirit.
- Perfectionism.
- Rebellion — fear of rejection can lead some to rebel against any expectations they feel are being placed on them to avoid messing up and feeling embarrassed.
- Pretense.
- Controlling of others — fear can drive us to want to control circumstances and people.
- Addictive behaviors — may begin as an attempt to calm anxiety.
- Anger — this relates to control. When we can't control things, we may lash out.
- Co-dependency/ people pleasing.

Do you recognize any of these traits in yourself? Oh, dear friend, fear is such a heavy burden to carry. It consumes our thoughts, drives our actions, and is absolutely exhausting. I remember trying so hard to control everything in my world so my husband wouldn't react, or my children wouldn't mess up, but in the end I realized my attempts to control were futile. In this world, things beyond our control happen on a regular basis. The idea of control is just an illusion. Only God, who knows the beginning to the end, is in control, but He doesn't try to micromanage us. He gives us freedom to choose and exercises His control by working all things, including our mess ups and reactions, together for His good purposes (Romans 8:28-32, Ephesians 1:11, 2 Corinthians 4:16-18). He offers rest for your weary soul (Isaiah 40:28-31, Matthew 11:28), and that rest comes from knowing His great love for you. I pray that as you begin to mediate on His goodness you will be able to joyfully surrender every fear to His loving care.

KEYS TO OVERCOMING FEAR

1. *Recognize that God is in control and that He loves you.* He is sovereign, and even when bad things happen, He promises to work them together for your good, because you are His child. As you learn to trust God, your fear will subside. Understanding His sovereignty and ability to redeem is critical for emotional well-being. Although He does not take away our abusers' freedom to sin, He lovingly weaves everything we experience into His good redemptive plan (Genesis 50:19-20). Note: This does not mean we stay in a dangerous situation.
2. *Realize that His Spirit can enable us to overcome fear and anxiety.* You are not alone. He promises to empower you! (2 Timothy 1:7, John 14:26-27, Romans 8:15-16, 26-27).
3. *When we choose to line our thinking up with His truth, our emotions will follow.* This may take time, as my trauma therapist friend, Tabitha Westbrook, says, "Feelings are the caboose of the train," meaning it takes our emotions time to catch up with our thinking, but it does inevitably happen as we commit ourselves to Him. For further study on changing your thought life see Philippians 4:6-9; Isaiah 26:3, 1 Peter 1:6-9, 13; 2 Corinthians 10:3-5, Proverbs 23:4, Romans 8:6, and Psalms 42 & 43.
4. *Abide in His presence and praise Him (Isaiah 41:10, Psalm 3:3, 16:11, 23:4-6, 46:4-5).* Worship makes Him bigger than our problems—we tend to do the opposite by giving our problems first place in our thoughts. Praise and worship music, time spent in nature, and intentional gratitude can help to put Him in His proper place. As we lift Him up He draws us closer and gives us peace that surpasses human comprehension (Psalm 22:3, Philippians 4:7).

5. *Refuse fear, embrace faith, and depend on His Spirit.* This is a moment-by-moment process, filled with choices. You won't always get it right, but as you pour your fears out to Him, proclaim your trust in Him, and depend on His Spirit, your life will change. Journaling through this process or making an audio journal will be helpful. Proclaiming your choice to believe out loud, even before you fully do, will get the truth into the deepest parts of your being.
6. *Get help for trauma-related fear and panic.* See Lesson 5, "Healing From Trauma," for some practical recommendations.

I'd like to close with Psalm 56, that has long been one of my favorites. Notice how the psalmist *chooses* to deal with his fear. I have recited these words many times as I have made the choice to believe rather than fear. If you are struggling with fear, I hope you will pray this psalm now:

> Be merciful to me, my God, for my enemies are in hot pursuit; all day long they press their attack. My adversaries pursue me all day long; in their pride many are attacking me. When I am afraid, I put my trust in You. In God, whose word I praise—in God I trust and am not afraid. What can mere mortals do to me? All day long they twist my words; all their schemes are for my ruin. They conspire, they lurk, they watch my steps, hoping to take my life. Because of their wickedness do not let them escape; in Your anger, God, bring the nations down. Record my misery; list my tears on Your scroll—are they not in Your record? Then my enemies will turn back when I call for help. By this I will know that God is for me. In God, whose word I praise, in the Lord, whose word I praise—in God I trust and am not afraid. What can man do to me? I am under vows to you, My God; I will present my thank offerings to You. For You have delivered me from death and my feet from stumbling, that I may walk before God in the light of life.

LESSON 7 EXERCISES

For you did not receive a spirit that makes you a slave again to fear, but you received a Spirit of adoption. And by Him we cry, "Abba, Father." — Romans 8:15

1. The first step to overcoming the vicious cycle of fear is to replace your unhealthy fears with a proper fear of the Lord. "The fear of the Lord—that is wisdom. And to turn from evil is understanding" (Job 28:28). Are you struggling with anxiety or fear in your thought life? If so, write it out. Be honest and list your fears. If the worst were to happen, what would that mean for your life? What would it mean about God?

2. Philippians 4:6-7 encourages us, "Do not be anxious about anything, but in every situation, by prayer and petition, with thanksgiving, present your requests to God. And the peace of God, which transcends all understanding, will guard your hearts and your minds in Christ Jesus." When you bring your thoughts to the Lord, He will help change your way of thinking. Proclaim Him as Lord over your circumstances and your thoughts. In time you will find that His incredible "peace that passes all understanding" is guarding your heart and mind.

   Write out some of the fears you listed above and, "by prayer and petition, with thanksgiving, present your requests to God." Remember to include thanksgiving as you pray. What can you thank Him for as you pray?

3. "Finally, brothers and sisters, whatever is true, whatever is noble, whatever is right, whatever is pure, whatever is lovely, whatever is admirable—if anything is excellent or praiseworthy—think about such things" (Philippians 4:8).

   With this passage in mind, ask God to show you areas of your thought life that need to be renewed. Begin by identifying untrue thoughts. Write them below and commit them to Him.

4. Use the following verses to help redirect your thoughts.
   - "For God has not given us a spirit of fear, but of power and of love and of a sound mind" (2 Timothy 1:7 — NKJV).

   - "If any of you lacks wisdom, let him ask of God, who gives to all liberally and without reproach, and it will be given to him" (James 1:5).

   Use words from these verses to write and pray a personal declaration of the truth over your life. Focus on the abundant life Jesus promises you!

5. Read the following biblical examples of Daniel and Esther, who handled fear God's way. Write out any insights that come to you as you read and consider how they might relate to your own situation.
   - Daniel 6:6-12, 21-23

   - Esther 4:10-16, 5:1-3

6. Take time to look at the stories of Gideon, Moses, and Jeremiah when they were called to ministry. (Judges 6-8; Exodus 3-4, Jeremiah 1). Write out your observations on how they handled their fear. How could their examples apply in your life right now?

7. Choose a passage below and write it out. Personalize it, memorize it, and meditate on it often.
    - **Psalm 34:4-5** — "I sought the Lord, and He answered me; He delivered me from all my fears. Those who look to Him are radiant; their faces are never covered with shame."
    - **Isaiah 41:10-14** — "So do not fear, for I am with you; do not be dismayed, for I am your God. I will strengthen you and help you; I will uphold you with My righteous right hand. "All who rage against you will surely be ashamed and disgraced; those who oppose you will be as nothing and perish. Though you search for your enemies, you will not find them. Those who wage war against you will be as nothing at all. For I am the LORD your God who takes hold of your right hand and says to you, Do not fear, Do not be afraid, you worm Jacob, little Israel, do not fear, for I myself will help you," declares the LORD, your Redeemer, the Holy One of Israel."
    - **Psalm 27:1-5** — "The Lord is my light and my salvation; whom shall I fear? The Lord is the stronghold of my life; of whom shall I be afraid? When evildoers assail me to eat up my flesh, my adversaries and foes, it is they who stumble and fall. Though an army encamp against me, my heart shall not fear; though war arise against me, yet I will be confident. One thing have I asked of the Lord, that will I seek after: that I may dwell in the house of the Lord all the days of my life, to gaze upon the beauty of the Lord and to inquire in His temple. For He will hide me in His shelter in the day of trouble; He will conceal me under the cover of His tent; He will lift me high upon a rock."
    - **Romans 8:15** — "For you did not receive the spirit of bondage again to fear, but you received the Spirit of adoption by whom we cry out, "Abba, Father." The Spirit Himself bears witness with our spirit that we are children of God" (NKJV).

I'd recommend repeating this process by reading through Psalms.
I particularly like Psalms 23, 27, 34, 55, and 56 for fear.

Notes

LESSON 8

DEALING WITH ANGER

Life in this world is often unfair. Abuse is unfair. Our natural response, often a righteous one, is anger. So, how do we deal with anger without responding sinfully? When we suffer wrongfully at the hands of others, we must choose to respond rather than react. Often, the natural response of our flesh is a desire for vengeance. But if we want to find healing for the deep hurts we've experienced, we must choose to find it on God's terms rather than our own, always remembering that His ways lead to freedom. Jesus displayed anger, but His was righteous. Frequently, ours is not. Becoming upset over violence and injustice is not only understandable, but it is also normal. The problem isn't becoming angry as much as it is failing to deal with it quickly. When we stay in a state of anger and allow it to control us, we are headed for trouble. It seems that unresolved anger opens our lives to Satan's destructive schemes (Ephesians 4:26-27). Jesus' anger was not self-centered, but kingdom centered. Our goal should be to follow His example when dealing with anger. Doing that will require a willingness to commit your responses to Him. It will mean being honest with yourself, and no longer minimizing or making excuses for the abuse—although this might make you angrier temporarily. Entrusting the full weight of the burden to God is an important step in the healing process. Pour out your complaint to God quickly, and do not let it fester. Ask Him to fight your battles, and continually commit your struggles to Him. Sure, there may be actions you will need to take to protect yourself and your children, but you won't have to try to force your version of justice anymore. In time, you will want to choose to forgive your abuser, recognizing that it will set you free and leave justice in God's hands. I recognize that this can be a slow and difficult process but remember that doing things God's way will set you free and help you avoid further abuse in the future. (See the "Anger" portion of Chapter 12 in *CTP*).

Take an honest look at yourself. Do you find yourself engaging in these harmful responses in your relationships?

- Do you criticize, use name-calling, curse, nag, yell, threaten, throw things, belittle, or even get physical and slap or punch when you are upset with others?
- Do you punish them with the silent treatment or gossip about them to others (Please note that getting help is not gossip)?
- Do you hold your anger inside and ruminate on the harm you've experienced?

If you find yourself resorting to these or other sinful responses, would you be willing to let go of your desire for control and allow the Lord to change you? This often involves changing our view of God. If you don't believe He is good, and on your side, you won't be able to trust Him for the outcome. Most of us who have experienced abuse find ourselves questioning His goodness. We may even struggle with anger at Him. I know I did, because there was so much injustice. For a long time, my husband's unceasing cruelty was allowed to continue without consequence. It felt like he had God's favor, and I had been abandoned. However, as I began to meditate on Scripture about God's nature and His faithfulness to those who are suffering, I began to recognize how wrong my view of Him had become. Examine your view of God. Is it faulty? Do you identify with Jesus, but feel distant from the Father? Correct any thinking that is contrary to God's truth. Look at Jesus's choice to enter human suffering and consider how God redeemed suffering in Scripture. There are so many stories to ponder including Joseph, Esther, Ruth, David, the apostles, and many more. Resolve to believe that God will redeem your sorrows. Remember that He is for you, and that even though He will not violate the free will of your abuser, He is sovereign and wants to use your trials for good purposes.

KEYS TO OVERCOMING ANGER

1. *Recognize the unhealthy extremes.* Anger itself is not a sin but allowing it to consume and control you is.
2. *Surrender it to God*—admit the worst of it all and commit it to Him. Pour out your anger to the Lord, and perhaps a wise Believer (Psalm 142).
3. *Recognize His Sovereignty.* Know that He is powerful enough to work out His good intentions for you even when people act against His will. Our Lord is a Redeemer, and He desires to use our troubles for His redemptive purposes (Romans 8:28-29).
4. *Know His Love and Character.* It is almost impossible to let go of anger if you don't understand that "He cares for you" (1 Peter 5:7). Believing He is sovereign is worthless if you do not believe He loves you and is for you. It is very helpful to meditate on Scriptures that reinforce His loving intentions toward you. Remember that, even though you may not feel it yet, nothing can separate you from His love (Romans 8:35-39).
5. *Identify with Christ who suffered on your behalf.* Many times, abuse victims have a disconnect between Jesus and the Father. Jesus said, "Anyone who has seen Me has seen the Father" (John 14:9). See also Hebrews 4:15, Isaiah 50:6, 53:3, Psalm 22:14-18, Matthew 23:37- 39, 26:6-7, Luke 22:63-65, 24:20, Isaiah 49:15-16, Zephaniah 3:17, and Isaiah 66:13.
6. *Choose to forgive.* This does not mean you have to trust or reconcile. Rather, it means putting the offender in God's hands and setting yourself free. Sometimes, it's an act of the will and you'll find yourself having to repeat the process as you continue to experience hurt. You may find this extra hard to do, because it seems you're letting him off the hook, but I believe it is putting Him on God's "hook," and He's far better able to handle it than you. Do not take revenge, my dear friends, but leave room for God's wrath, for it is written: "It is Mine to avenge; I will repay," says the Lord (Romans 12:19).
7. *Be humble.* Humility is a key to victory. "God opposes the proud but gives grace to the humble" (James 4:6). Sometimes, in our anger we think we know better than God. We demand answers and want to control everything, because He seems to be asleep on the watch. Job challenged God's justice and accused Him of divine neglect—he poured out his anger to Him, but Scripture tells us that "in all this, Job did not sin by charging God with wrongdoing" (Job 1:22). God's response was simply to let him know that He is intimately familiar with every molecule and creature in this world, and that He still reigns over the universe. While Job never understood why he suffered, He recognized that God's purposes are good. When He encountered God's majesty he proclaimed, "Behold, I am insignificant; what can I reply to You? I lay my hand on my mouth..." Job 40:3-5. It is wise to accept the fact that we will never have all the answers here on Earth, but we belong to One who does and who loves us dearly.

8. *Resolve to leave it in His hands.* It is a choice that you may have to do again and again. This is not always a simple process. Be determined!

I can think of no better way to end this lesson than by posting some passages on anger below. My prayer is that you will choose to deal with anger God's way. As you do, I trust that His Holy Spirit will strengthen you and enable you to overcome your anger.

SCRIPTURES ABOUT ANGER

- In your anger do not sin: Do not let the sun go down while you are still angry, and do not give the devil a foothold... Get rid of all bitterness, rage and anger, brawling and slander, along with every form of malice. Be kind and compassionate to one another, forgiving each other, just as in Christ God forgave you. — Ephesians 4:26, 31-32
- Be still before the Lord and wait patiently for Him; do not fret when people succeed in their ways, when they carry out their wicked schemes. Refrain from anger and turn from wrath; do not fret, it leads only to evil. — Psalms 37:7-8
- An angry person stirs up conflict, and a hot-tempered person commits many sins. — Proverbs 29:22
- Do not be quickly provoked in your spirit, for anger resides in the lap of fools. — Ecclesiastes 7:9
- Do not repay anyone evil for evil. Be careful to do what is right in the eyes of everyone. If it is possible, as far as it depends on you, live at peace with everyone. Do not take revenge, my dear friends, but leave room for God's wrath, for it is written: 'It is mine to avenge; I will repay,' says the Lord. — Romans 12:17-19
- But now you must also rid yourselves of all such things as these: anger, rage, malice, slander, and filthy language from your lips. Do not lie to each other, since you have taken off your old self with its practices and have put on the new self, which is being renewed in knowledge in the image of its Creator. — Colossians 3:8-10
- My dear brothers and sisters, take note of this: Everyone should be quick to listen, slow to speak and slow to become angry, because human anger does not produce the righteousness that God desires. — James 1:19-20
- Fools give full vent to their rage, but the wise bring calm in the end. — Proverbs 29:11

LESSON 8 EXERCISES

1. Read the "Anger" section of Chapter 12, "Managing Your Emotions" in *CTP*. Is there a particular step in working through anger that you need to work on? Write out your insights.

2. We all learn to deal with anger in different ways depending on how we were raised. How did your family deal with anger—did they stuff it, blow up, or find some other way to show it?

3. Healthy people learn to talk things out without resorting to extreme behaviors like blowing up or clamming up. How do you most often deal with your anger?

4. What is your biggest struggle when it comes to dealing with anger?

5. Were there some practical steps you got from this lesson that you would like to implement in your life? Write them out.

6. Was there something helpful you learned that you would like to teach your children or loved ones? List them here.

7. This week, read the passages on anger listed above and journal about how they apply to you. What changes do you need to make? Examine your own life in light of these passages. Also, if you continue to find yourself angry, go back to the "Keys to Overcoming Anger" in the lesson, look up the passages there, and journal any insights you receive as you go.

Notes

LESSON 9

MANAGING SADNESS AND GRIEF

Nothing is sadder than feeling despised and rejected by the one person you have chosen to love and honor above all others. Many times, over the years I struggled with suicidal thoughts because my husband's opinion of me was so low. Like most young women, I dreamed of living happily ever after with a man who adored me. Instead, I felt worthless and hopeless. Nothing I said or did could stop the criticism and contempt he regularly directed toward me, and it was devastating. I had made him and our marriage the center of my universe, so having to walk away from both left me shattered. Sorrow overwhelmed me until I learned to surrender it to God. Grief is usual in these situations, but we have a choice about how we will grieve. Either we can become self-focused and filled with self-pity, or we can connect with Him in our despair, and discover His ability to redeem.

GRIEVE WELL

There's a grieving process that you must go through when coming out of abuse. You've had to face the truth that the person you promised to love and honor above all others has spurned the same promise he made to you. The knowledge that your spouse has chosen his actions against you can weigh as heavily as death. And that's often not the end of the story—there is pain upon pain, loss upon loss, when dealing with abuse. Many lose not only their marriages, but often other relationships as well. Many face financial ruin; some even lose custody of their children. Nothing is off limits with an abusive person; they attack whatever is dear to us, and are indifferent to the soul-deep sorrow they cause. It's normal to grieve such significant loss, but it's essential to try to avoid getting stuck in the grief. God longs to share in your sorrows and carry them for you. He understands the grief and rejection you've experienced and wants to hold you together when you feel you're falling apart.

God is not so cruel that He expects us to just deal with our pain and move on. Jesus wept at the tomb of His friend Lazarus and lamented the rejection He experienced from His own people (Matthew 23:37-39). He longs to relieve your burdens, dear friend, and to carry your griefs and sorrows (Isaiah 53:4). Knowing that you do not have to carry the burden alone and that you can bring your heavy burdens to Him is so important. We do not have to grieve "as those with no hope" (Thessalonians 4:13). He is our hope! The image of God as a comforter in Zephaniah 3:17 was particularly precious to me; "He will quiet you with His love, He will rejoice over you with singing." I often curled up into a ball and imagined myself lying on His lap as I poured my hurts out to Him. I knew in my spirit that He was rejoicing because I was bringing my burden to Him. I still treasure those times of grieving in His arms because He was so faithful. I came to know Him on a deeper level than I ever had before. The process of healing from sadness and grief is much the same as it is for anger. We must learn to trust His goodness.

As it turned out for me, unresolved anger turned inward and manifested as depression, but I've seen it happen the other way around too. Some people mask their sadness by lashing out in anger. The two are very much interconnected, but the cure is the same either way—pour your heart out and roll the burden onto Him. There's healing power in praising Him during your pain. Like Job, I remember being determined to praise Him no matter what (Job 13:15), and something beautiful happened: He sustained me and He comforted me. He proved His goodness and faithfulness amid intense suffering, and I came to know Him as I never had before. Despite the pain it took to get there, I wouldn't trade that experience for anything; it felt like losing everything and gaining everything all at the same time. I pray that you will choose to cling to truth rather than your feelings. This doesn't mean that sadness will automatically disappear, but you will find healing as you move closer to Him. Grief comes in waves. Just when you think you're recovering, another wave— a memory or trigger— comes and knocks you over. But just as we can get past the breakers by moving forward in the ocean, we can move past grief by seeking and moving towards our loving Redeemer.

Since the first edition of this book, several articles and books on the biblical lament have surfaced identifying a four-step process: 1) turning to God, 2) bringing your complaint, 3) asking boldly, and 4) choosing to trust.[68] Lament requires raw honesty before the Lord, and many survivors I have worked with have learned to hide or bury their true feelings, but Jesus wisely proclaimed that truth sets us free (John 8:32). So much freedom happens when we can finally admit the truth about what happened to us, as well as the truth about God's character, love and, desire to redeem our pain.

BELIEVE HIS WORD AND DRAW NEAR

Living with abuse changes our thinking. It makes us think we are less than who God says we are, and very often, it makes us doubt His goodness. As mentioned earlier, connecting to God and grieving "in His arms" brought me great comfort, but before I could do that, I had to really trust He was good, and that He deeply loved me. I had to know He was for me, not against me, and that I was his precious child. Building intimacy with Him is crucial to healing from grief.

Praise God for His Word, because as I sought Him in those pages, I found that the Perfect One loves and cherishes me unconditionally. Scripture tells us that He lives to intercede for us (Hebrews 7:25). He is our Advocate in heaven, and nobody has the right to condemn His children. "Who then can condemn us? No one—for Christ Jesus died for us and was raised to life for us, and He is sitting in the place of honor at God's right hand, pleading for us" (Romans 8:34). If you doubt His goodness, countering those thoughts with truth is crucial. Choose to trust in His sovereign ability to redeem your life and believe the good things He says about you over the cruel things a man has said. If you find yourself still struggling with this, revisit Lesson 1, "Knowing God," as well as the "God's Love" section of the Scripture Database at the back of the book.

---

[68] Vroegop, Mark, "Dare to Hope in God How to Lament Well," at https://www.desiringgod.org/articles/dare-to-hope-in-god accessed July 15, 2024. Also see Vroegop's book, *Dark Clouds, Deep Mercy: Discovering the Grace of Lament*, Crossway, Wheaton, Illinois, 2019.

AVOID THE SELF-PITY TRAP

I must admit that, in my life, I have had more than my fair share of pity parties. Life has not always been easy, and people have not always been kind. Clearly, I have had plenty of good reasons to feel sorry for myself, and on many occasions I have done just that. In fact, I spent several years doing it so much that I slipped in and out of depression on a regular basis to the point of becoming suicidal. Thankfully, God intervened in my life, and I found a way to escape the negative thoughts and feelings that consumed me. Sadly, over the years, I have worked with many women who were stuck in self-pity.

By nature, I am an encourager, but I've learned that people like this cannot be encouraged. It makes no sense, but it seems as though they enjoy being miserable. And if that were not enough, they also seem to love dragging everyone else into their wretched state. They like to blame others for their misery and try to make them responsible for improving their lot in life. In fact, over my years of working with victims of domestic violence, I've found that most abusive people are consumed with self-pity, and they manage to use it to control their victims. The problem is you can never please someone like this. Nothing you do is ever enough.

In Scripture we see an example of this harmful attitude in John 5:1-15. When Jesus asked the paralytic at the pool of Bethesda if he wanted to be well, he simply blamed others that he wasn't. After Jesus healed him, he reported Him to the religious officials rather than thanking Him. In the end, Jesus warned him to "stop sinning or something worse may happen to you." When I read this story, I am amazed that this man received such a great miracle, and yet, according to the Biblical account, did not show an ounce of gratitude. *At the heart of those ruled by destructive self-pity, you will usually find ingratitude.* Their eyes are so focused on self that they become blind to the blessings they do have, and their lack of gratitude is like poison. It spews to everyone around them as they use their misery to try to control those who love them. They want people to feel sorry for them and bend over backwards to make them happy, but it's nearly impossible to help someone who has decided that their pain is greater than God's provision. They would much rather drag you into their misery than to allow you to help them out of it.

The way to escape the harmful trap of self-pity is to *choose to be grateful rather than self-focused.* Our lives will make a positive impact on the world when we do. However, people consumed with self-pity usually do the exact opposite. They are takers rather than givers. Jesus said it is more blessed to give than to receive, and to be blessed in Biblical terms means to be happy. We can choose to allow misery to rule us, or we can choose to be grateful for the blessings we have. Ephesians 1:3 tells us that God has blessed us with every spiritual blessing, and Romans 8:37 says that as His children, we are more than conquerors. Scripture is filled with God's good intentions toward His children, but we must choose to believe what He says about us. It's not always easy to do that, but when we choose His way above our own, He will enable us to overcome the toxic trap of self-pity.

TIPS FOR MANAGING SADNESS AND GRIEF

- *Pour out your grief to Him* (Psalm 62:8). Be honest and admit to the full extent of what happened to cause you sorrow. This can be confusing after abuse. Many times, we are lamenting what should have been rather than what was. Journaling, reading, and praying Psalms of lament, singing comforting songs, and other activities listed in Lesson 5 can be immensely helpful.
- *Meditate on Scriptural truths related to His character and goodness.* Choose to trust His love and care for you (Psalm 42:5,8).
- *Commit your heartache to Him, and trust that He will help carry it* (Psalm 147:3, Isaiah 53:4). This is a commitment you will need to make many times in the grieving process.
- *Schedule times to grieve.* I learned this from a local grief counselor. She told me that sometimes people are afraid to cry because they are afraid they won't be able to stop. However, setting time limits on your grief can be helpful. Even if you can't cry yet, take time to express the grief you feel either vocally or in writing.
- *Allow yourself to cry* (Psalms 42:3, 56:8). Research has shown that tears can release toxins, reduce pain, relieve stress, and aid sleep.[69]
- *Help your children express their grief too.* It's important to encourage your children to express their grief, and to talk to God about it. You can be honest with them about what has happened without sharing too many details or dragging them into adult conversations. Focus on helping them express the sadness they feel and let them know that Jesus wants to help carry their sorrows (Isaiah 53:4).[70]
- *Practice gratitude when you find yourself slipping into self-pity.* Intentionally recognizing and thanking God for your blessings can be extremely helpful in reducing unhealthy self-focused grief. In addition, worship music and praise are powerful ways to help move our focus from ourselves to God.

---

[69] Burgess, Lana, "Eight benefits of crying: Why it's good to shed a few tears," on www.medicalnewstoday.com, July 13, 2023, accessed July 15, 2024.

[70] For younger children, Darby Strickland's book, *Something Sad Happened* (New Growth Press, 2024) is helpful for initiating conversation about traumatic events and God's care.

LESSON 9 EXERCISES

1. What has living with abuse taken from you? List the losses you have suffered. (These losses can be physical, relational, emotional, or spiritual.) Pour your complaint out to God, then apply His truth to your situation. Considering those losses, can you relate to the following passage? Is there anything you have gained in this process?

   "What is more, I consider everything a loss because of the surpassing worth of knowing Christ Jesus my Lord, for whose sake I have lost all things. I consider them garbage, that I may gain Christ…" (Philippians 3:8).

2. Do you often find yourself asking "why" questions? Why me? Why did this happen? Why didn't I get out sooner? There are an infinite number of questions like this, but continually asking them can prolong your sense of despair. One thing I learned as I was processing through the abuse was that it was far more productive to ask "what" and "how" questions. "Lord, what do You want to teach me in all of this?" "How will You use it for good in my life?' "How should I respond to what has happened?" These types of questions will move you from focusing on your losses and your past— which can't be changed— to concentrating on finding God's redemptive purposes for your present and future.

   In the response space below, think of a "why" question that has plagued you and rewrite it as a "what" or "how" question aimed at finding God's good intentions for you.

3. First Thessalonians 4:13 tells us that Believers do not grieve like unbelievers do, because we have hope. Are you struggling to find hope in your grief? If so, write out a prayer asking Him to restore your hope. If you have hope, write out a prayer describing your reasons for hope and thanking Him.

4. Unresolved anger can turn inward and manifest as depression, but I've seen it happen the other way around. Some people mask their sadness by lashing out in anger. Can you identify a connection between your own sadness/depression and anger? If so, describe it below.

5. God redeems and restores the worst of our sorrows when His people turn to Him. He restored wayward Israel, even after they betrayed Him for foreign gods. It's always His desire to heal and restore His people, especially when they have suffered oppression. Read the following passages and write out a prayer based on one of them, asking Him to restore your hope and redeem your griefs.

   Joel 2:25-27 — "I will repay you for the years the locusts have eaten—the great locust and the young locust, the other locusts and the locust swarm—My great army that I sent among you. You will have plenty to eat, until you are full, and you will praise the name of the Lord your God, Who has worked wonders for you; never again will My people be shamed. Then you will know that I am in Israel, that I am the Lord your God, and that there is no other; never again will My people be shamed.

   Jeremiah 31:3-4 — The Lord appeared to us in the past, saying: "I have loved you with an everlasting love; I have drawn you with unfailing kindness. I will build you up again, and you, Virgin Israel, will be rebuilt. Again, you will take up your timbrels and go out to dance with the joyful.

6. Going through abuse and divorce can seem just as hard, or even harder, than losing a spouse to death because we realize that our partners chose actions that deliberately hurt us. They may also continue to torment us long after the relationship ends. Many times, we see a new relationship as the answer, but that isn't wise if we haven't healed and allowed the Lord to bind up our wounds (Psalm 147:3). Are you stuck in grief? Are you trying to find comfort somewhere besides God? What do you need from God as you continue to process your grief? Write out your answers in a prayer below.

7. It is so much easier to grieve when you know you are being held by the One Who loves you most. He sees your pain and grieves with you. He promises to never leave nor forsake you, and He collects every tear you shed (Psalm 56:8).

   Read the following passages and write down anything that speaks to your heart. Ask Him to make this truth your reality.
   - **Zephaniah 3:17** — "The Lord your God is in your midst, a mighty one Who will save; He will rejoice over you with gladness; He will quiet you by his love; He will exult over you with loud singing."
   - **Psalm 119:76** — "May Your unfailing love be my comfort, according to Your promise to Your servant."
   - **Romans 8:38-39** — "For I am convinced that neither death nor life, neither angels nor demons, neither the present nor the future, nor any powers, neither height nor depth, nor anything else in all creation, will be able to separate us from the love of God that is in Christ Jesus our Lord."
   - **Psalm 34:18** — "The Lord is close to the brokenhearted and saves those who are crushed in spirit.

Notes

LESSON 10

OVERCOMING SHAME, GUILT, AND REGRET

"How can I ever forgive myself?" It's a question I've heard many times in my years of counseling. In fact, I get it! I know very well how it feels to be plagued with guilt and remorse over a bad decision. When I finally broke free from a 23-year abusive relationship, I lived with regret daily. I couldn't believe I had been stupid enough to believe the lies that had kept me bound for so long and couldn't believe how I had foolishly disregarded the harmful impacts on my children. As much as I tried to tell myself that I did the best I could at the time, I was overwhelmed with remorse. The fact that I was still living with the consequences of my failures seemed to make it even harder to let myself off the hook. As with the many other struggles I faced as a survivor of abuse, I went to Scripture to find the answer to overcoming the guilt and shame I carried. Interestingly, I found nothing there that spoke to a need to forgive myself. The Bible urges us to forgive one another and to receive God's forgiveness, but never once does it tell us to forgive ourselves. Instead, it reminds us that "there is no condemnation for those who are in Christ Jesus" (Romans 8:1). It also lets us know that if we confess our sin, He is faithful to forgive and cleanse us (1 John 1:9).

My study of Scripture led me to conclude that rather than focusing on myself and my mistakes, I needed to focus on what He had accomplished on my behalf. I recognized that condemning myself for things I had no power to change was the equivalent of saying His work on the cross was not adequate for my sin. It was choosing to walk in condemnation, even though He had set me free from it. Although I finally realized I had no right to continue to condemn myself, I was still overwhelmed with sorrow about the consequences of my choices earlier in life. For many years after I left the abuse, I watched my children continue to struggle because of their tumultuous upbringing, and my own failures as a parent. Over time, I finally learned to establish boundaries with them, but it seemed to be too little too late. In the long run, all I could do was surrender them to His loving hands. My fear-motivated attempts to control them seemed to push them further away. One day, as I was crying out to God about it, I sensed in my spirit that He was not done with them yet and that He was even sovereign over my mistakes and failures. I realized that just as He was using my pain and suffering for His good purposes, He would do the same with my kids. It took many years to see things turn around, but as I have surrendered them to His loving hands, He has worked in amazing ways.

GUILT

Guilt simply says, "I've done something wrong. I made a mistake." It generally acknowledges that we have violated a standard, but we know that abusive people love to manipulate us into feeling guilty— even when we have done nothing wrong. It's important to examine your feelings of guilt to see if they are really warranted. Did you violate God's standard, or was it an elusive requirement set up by someone seeking to confuse and control you? Legitimate guilt can be beneficial in leading us to repentance. It is not as harmful as shame, so we must guard against false guilt that can turn into shame. Shame condemns and leads to worldly sorrow that alienates us from God, but godly sorrow leads to repentance that restores us to Him (2 Corinthians 7:9-10). If you still feel unforgiven after confession and repentance, perhaps your guilt has morphed into shame.

SHAME

While "guilt is an awareness of failure against a standard. Shame is a sense of failure before the eyes of someone."[71] People with shame carry a crushing sense of being intrinsically flawed and unacceptable. We have all failed before God, He took on our shame at the cross making us blameless in His eyes. However, people with shame have much harsher standards than He does. Shame not only warps our view of ourselves, but also our view of God. In his book, *Shame Interrupted*, Ed Welch speaks candidly to those who struggle with shame. "Think of yourself as someone who has a delusion. Shame is not your delusion. Shame is very real. But your knowledge of God's defy-all-expectations holiness is a delusion."[72] In other words, your view of God's holiness— the one that says you are worthless and defective— is based on an internal narrative that denies His truth. Knowing His amazing grace and our identity in Him are essential to overcoming shame, but we must choose to believe what He says over our own feelings or our abusers' opinions of us. "Can you say, 'Lord, I believe You more than I believe me?'"[73] I realize this sounds simplistic after trauma, and it can take a considerable amount of time, but it is not impossible. I believe the principles set forth in earlier lessons regarding choosing to believe, engaging in Biblical meditation, and renewing your mind will help alleviate feelings of shame over time. Intentionally shifting your mindset from self to the One who knows you best can begin a healing process that He will be faithful to complete (Philippians 1:6).

While many suggest positive self-affirmations and building self-esteem, I believe that these actions merely keep the focus on ourselves, reminding us of just how broken we are. We need Someone greater than ourselves to pull us out of the mire of shame. Remember when I talked about putting off and putting on back in Lesson 5? It's much easier to replace behaviors or attributes with new ones than to just stop them. When we live with shame, we miss the grace of God. In fact, we live under self-imposed standards that nullify it. We fail to believe that our Most Holy God came to Earth and took on the unholy burden of our sin and shame to set us free. "For He made Him who knew no sin to be sin for

---

[71] Powlison, David & Julie Lowe (2012, July,16). What is the difference between guilt and shame? On the CCEF Podcast. https://www.ccef.org/re- sources/podcast/what-difference-between-guilt-and-shame.

[72] Welch, Edward T., *Shame Interrupted: How God Lifts the Pain of Worthlessness and Rejection*, (Greensboro, NC, New Growth Press, 2012) 94.

[73] Ibid, 62.

us, that we might become the righteousness of God in Him" (2 Corinthians 5:21). That, my friend, is abounding grace. He took any punishment you ever deserved, and He bore your shame. The question is, will you choose to receive His grace and reject your shame? It will take time, but I pray that, as you resolve to believe Him above the false narrative of shame,[74] you will come to know His amazing grace that demolishes shame.

REGRET

Although regret is often associated with guilt and shame, it is different. The Cambridge Dictionary defines regret as "a feeling of sadness about something sad or wrong or about a mistake that you have made, and a wish that it could have been different and better." Regret is the constant companion of most abuse survivors. We regret getting into the relationship, not leaving soon enough, not responding wisely enough, and most lamentably, how the abuse impacted our children. The latter of those regrets is by far the most common, and the most severe. It was something I struggled with for years. I regretted it so much that I carried a tremendous amount of guilt long after I got out of the abuse. I prayed and cried out to God for them. He assured me He would not waste their struggles. Nothing is impossible for Him; He would use even their pain for good and redeem their stories.I prayed and cried out to God for them. He assured me He would not waste their struggles. Nothing is impossible for Him; He would use even their pain for good and redeem their stories. I realized that just as He was using my pain and suffering for His good purposes, He could do the same with my kids. It finally dawned on me that He loved them even more than I did so I could entrust them to Him. It took many years, and many hard decisions, but eventually things began to turn around. As I relinquished my desire to control the outcome to His loving care, He worked in amazing ways. I pray that if you are consumed with regret, you will choose to lean into His goodness and release every burden to His loving care (1 Peter 5:7).

THE PATH FORWARD

If you find yourself overwhelmed with the weight of regret from your past, two truths will set you free. First, you must choose to believe God's proclamation that you have been set free from condemnation by Jesus' finished work on the cross. Second, you need to trust His goodness and sovereignty. He will somehow use the pain and sorrow you experienced for His good purposes (Romans 8:28). He specializes in turning ashes into beauty (Isaiah 61:3). As you choose to embrace Him in your pain, you will experience the reality of this truth. Full surrender to our good God will never disappoint, but holding on to shame and self-condemnation will keep you in bondage. Freedom is a choice, and you will find it as you shift your focus from yourself—and your mistakes—to His abundantly sufficient grace.

---

[74] Since shame is so deeply imbedded in our brains, especially for those who experienced abuse as children. Finding freedom takes time. It's a process that begins with recognizing the truth of how shame has impacted you, and the common lies you have come to believe about God, yourself, and others. People with shame often misinterpret the motives of others and see allies as enemies. It is important to recognize this tendency. A good way to recognize and untangle the lies of shame is to work through Ed Welch's book, *Shame Interrupted*, with a counselor or trusted friend.

It may be hard to believe after living in abuse, but as His child, our Lord delights in you (Psalm 149:4, Zephaniah 3:17). He doesn't see your mistakes, failures, or even your sins. Your standing with Him has nothing to do with what you've done, and everything to do with what He's done out of His great love for you. Abusive people love to use guilt and shame to control us, but the remedy is to correct our perception of God and refuse to allow it to be marred by human experience. People may hold grudges and seek revenge, but God is not a man that He should lie (Numbers 23:19). Unlike our abusers, He does not require us to earn His favor. By its very definition, grace is freely given because of God's underserved favor. Our response should be profound gratitude, and gratitude paves a powerful path to victory. "Enter His gates with thanksgiving and His courts with praise; give thanks to Him and praise His name (Psalm 100:4). When you find yourself struggling, I urge you to stop and enter His gates with thanksgiving and praise. It will put things in proper perspective, and the weight of His glory will overwhelm the weight of guilt, shame, and regret in your life. "For our light and momentary troubles are achieving for us an eternal glory that far outweighs them all" (2 Corinthians 2:17).

TRUTHS TO REMEMBER

1. *God has graciously provided a solution for the guilt of our sin.* See John 1:14 & 16; Romans 8:1-2, 31-34, 1 John 1:9, Colossians 1:21-22, and 2 Corinthians 5:19 & 21. The cross is not just effective for our salvation, but for our daily walk! We are not only saved by grace, but we must also live each day by grace. We desperately need it and need to learn to depend on Him.
2. *There is a difference between condemning guilt and godly sorrow that leads to repentance.* Shame and false guilt result in worldly sorrow that leads to alienation from God, but godly sorrow leads to repentance and restored relationship with Him.
3. *We need to correct our perception of God because our understanding of Him can be marred by our human experience.* Perhaps our abusers have made us think God is harsh or distant. People may hold grudges and seek revenge, but God is not a man that He should lie (Numbers 23:19).
4. *We have an enemy who loves to accuse and condemn us.* We must reject his condemnation and embrace God's grace instead. See Revelation 12:10, Zechariah 3:1, Job 1:6-11, and Titus 2:11-12.
5. *We must shift our focus from self to God to find freedom from shame.* Believers have been restored to relationship with God, but sometimes we suffer from spiritual amnesia. This is why it is vital that we stay in His Word and in His presence.
6. *He does not require us to earn His favor.* By its very definition, grace is God's underserved favor (Ephesians 2:8, 2 Timothy 1:9).
7. *He gives us the grace we need to walk in a manner worthy of His calling despite our frailties.* See 2 Corinthians 12:8-10, Romans 8:26, Galatians 5:13-16, 22, 23, and 1 Corinthians 10:13, Matthew 11:28, and Romans 8:11-12.
8. *We must keep our eyes on Him, rather than our circumstances and ourselves.* See Peter's experience in Matthew 14:22-33. As with Peter on the water, we will most certainly fail when we take our eyes off Jesus. Still, even if we blow it, His grace and mercy are there to pick us up. He will even use our failures to teach us if we let Him.
9. *He specializes in turning ashes into beauty* (Isaiah 61:3). As you choose to embrace Him in your pain, you will experience the reality that He is a redeemer. Complete surrender to our good God will never disappoint, but holding on to shame and self-condemnation will keep you in

bondage. Freedom is a choice, and you will find it as you shift your focus from yourself and your mistakes to His abundantly sufficient grace.

SCRIPTURES TO COMBAT SHAME

- He has not dealt with us according to our sins, nor rewarded us according to our iniquities. For as high as the heavens are above the earth, so great is His lovingkindness toward those who fear Him. As far as the east is from the west, so far has He removed our transgressions from us. Just as a father has compassion on his children, so the LORD has compassion on those who fear Him. For He Himself knows our frame; He is mindful that we are but dust. – Psalm 103:10-14
- There is therefore now no condemnation to those who are in Christ Jesus, who do not walk according to the flesh, but according to the Spirit. For the law of the Spirit of life in Christ Jesus has made me free from the law of sin and death… What then shall we say to these things? If God is for us, who can be against us? He who did not spare His own Son, but delivered Him up for us all, how shall He not with Him also freely give us all things? Who shall bring a charge against God's elect? It is God who justifies. Who is he who condemns? It is Christ who died, and furthermore is also risen, who is even at the right hand of God, who also makes intercession for us. – Romans 8:1-2, 31-34
- And you, who once were alienated and enemies in your mind by wicked works, yet now He has reconciled in the body of His flesh through death, to present you holy, and blameless, and above reproach in His sight. – Col. 1:21-22
- That is, that God was in Christ reconciling the world to Himself, not imputing their trespasses to them, and has committed to us the word of reconciliation… For He made Him who knew no sin to be sin for us, that we might become the righteousness of God in Him. – 2 Corinthians 5:19, 21
- If you, Lord, kept a record of sins, Lord, who could stand? But with You there is forgiveness, so that we can, with reverence, serve You. – Psalm 130:3-4.
- As Scripture says, "Anyone who believes in him will never be put to shame. – Romans 10:11
- Do not be afraid; you will not be put to shame. Do not fear disgrace; you will not be humiliated. You will forget the shame of your youth and remember no more the reproach of your widowhood. –Isaiah 54:4

LESSON 10 EXERCISES

1. If living through abuse has left you filled with shame, guilt, and regret, list the things that you struggle with below.

2. How do you deal with shame, guilt, and failures? Do you try to justify yourself? Do you alienate yourself from God? Do you try to win His favor? What steps can you take to change unhealthy responses?

3. Holding on to false guilt can be a huge hindrance to the healing process. One way to know you're stuck in guilt is by paying attention to the thoughts you are having about yourself. Do you find that you're beating yourself up because of decisions you made in the past? Self-talk that can hurt you sounds like, I should have…, I could have…, Why did/didn't I…, and the like. Write down any questions like this that have haunted you and ask God to free you from the lie that your decisions are irredeemable.

4. In order to overcome feelings of guilt and shame, we must recognize our restored identity in Christ, and we must surrender ourselves fully to Him. Read the following passages, jot down the main point, and note how that might relate to overcoming feelings of shame.
   - Matthew 16:25 — For whoever wants to save their life will lose it, but whoever loses their life for me will find it.

   - Galatians 2:20 — I have been crucified with Christ and I no longer live, but Christ lives in me. The life I now live in the body, I live by faith in the Son of God, who loved me and gave himself for me.

5. In Him, we have a glorious identity. Look up the following passages and put your name in each verse. Note what God says about you below.

   - You are fully known and loved. See Psalm 139 and Luke 12:4-7.
   - You are reconciled, holy, and beyond reproach in Him. See Colossians 1:21-22.
   - You are blessed with every spiritual blessing. See Ephesians 1:3-14 and list them.
   - God is for you, and you are more than a conqueror! See Romans 8:31-39.
   - You've been chosen by the king, even though you had nothing. See 1 Corinthians 1:26-30.
   - God created people in His own image to have intimacy/fellowship with Himself, but when Adam and Eve sinned, we lost that identity as His children. However, He loved us enough to pursue us—even after we rejected Him. Thank God that Jesus regained that identity for us. He became sin on our behalf so we could become "the righteousness of God" (2 Corinthians 5:21, 8:9).

6. Write out a prayer and release your regrets to God. Be sure to claim His truth over yourself and release yourself from the things you listed in question number 1.

7. God is a healer. In His presence we find comfort and healing. He is also a redeemer, and that means He can and will use painful events for good when we turn to Him. Holding on to Him as we grieve builds intimacy with Him that will see us through the toughest storm and bring us out victoriously on the other side. Read Isaiah 61:1-7 below:

- "The Spirit of the Sovereign Lord is on me, because the Lord has anointed me to proclaim good news to the poor. He has sent me to bind up the brokenhearted, to proclaim freedom for the captives and release from darkness for the prisoners, to proclaim the year of the Lord's favor and the day of vengeance of our God, to comfort all who mourn, and provide for those who grieve in Zion—to bestow on them a crown of beauty instead of ashes, the oil of joy instead of mourning, and a garment of praise instead of a spirit of despair."

Thank God for His desire to rebuild your life and turn back your shame. Commit yourself to Him and write out a prayer asking Him to turn the ashes of your past into beauty and to replace your mourning with joy.

For further study, look up the following verses and write out how they apply to the guilt and regret you've experienced.
- Romans 8:1-2, 31-34

- Psalm 103: 10-14

- Isaiah 50:2

- Psalm 55:18

- Genesis 50:20

- Jeremiah 29:11-13

Notes

LESSON 11

THE POWER OF DISENGAGEMENT
Wise Responses to Abusive People

*Do not answer a fool according to his folly, or you will
also be like him. Answer a fool as his folly deserves,
that he not be wise in his own eyes.*
~ Proverbs 26:4-5, NASB

One thing I learned when I was coming out of abuse was that the more I responded or engaged with my husband, the worse he got. It was like adding fuel to the flame. Eventually, I learned that I had to deal with him as I would a stranger and keep it "business only" when talking about the kids and such. As much as I wanted to defend myself against his untrue and unfair accusations, I learned that doing so just pulled me back into the madness. I believe the Bible has much to say about understanding and dealing with foolish, self-centered people.

- "A fool's mouth lashes out with pride, but the lips of the wise protect them" (Proverbs 14:3).
- "Like a maniac shooting flaming arrows of death is one who deceives their neighbor and says, 'I was only joking!'" (Proverbs 26:18-19).
- "Do you see someone who speaks in haste? There is more hope for a fool than for them" (Proverbs 29:20).
- "Sin is not ended by multiplying words, but the prudent hold their tongues" (Proverbs 10:19).
- "Do you see a person wise in their own eyes? There is more hope for a fool than for them" (Proverbs 26:12). One common trait among abusive people is that they rarely admit they are wrong. I'd say that's the epitome of being wise in their own eyes.
- "Enemies disguise themselves with their lips, but in their hearts, they harbor deceit. Though their speech is charming, do not believe them, for seven abominations fill their hearts" (Proverbs 26:24-25). We may not want to call them our enemies, but the truth is apparent by their actions rather than by what they say to us.

- "A hot-tempered person must pay the penalty; rescue them, and you will have to do it again" (Proverbs 19:19). If we cover up for them and protect them from the consequences of their destructive ways, it perpetuates the abuse.
- "People will be lovers of themselves, lovers of money, boastful, proud, abusive, disobedient to their parents, ungrateful, unholy, without love, unforgiving, slanderous, without self-control, brutal, not lovers of the good, treacherous, rash, conceited, lovers of pleasure rather than lovers of God—having a form of godliness but denying its power. Have nothing to do with such people" (2 Timothy 3:2-5). Or at least, don't let them drag you into their madness. Jesus refused to allow the religious leaders to pull Him into power struggles (See Mark 11:27-33). He refused to allow the religious leaders to trap Him with their questions. He also used their desire to look good in front of others to silence them. Up until His time to die, He withdrew from them and escaped their grasp when they sought to harm Him.

HOW TO RESPOND TO OPPRESSIVE PEOPLE

Oppression in marriage may involve blatant aggression like yelling, insulting, or name-calling, but it may also be subtler and take the form of disrespectful jokes, relentless criticism, blame, and accusations. Many oppressors use spiritual language to demean or belittle. They play mind games, like gaslighting and manipulation, to keep their victims confused. If you are feeling bullied, the way you respond is crucial. Always try to maintain a calm demeanor. Abusive people gain more power when they can upset you, and many times they enjoy it. Since the original publication of this book, some helpful acronyms have been devised to help survivors respond wisely to coercively controlling tactics. I've listed a few that I like below.

- BIFF means keep your response *brief, informative, factual*, and *friendly*. While popular wisdom in 2018 suggested that victims of abuse keep their responses business like and just stating facts (Gray Rock Method), the way some approached it was too business-like and backfired by making abusers angrier. Furthermore, victims who approached this method with too much indifference were seen as uncaring in the eyes of judges and people helpers. As Believers, our speech should "always be full of grace, seasoned with salt, so that [we] may know how to answer everyone" (Colossians 4:6). Being kind as we set limits on sin is wise. It doesn't always work, but it may help diffuse our partners' rage (Proverbs 15:1).

- JADE stands for don't *justify, argue, defend,* or *explain* to an abusive person. Coercively controlling people cannot be won over by words. Like with most people with persistent and destructive sin patterns their perspective on life is warped. They do not see God, others, or themselves clearly. Abusive people typically assume that, even the most supportive spouses have wicked motives and there is nothing that can be said or done to change that perspective. You may be able to calm them temporarily by complying with their demands, but I have never seen a hot-tempered person won over through words. "Sin is not ended by multiplying words, but the prudent hold their tongues" (Proverbs 10:19).

While there are times when nothing can stop the rage aimed at us by abusive people, our response can make a difference. Disengaging, choosing not to react, and attempting to keep the topic of conversation away from volatile issues can be helpful. Below are some practical tips on dealing with unwanted verbal attacks.

1. *Refuse to engage emotionally.* Abusive people want to see us lose control of our behavior. They want us to react and get upset. It's so important to control your own behavior—it takes the power away from them.
2. *Don't let them drag you into an argument.* You can't win an argument with an abusive, self-absorbed person who is determined to win no matter what it takes.
3. *Do not defend yourself against accusations and insults.* If you do this, you give credibility to what they say. Instead, kindly say, "I'm sorry you feel that way, but that does not reflect what I meant" (or something like it to let them know you disagree with their perspective). You may repeat this statement and let them know it is your final word, but do not argue.
4. *Do not appeal to your abuser's sympathy.* Abusive people only use vulnerability as a weapon. Remember who God says you are no matter what they say! They do not have the right to judge or condemn you, and your response should honor Him.
5. *Respond with a calm and even voice no matter what they say or how they present to you.*
6. *Do not raise your voice or make comments under your breath.* This will almost certainly invite further wrath.
7. *Do not insult them.* Speak respectfully and avoid resorting to their methods.
8. *Assess the danger.* If you think your partner might become physically abusive, be sure to take precautions. Have a safety plan in place.
9. *Set boundaries.* When your partner begins to use abusive speech, let him know that it is not OK for him to talk to you that way. You can say, "I'll be happy to talk to you about a legitimate concern when you are calm, but I will not have a conversation while you are upset." Tell him you will leave if he does not stop the abusive talk and follow through if he continues with it.
10. *Leave if he crosses a boundary you set.* Try to remove yourself from the situation by going to another room. If that doesn't work, leave the house. If he tries to prevent your exit, call 911. Return only when you feel it is safe.
11. *If the situation remains unsafe, consider getting a protective order.* Your local DV program can help with this.
12. *Go no contact!* This can be so helpful for your healing. If possible, avoid all or most contact until you have done enough healing work to avoid reacting. If "no contact" is impossible, seek to distance yourself from situations that make you more vulnerable.
13. *Get counseling.* Find a counselor who understands domestic abuse and can help you navigate your responses, build strength, and replace faulty beliefs with truth.
14. *Find your satisfaction in God.* When a person has something we think we need, we give them power, and we are much more likely to react. Only God should have that sort of power in our lives.

For further reading, see *The Emotionally Destructive Marriage* (Part 3: Initiating Changes in Your Marriage), by Leslie Vernick.

LESSON 11 EXERCISES

1. This week take time to write out at least one example in your own situation where disengaging would have been more helpful. Examine how your responses aggravated the situation.

2. Consider the example you wrote down in question one, then write out what you might have said or done instead.

3. When we haven't had practice with disengaging, it's good to think through how that might look. Consider a potential interaction with your abuser. Think of something that has ended up in an argument in the past when you felt attacked or unjustly accused. Write out several potential responses you might give or actions you can take. Rehearse specific responses in writing. Without practicing new ways of responding, you will find it much easier to resort to old and ineffective ways of reacting.

4. Have you been reactive in your relationship—meaning, have you let your emotions guide you rather than logic and God's truth? If so, write out your confession to God and ask Him to help you change. Commit to asking Him for help when your emotions get out of hand.

NOTES

IF YOU ARGUE WITH A FOOL

If you argue with a fool, he will be energized by the drama. The energy will fuel him while it simultaneously drains you. You will end up nowhere positive.

> Folly is a joy to him who lacks sense, but a man of understanding walks straight ahead.
> – *Proverbs 15:21*

> As charcoal to hot embers and wood to fire, so is a quarrelsome man for kindling strife.
> – *Proverbs 26:21*

> If a wise man has an argument with a fool, the fool only rages and laughs, and there is no quiet.
> – *Proverbs 29:9*

If you try to reason with him, he won't really hear or understand a word you say. His values and world view are in opposition to yours. He'll actually be delighted if you become unhinged; it makes him not look so bad.

> The way of a fool is right in his own eyes, but a wise man listens to advice.
> – *Proverbs 12:15*

> A rebuke goes deeper into a man of understanding than a hundred blows into a fool.
> – *Proverbs 17:10*

> A fool takes no pleasure in understanding, but only in expressing his opinion.
> – *Proverbs 18:2*

If you try to explain how his behavior hurt you, he will secretly gloat that you are at his mercy and that his tactics worked. Your vulnerability makes him feel powerful. And then somehow, he will blame you for his behavior. Like a magician, he will flip the conversation to make him the victim.

> With his mouth the godless man would destroy his neighbor, but by knowledge the righteous are delivered.
> – *Proverbs 11:9*

> Whoever is righteous has regard for the life of his beast, but the mercy of the wicked is cruel.
> –*Proverbs 12:10*

> When a man's folly brings his way to ruin, his heart rages against the Lord.
> – *Proverbs 19:3*

If you try to get help for him, it will probably backfire. He will focus on your faults and downplay his. He actually doesn't want to be emotionally healthy: that's boring and average to him - he believes he's super special and entitled! The fact is you can't ever love him to health. He has to want to change.

> A scoffer does not like to be reproved; he will not go to the wise.
> – *Proverbs 15:12*

> A man of crooked heart does not discover good, and one with a dishonest tongue falls into calamity.
> – *Proverbs 17:20*

> A man of great wrath will pay the penalty, for if you deliver him, you will only have to do it again.
> – *Proverbs 19:19*

If you do happen to hear him apologize, it's because he's sorry he got caught. He has no intention of changing his ways. It will happen again and he will be more covert next time. He has proven himself untrustworthy. He's a really good liar.

> Doing wrong is like a joke to a fool, but wisdom is pleasure to a man of understanding.
> – *Proverbs 10:23*

> Deceit is in the heart of those who devise evil, but those who plan peace have joy.
> – *Proverbs 12:20*

> A desire fulfilled is sweet to the soul, but to turn away from evil is an abomination to fools. – *Proverbs 13:19*

> The wisdom of the prudent is to discern his way, but the folly of fools is deceiving.
> – *Proverbs 14:8*

If you try to reach out emotionally, he'll play games with your heart, drawing you in with sweet gestures, words, and gifts. But then he will blindside you by treating your heart like trash; gas lighting, ignoring, stonewalling you, and betraying your trust. It will make you wonder what's wrong with you and you'll feel crazy, as if you're in a tailspin. He has no concept of true love, even though he says how much he loves you. His words and actions will contradict each other.

> Many a man proclaims his own steadfast love, but a faithful man who can find?
> –*Proverbs 20:6*

> Do not eat the bread of a man who is stingy, do not desire his delicacies, for he is like one who is inwardly calculating. 'Eat and drink!' he says to you, but his heart is not with you.
> – *Proverbs 23:6-7*

A lying tongue hates its victims, and a flattering mouth works ruin.
– Proverbs 26:28

A man who flatters his neighbor spreads a net for his feet.
– Proverbs 29:5

If you set boundaries for your own health, peace, and sanity, he will tell you how mean, selfish, and unforgiving you are. How dare you be happy without him! Any suffering he feels by your backing away is all your fault! How could you do this to him? (He's the victim, remember?)

Whoever pursues righteousness and kindness will find life, righteousness, and honor.
– Proverbs 21:21

An evil man is ensnared in his transgression, but a righteous man sings and rejoices.
– Proverbs 29:6

If you try to find common ground of truth and reasonableness, know that you are not on an equal playing field in his mind. This is a game he believes he must win. The game is called "You Lose." He makes and breaks the rules, which is why he will always win. The only way to "win" is to not play.

Whoever walks with the wise becomes wise, but the companion of fools will suffer harm.
– Proverbs 13:20

Make no friendship with a man given to anger, nor go with a wrathful man, lest you learn his ways and entangle yourself in a snare.
– Proverbs 22:24-25

Trusting in a treacherous man in time of trouble is like a bad tooth or a foot that slips.
– Proverbs 25:19

His lies and charades may make you want to react in anger and argue with him. But please don't. You can't reason with a fool, nor can you fix him. Put your limited energies into finding your own health and freedom.

Leave the presence of a fool, for there you do not meet words of knowledge.
– Proverbs 14:7

Drive out a scoffer, and strife will go out, and quarreling and abuse will cease.
– Proverbs 22:10

The prudent sees danger and hides himself, but the simple go on and suffer for it.
– Proverbs 27:12

Used with permission from Shari Ellis.
All Scriptures are taken from the ESV translation of the Bible.

LESSON 12

LEARNING TO SET HEALTHY BOUNDARIES

Am I now trying to win the approval of human beings, or of God? Or am I trying to please people? If I were still trying to please people, I would not be a servant of Christ.
~ *Galatians 1:10*

I used to tell people I had lived most of my life with a doormat theology. Between my parents' social gospel of service and deferring to others, and the strict teaching I'd heard on marital submission as a teenager, the very act of saying no to people was distressing for me. I felt obligated to help anyone who needed help, and if I had to say no, I felt obliged to apologize and then thoroughly explain why I couldn't help. It was a problem in parenting too. While I did set boundaries with my kids, I was horrible at enforcing them, especially once they started begging for something. It was really tough to say no to them, but it was almost impossible to say no to their dad. In *Called to Peace* I described how reading the book *Love Must Be Tough* helped me to set boundaries with consequences so that the violence in our home stopped for several years. However, I later slipped back into my old compliant ways, which quickly served to rekindle the violence in our home. Throughout my years of working with survivors of domestic abuse, I have found that most of them have similar stories and have learned to bow down to the demands of their abusers. While compliance is a typical response to the trauma of abuse, it can be especially complicated for Christian wives. We believe that it is our duty to submit, even when our husbands' demands are selfish and cruel. Unfortunately, the result of this mindset is to subject our children and ourselves to great harm. Jesus never expects us to promote sin, but that is what we're doing when we allow people to intimidate, manipulate, and control us.

Some people see boundaries as selfish and unbiblical, but I believe they are both biblical and loving. Disengagement can help diffuse tension in stressful conversations with controlling people, and boundaries can help set the tone for those conversations by setting parameters for the interactions. Boundaries are not rules. Rather, a boundary is a limit you set for someone who is mistreating you to let them know what you will and will not tolerate. This limit gives an offender the opportunity to choose respect and love over selfish and destructive desires. It is saying, "It is not ok for you to do this to me," versus "You are not allowed to do that." In the beginning, you may need to calmly repeat your boundary multiple times, continually assessing for potential danger. After you set the limit, you must commit to removing yourself or some privilege of the relationship to let them know you are serious.

Unfortunately, imposing boundaries on someone early in a relationship is easier than later. This is particularly true because controlling people do not like to give up ground they have taken. Be prepared! When you start to establish boundaries in your relationship, you are likely to find your partner will become even angrier, so you must have a safety plan in place. Do not hesitate to call 911 if you are in danger. Consequences are one of the best ways to teach boundaries to those who refuse to accept them.

FEAR OF MAN VS. BOUNDARIES

Most of the time, even when refusing mistreatment is the most God-honoring and loving response, fear may paralyze us. We might fear the loss of a relationship, an angry reaction, or disapproval. Scripture addresses this type of fear and warns against it. "The fear of man brings a snare, but one who trusts in the Lord will be protected" (Proverbs 29:25). Fear of man can lead us to serve people rather than God, resulting in bondage. I should also note that fear is a trauma response developed over time and after numerous incidences of abuse. Our response is natural, and often aggravated by the effects of trauma, but allowing it to control us is harmful. That is why both trauma work and learning to set boundaries is so important. We simply can't afford to be ruled by fear that allows someone to keep sinning against us, and I believe that setting boundaries is the most loving thing we can do for those who harm us. Boundaries protect us, and when done well, they can even protect our relationships as we set limits on destructive sin patterns.

WHAT DOES THE BIBLE SAY?

If we look at boundaries as setting limits on someone sinning against us, we can say God is the One who created them. He has set limits for His children since the beginning of creation, and those who violate His boundaries both grieve His heart and hurt themselves. His purposes are always loving, and love "does not dishonor others, it is not self-seeking, [and] it is not easily angered" (1 Corinthians 13:5). When we set boundaries we are creating an opportunity for those we love to choose love over self-centeredness. We see this example in Scripture in the way Jesus responded to the religious leaders. He never tried to justify or defend Himself. He didn't argue or explain His positions. Instead, He called them to examine themselves and their warped view of Scripture. He aimed His toughest words at their hypocrisy and oppressive treatment of others. In calling them out, He summed up their character, "For they don't practice what they teach. They crush people with unbearable religious demands and never lift a finger to ease the burden. "Everything they do is for show. On their arms they wear extra wide prayer boxes with Scripture verses inside, and they wear robes with extra-long tassels. And they love to sit at the head table at banquets and in the seats of honor in the synagogues" (Matthew 23:3-6). Anyone familiar with the dynamics of coercive control will immediately recognize this portrayal of the scribes and Pharisees as characteristic of abusive people. Oppression, deception, and hypocrisy grieve and anger the heart of our God. His Word is filled with admonitions against them. See Proverbs 14:26, Zechariah 7:10, Matthew 15:7-9, 1 John 2:4, Proverbs 12:22, and 1 Peter 2:1.

Not only does God hate destructive sins like oppression and deception, but He also warns His children to be on guard against people who practice them. Below are just a few examples in Scripture.

- I wrote to you not to associate with anyone who is called a brother if he is sexually immoral, or greedy, or an idolater, or verbally abusive, or a drunkard, or a swindler. Do not even eat with such a person. For what business is it of mine to judge people outside the church? Do you not judge those inside? God will judge the people outside the church. "Remove the wicked man from among yourselves." – 1 Corinthians 5:9-13
- Don't have anything to do with foolish and stupid arguments, because you know they produce quarrels. – 2 Timothy 2:23
- Alexander the metalworker did me a great deal of harm. The Lord will repay him for what he has done. You too should be on your guard against him, because he strongly opposed our message." – 2 Timothy 4:14-15
- Do not make friends with a hot-tempered person, do not associate with one easily angered… – Proverbs 22:24

These passages demonstrate the wisdom of boundaries in response to oppressive and toxic people. There are also many Scriptural examples of people fleeing harm. Only Jesus, after eluding the clutches of the religious leaders many times prior, willingly chose to subjugate Himself to harm according to the Father's perfect plan and timing. Dear friend, you are not called to be your husband's savior; only Jesus can save a soul. Perhaps you think that suffering oppression will win your husband's heart, but after nearly 30 years of doing this ministry, I have never seen it. In fact, of the rare cases I have seen marriages restored after abuse, every single one of them happened after the injured spouse learned to set boundaries and follow through with consequences. That is how God dealt with His own wayward spouse, Israel, in the Old Testament (Jeremiah 2:32, 3:8, 14:10-12,15:2). God turned His face and blessings from His chosen people, gave them a writ of divorce, and allowed them to go into captivity. Still, His heart was for restoration, but He knew that allowing them to continue in their sin would never accomplish it. The same is true for wayward husbands. Most need consequences to come to the end of themselves and be willing to sincerely yield their lives to God. I pray He will give you the strength to follow His lead by learning to set limits on sin.

PRACTICAL TIPS FOR SETTING BOUNDARIES

1. *Assess your situation.* How is it impacting you, and what needs to stop?
2. *Create your boundaries along with consequences for violating them.* A wise counselor or therapist can be helpful with this.
3. *Kindly inform your partner or others of your boundary.* It may sound something like this, "I care about you, but the way you are treating me is hurtful. It is not ok for you to curse at me and belittle me. From now on, when you do that, I will separate myself from you and go somewhere I feel safe." Usually, the consequence is limiting access to yourself.
4. *Remember, boundaries are not rules for others.* They are limits you set to protect yourself from mistreatment.
5. *Be firm but kind and calm when informing others of your boundary.* Don't be harsh when setting the limits. Pray as you are speaking.
6. *Biblical boundaries are motived by love,* and a desire to honor God, rather than to control others.

7. *Boundaries help us better practice self-control because we are not being manipulated and controlled by the whims of others.*
8. *Relationships with boundaries are healthier than those with none.* The goal of good boundaries is to protect us and perhaps even our relationships.
9. *Setting boundaries is not meant to threaten or punish.*
10. *Practice what you will say before setting the boundary.* This is especially true for abuse survivors who have had very little practice in doing it. With practice, it will become much easier over time.
11. *Boundaries without consequences don't work.* If your abuser continues to violate your boundaries, you will need to come up with more effective consequences, such as short-term separation or calling the police if your safety is threatened.
12. *Boundaries may or may not impact the other person.* They may not achieve the desired results, and you will need to have a plan of action if that is the case.

If you struggle withstanding mistreatment, I highly recommend Leslie Vernick's book *The Emotionally Destructive Marriage*. In it she suggests the following principles for building core strength and resisting sin. You must be:

- Committed to truth and reality. The lies we tell ourselves are often far more damaging than the ones our abusers tell us.
- Open to growth, instruction, and feedback.
- Responsible for yourself and respectful toward others without dishonoring yourself.
- Empathic and compassionate toward others without enabling people to continue to abuse and disrespect you.[75]

Vernick says you must learn to speak up firmly and kindly, and you must set limits. If the destructiveness continues, you can:

- End the conversation (keep your cell phone with you if you need to call the police).
- Do not drive anywhere together.
- Exit a situation when he starts to escalate.
- Go to the church for discipline and accountability (if the church gets abuse).
- Withdraw sexual privileges.
- Separate.
- Call the police.

For more on the importance of boundaries, see *The Emotionally Destructive Relationship, How to Act Right When Your Spouse Acts Wrong*—particularly under subtitle, "The Gift of Consequences" in Chapter 9—& *The Emotionally Destructive Marriage*, both by Leslie Vernick, and *Good Boundaries and Goodbyes* by Lysa Terkeurst.[76]

---

[75] Vernick Leslie, *The Emotionally Destructive Marriage*, 105.

[76] TerKeurst, Lysa, *Good Boundaries and Goodbyes: Loving Others Without Losing the Best of Who You Are*, (Nashville, TN, Thomas Nelson, 2022).

LESSON 12 EXERCISES

1. Read Romans 12:17-19 below.
   - Do not repay anyone evil for evil. Be careful to do what is right in the eyes of everyone. If it is possible, as far as it depends on you, live at peace with everyone. Do not take revenge, my dear friends, but leave room for God's wrath, for it is written: "It is mine to avenge; I will repay," says the Lord.

   How does God instruct us to deal with difficulties in our relationships? Is this different than your way of dealing with them? Since it is not always possible to live in peace in the physical world, allow the Lord to lead you to rest and let your heart and mind be filled with His peace. Make sure you set the boundaries you need to protect yourself from dangerous and demanding people. Write out a prayer asking God to help you do this.

2. Let the following passage speak to your heart. "Am I now trying to win the approval of human beings, or of God? Or am I trying to please people? If I were still trying to please people, I would not be a servant of Christ" (Galatians 1:10). Take time to assess where your heart is. Are you more concerned with pleasing God or people? Misplaced fear leads to misplaced devotion. To move forward, we must learn to put God on the throne of our lives rather than a man. Do you find yourself seeking the approval of man over God? If so, what has been the outcome?

3. There are many biblical examples of withdrawing from dangerous and demanding people. Below are just a few. All but Jesus's situation involved family members. Is there an example here you need to follow?
   - Jacob from Esau (Genesis 27:41-45)
   - David from Saul (1 Samuel 21-23) and Absalom (2 Samuel 15:14)
   - Jesus (Matthew 12:14-16; Luke 4:28-30)

4. Now, let's look at a few biblical examples of problems caused by somebody's failure to say no. Can you see how Eli, David, and Solomon could have considered their actions loving? Were their actions really loving? Have you made similar mistakes in failing to set boundaries? If so, write them out below.
   - Eli's failure to restrain his sons led to destruction. (1 Sam. 2:22-25 & 3:13)
   - David's failure to discipline his children led to their demise. (1 Kings 1:6)
   - Solomon tried to please his wives, and as a result turned his heart from God. (1 Kings 11)
   - Saul tried to please the people and ended up losing the kingdom. (1 Sam. 13:8-15)

5. There are also positive biblical examples of setting boundaries and standing up against sin in Scripture. Jesus is love incarnate, yet did not give in to the demands placed on Him by people. He often withdrew from the crowds to be alone and spend time with the Father. Read the following passages and try to imagine yourself in the same situation. Can you relate? How would you have felt if you had been facing the same thing? How can these examples help you the next time you have to take a stand against pressure from others or against sinful mistreatment? Look for specific steps you can take and list them below.
   - Daniel (Daniel 6:6-12, 21-23)
   - Jesus (Matthew 21:23-27 and Luke 23:8-9)

6. Take time to assess your own life. Is there an area where you are being harmed, and what kind of boundaries and consequences do you need to establish? Write them out below. Pray that God will give you wisdom in creating them, and courage to implement them.

Notes

LESSON 13

UNDERSTANDING FORGIVENESS
Putting Your Hurt in God's Hands

For many of us, forgiving our abusers can be the most difficult battle we face in the healing process, but it is a necessary step in overcoming the anger that comes with abuse. I knew I could not face the pain without God's help. I also knew His Word commanded me to forgive, but I needed a lot of help working through it. There were a few common misconceptions I had to overcome to truly forgive, and I've seen many other survivors struggle with them as well. As a child, I was taught to forgive and forget. When my siblings and I asked for forgiveness, we were taught to respond with, "That's ok. I forgive you." Then we were expected to hug and make up. Basically, that formed my view of how the process should look, but it was a very flawed perspective because it caused me to believe the myth that forgiveness would always lead to reconciliation. I also thought forgiving meant I simply had to minimize or dismiss the offenses as though they had never happened. Thankfully, I was wrong on both counts. Biblical forgiveness is placing the offender in God's hands and leaving justice to Him. It is letting go of our need for vengeance, but it does not dismiss the hurt as though it wasn't that bad or that it never happened. Romans 12:17-21 gives us instructions on dealing with those who harm us. We are not to repay evil with evil or take revenge, but we are instructed to leave room for God's wrath.

We must trust that God will handle the situation in His time with His perfect justice. When tempted to stoop to our abuser's level by taking revenge, we can remind ourselves of His promises to fight our battles and enact justice on our behalf (2 Thessalonians 1:6, Romans 12:19). Usually, when we refuse to let go of our anger and desire for retaliation, it is because we don't trust that His way of dealing with it is better than ours. Sadly, refusing to forgive damages us more than it does those who hurt us. I've heard it said that unforgiveness is like drinking poison and hoping the other person dies. I know I was miserable until I was finally able to forgive, and although it can be a grueling process, being willing is half the battle. Making the choice to release the burden to Him begins the process. Our feelings may not change immediately, but as we continue to release it, and ask Him to take it, our emotions will eventually catch up. Peace comes when we realize He always has our best interest at heart, and that He will enact justice on our behalf. Regardless of how things may look in the present, there will come a day when your abuser will have to bow before Him, perhaps in great fear and trembling, and confess that He is Lord (Philippians 2:10-11). He will make all things right in due time. Until that time, peace is found in surrendering the burden of the offenses suffered to His loving care. When we can do that, we will soon find ourselves set free.

PROBLEMS WITH UNFORGIVENESS

- Unforgiveness toward another person hurts you more than it hurts them and eventually poisons every relationship in your life, including the most important one—your relationship with God.
  - But when you are praying, first forgive anyone you are holding a grudge against, so that your Father in heaven will forgive your sins, too. – Mark 11:25
- Holding on to anger, and a desire for revenge, is failing to deal with it God's way. It gives Satan a foothold in your life.
  - If you are angry, don't sin by nursing your grudge. Don't let the sun go down with you still angry—get over it quickly; for when you are angry, you give a mighty foothold to the devil. – Ephesians 4:26-27
- We are commanded to let go of our unrighteous anger and to forgive.
  - Do not nurse hatred in your heart toward anyone. Confront people directly so you will not be held guilty for their sin. Do not seek revenge or bear a grudge but love your neighbor as yourself. I am the Lord. – Leviticus 19:17-18 (NLT)
- Unforgiveness is usurping God's role as Judge.
  - Don't speak evil against each other, dear brothers and sisters. If you criticize and judge each other, then you are criticizing and judging God's law. But your job is to obey the law, not to judge whether it applies to you. God alone, Who gave the law, is the Judge. He alone has the power to save or to destroy. So, what right do you have to judge your neighbor? – James 4:11-12
  - Do not judge others, and you will not be judged. For you will be treated as you treat others. The standard you use in judging is the standard by which you will be judged. – Matthew 7:1-2
- Unforgiveness can lead to depression and other problematic emotions.
- It is self-focused. People who have not forgiven still carry a lot of anger and pain—their hurt drives their lives, rather than His Spirit. Focusing on how someone has hurt us takes our focus away from what Jesus has done for us. Resentment wears us down, but gratitude sets us free.
- Unforgiveness gives the person who hurt us continued power over us because they continue to occupy so much space in our minds.

FORGIVENESS DEFINED

- It is not a feeling; it is an act of obedience.
- It is not minimizing or dismissing the offenses.
- It may not lead to reconciliation! Trust is earned, forgiveness is freely given.
- It is not forgetting the offense; it is releasing your desire to control the outcome to God.
- It is a choice of the will to obey God and to choose His path above your own.
- It is leaving the offender in God's hands and choosing to bless rather than curse, while trusting God for justice (Romans 12:17-21).

THE FORGIVENESS PROCESS

1. *Be honest; pour out your hurts to the Lord* (and perhaps to a wise Believer).
   - I cry aloud to the Lord; I lift up my voice to the Lord for mercy. I pour out before Him my complaint; before Him I tell my trouble. – Psalm 142:1-2
2. *Trust His sovereignty and goodness.* Recognize that He promises to work it together for your good. Be patient with yourself. It takes time to change your perspective, but as you choose to proclaim His truth over your life, I am confident that He will empower you to overcome lingering doubts.
   - And we know that God causes everything to work together for the good of those who love God and are called according to His purpose for them. For God knew His people in advance, and He chose them to become like his Son, so that His Son would be the firstborn among many brothers and sisters. – Romans 8:28-29. (NLT)
   - You intended to harm me, but God intended it for good to accomplish what is now being done... – Genesis 50:20
3. *Remember His great mercy and forgiveness towards you.*
   - But God showed His great love for us by sending Christ to die for us while we were still sinners. – Romans 5:8
   - See the parable of the unmerciful servant in Matthew 18:21-34
4. *Choose to obey His Word and forgive.*
   - I weep with sorrow; encourage me by Your word. Keep me from lying to myself; give me the privilege of knowing Your instructions. I have chosen to be faithful; I have determined to live by Your regulations. I cling to Your laws. Lord don't let me be put to shame! I will pursue Your commands, for You expand my understanding. – Psalm 119:28-32 (NLT)
5. *Entrust the offender to God and His justice.*
   - Though the tide of battle runs strongly against me, for so many are fighting me, yet He will rescue me. God Himself—God from everlasting ages past—will answer them! For they refuse to fear Him or even honor His commands. As for my companion, he betrayed me—I who was at peace with him. He broke his promises. His words were smooth as butter, but in his heart was war. His words were sweet, but underneath were daggers. Give your burdens to the Lord. He will carry them. He will not permit the godly to slip or fall. He will send my enemies to the pit of destruction. Murderers and liars will not live out half their days. But I am trusting You to save me. – Psalm 55:18-23
   - But I said to them, "Don't be afraid! The Lord God is your leader, and He will fight for you with His mighty miracles, just as you saw Him do in Egypt. And you know how He has cared for you again and again here in the wilderness, just as a father cares for His child!" – Deuteronomy 1:29-31
6. *Remember it is a process made up of minute-by-minute choices.*
   - We are destroying speculations, and every lofty thing raised up against the knowledge of God. We also capture every thought and make it obedient to Christ. – 2 Corinthians 10:5
   - I can do all this through Him who gives me strength. – Philippians 4:13
7. *Be proactive in filling your mind with truth from God's Word.*
   - I have thought much about Your words and stored them in my heart so that they would hold me back from sin. – Psalm 119:11 (NLT)

8. Act kindly—bless, love, pray. Some people are best loved from a distance. It is more loving to cut off relationship than to allow someone to sin against you continually. God allows consequences for those he loves, and we should do the same.
- But I tell you, love your enemies and pray for those who persecute you, that you may be children of your Father in heaven. He causes his sun to rise on the evil and the good and sends rain on the righteous and the unrighteous. — Matthew 5:44-45

Helpful Resources: *Lord, Heal My Hurts* by Kay Arthur and *Forgiving What You Can't Forget: Discover How to Move On, Make Peace with Painful Memories, and Create a Life That's Beautiful Again* by Lysa TerKeurst, and *Making Sense of Forgiveness: Moving from Hurt toward Hope* by Brad Hambrick.

LESSON 13 EXERCISES

1. Where are you in your forgiveness journey? Write out anything you think is holding you back from fully experiencing the freedom that comes from true Christ-like forgiveness. This could be unresolved feelings, memories, or a lack of trust in God. Remember you don't have to trust or reconcile with the one who hurt you to forgive.

2. To overcome unforgiveness and its damaging consequences in your life, you must determine to do it God's way rather than your own. So far, how have you handled the offenses you've endured? How will you do things differently going forward?

3. In the *CTP* book, Chapter 12, read the Forgiveness section, and write out a prayer to the Lord asking Him to help you release the offenses you are struggling with most.

4. Unforgiveness hurts us more than it hurts our abusers. Can you identify ways it has hurt you? If so, describe how it has impacted you.

5. When it comes to oppression and abuse, we may have to forgive the one who harmed us more than once. This excerpt from my journal in 1996 describes one of the many times I had to choose to forgive again.

This anger business is sort of like indigestion. Every time you think you're done with it, it comes back up again. Today I was doing some packing, and it just reminded me of all the things I've lost, and lately I've thought how senseless it has all been. It seems sometimes that I've spent 20 years of my life losing to him. I've lost possessions galore, but even worse than that, I let him steal my self-respect, my principles, my happiness, my life. I feel so used by him. I just wish I had woken up sooner. But then I know that the one thing that I have gained has been worth the struggle. Knowing my weak and selfish nature, I would have probably only played at my faith had I not gone through all the bad times.

Can you relate to this post? Write out offenses that still plague you, a prayer committing them to God, as well as any possible good you see coming from the pain you've endured.

6. The truth is that God will redeem your sorrows and your troubles. Remember that He is for you! Read the following passage and consider how it might apply to the hurts you've had trouble forgiving.

    - Genesis 50:15-20 — When Joseph's brothers saw that their father was dead, they said, "What if Joseph holds a grudge against us and pays us back for all the wrongs we did to him?" So they sent word to Joseph, saying, "Your father left these instructions before he died: This is what you are to say to Joseph: I ask you to forgive your brothers the sins and the wrongs they committed in treating you so badly.' Now please forgive the sins of the servants of the God of your father." When their message came to him, Joseph wept. His brothers then came and threw themselves down before him. "We are your slaves," they said. But Joseph said to them, "Don't be afraid. Am I in the place of God? *You intended to harm me, but God intended it for good* to accomplish what is now being done, the saving of many lives.

    Do you believe God could use what you've been through for good? Do you see any signs of that happening already? Write out your thoughts, and a prayer for grace to see how He might be working behind the scenes in your life.

7. Take time to read the Scriptures below. Be encouraged and hopeful as you lean on God. Claim His promises to help you through the healing process as you choose to forgive. Write out a prayer asking the Lord to help you live in His hope and truth this week.
    - The righteous person may have many troubles, but the LORD delivers him from them all. – Psalm 34:19
    - He rescues me unharmed from the battle waged against me, even though many oppose me. – Psalm 55:18
    - My enemies will retreat when I call to You for help. This I know: God is on my side! – Psalm 56:9 (NLT)
    - "For I know the plans I have for you," says the LORD. "They are plans for good and not for disaster, to give you a future and a hope." – Jeremiah 29:11

Choose to forgive your abuser. Throw off unforgiveness and recognize that this will set you free!

LESSON 14

WORSHIP HIM

Perhaps receiving reader feedback on this lesson, and the corresponding chapter in the book, was the primary motivation for revising both books. Most of the feedback on the lesson was positive acknowledging how freeing it is to recognize the connection between idolatry and abuse. It helps us understand that God is not calling us to slavish servitude in our marriages. However, I also got some adverse feedback saying that the concept of calling our abusers idols is both shaming and victim blaming. I realize that some would prefer that I leave out idolatry language altogether; however, this concept was something that God laid on my heart, and it was immensely freeing. In fact, it was a vitally important key to my healing, one that I believe must be included in the books. Still, the huge dichotomy in the feedback made me realize I needed to explain my convictions on this subject better. At first, I did not fully understand why people were reacting to a concept that I, and many others, found so freeing, but conversations with survivors helped me see the problem. Apparently, many counselors particularly some in my own world, the biblical counseling arena,[77] have used idolatry language in a way that is undeniably condemning. The following accounts from two survivors connected with CTPM support groups, I'll call them Grace and Judy, demonstrate how destructive this sort of counseling can be.

---

[77] Please note that in recent years the biblical counseling world has improved significantly in its understanding of trauma and abuse, but there are still many among our ranks who lack understanding. That is why it is wise to vet any counselor you choose before committing to counseling. Also note that although many well-known abuse advocates suggest only licensed therapists can handle abuse-related trauma well, I have found that most licensed therapists are also deficient in this area. The Christian Trauma Healing Network (https://christiantraumahealingnetwork.org) and The Association of Biblical Counselors (https://christiancounseling.com) offer advanced training on abuse and trauma for counselors. In 2023, the Christian Counseling Education Foundation CCEF (www.ccef.org) devoted its entire annual conference to trauma. You may want to reach out to these organizations to find abuse/trauma informed counselors near you.

GRACE'S STORY

"[Our counselor] believed that every interaction between two people where sin was involved was because each of those individuals had their own idol for that instance. Everything was jointly an issue, every marital fight we relayed we were given the worksheet to pick our idol for that [conflict]. His was usually peace… Mine was perfection…"

Grace went on to describe two extremely dangerous situations involving her ex-husband. First, he threw their son up against a wall leaving bruises. Next, he began rage driving at 100 mph, while grabbing their 2-year-old son's leg and screaming that his crying was going to kill the entire family if he didn't be quiet.

Later in marriage counseling[78] when Grace told their counselor she was fearful for their lives during the rage driving incident, the counselor turned to her and asked if she recognized her "idol of control." When she said she had considered calling 911, the counselor said that proved her desire to be in control "by calling the authorities." He told her she should have "calmly explained to [her] husband how the situation had escalated, and [they] should take a few minutes to pray." This counselor clearly minimized extreme abuse, which later subjected her to further harm. He also wrongly stood in judgment over Grace calling her God-given response to danger an idol.

JUDY'S STORY

"My experience with "idolatry" in my abusive marriage was primarily through the women's ministry and "prominent" women at my old church. Submission (complete obedience), unconditional respect and sexual "availability" were main features of the beliefs of the church… Nearly every women's study and retreat was on biblical womanhood, and submission… I was taught that as a woman I was manipulative, wicked, a gossip, easily deceived and untrustworthy. [The book they used] gave me many examples of idolatry such as wanting to be treated well by my husband, having my own desires, feeling hurt by him, or being afraid of him, wanting my house a certain way, making a meal I liked, and wanting to feel loved by him. I was taught that all of these and more were idolatry, and petty selfishness."

"My marriage was destructive, and I thought it was all my fault. I was afraid to ask for help because I thought I would be put under church discipline for my disobedient and rebellious heart… What I realize now, is that these teachings made my husband my idol. They put him in the place of Christ, which is harmful not only to me, but to him. I was feeding the monster of his sinful behavior."

---

[78] Please note that marriage counseling is not recommended in cases of domestic abuse and coercive control, because it usually mutualizes problems and makes things far worse for victims. Moreover, abusers tend to weaponize any counsel given to their wives.

I completely agree with Judy! That's exactly what God showed me after I got out of the abuse. When we bow down in fear to anyone, it gives them control over us. After experiencing trauma and abuse, it is normal to find ourselves being controlled by fear of our abusers, especially when distorted interpretations of biblical headship and submission seem to indicate that our job as wives is to wholeheartedly bow down to whatever our husbands want. My interpretation of wifely submission meant that, no matter what he wanted, I had to yield to my husband—even when it served his selfish, sinful agendas. After getting out of the abuse, God convicted me that blind obedience to my husband's whims had unintentionally given him dominion over my life. Scripture certainly seems to confirm the connection between fear and idolatry. This passage in Isaiah demonstrates it.

> Whom have you so dreaded and feared that you have been false to Me, and have neither remembered Me nor pondered this in your hearts? Is it not because I have long been silent that you do not fear Me? I will expose your righteousness and your works, and they will not benefit you. When you cry out for help, let your collection [of idols] save you! The wind will carry all of them off, a mere breath will blow them away. But the man who makes Me His refuge will inherit the land and possess My holy mountain" (Isaiah 57:11-13).

"Whom have you so dreaded and feared that you have been false to Me…?" I'm not sure how much clearer that could be. At the heart of being unfaithful to God is usually a fear of something, or someone else. The bottom line is that when we live in fear of our partners, we unintentionally give them lordship of our lives. Another interesting line in this passage is "I will expose your righteousness and your works…" Their actions were motivated by a fear of punishment rather than love. The fear of the Lord is the beginning of wisdom because we are more concerned about pleasing Him than people or circumstances. Our "God is love. Whoever lives in love lives in God, and God in them. There is no fear in love. But perfect love drives out fear, because fear has to do with punishment. The one who fears is not made perfect in love" (1 John 4:16 &18). If fear of punishment has motivated your thoughts and actions, there's a good chance someone, or something else, has unconsciously taken control of your life. If you have filtered most of your thoughts through your husband or partner's possible reaction, then he has unconsciously become your lord. I am not saying that you didn't still love and worship God. I am saying that when the wrong kind of fear takes over, you can easily find yourself in slavish bondage. It is a matter of who has control of your life.

Destructive fear dreads losing control, and that is why the Israelites sacrificed to idols. They believed that appeasing them would make things run smoothly and that if they didn't sacrifice, things would go badly. When we live in fear of man, we have a similar mentality. "If I can just do _____" everything will be OK. We find ourselves spending inordinate amounts of time thinking about what might happen if we mess up, and about what has already happened. That is another way that abusers continue to control our lives. They consume our thought life like a negative form of meditation. Unfortunately, this trauma-related "meditation" can also be a somatic experience, meaning our bodies are reacting to what has happened. Even though logic may tell us we are safe, our bodies do not get the message. This is a natural, God-given response to danger, but people with post-traumatic stress (PTS) experience these symptoms in the absence of current danger. It is a perfectly understandable response to trauma. The problem is that faulty responses must be addressed over time if we want to find healing. Replacing this negative meditation on our abusers with true worship is a powerful and healing step (see Lesson 5).

PURE WORSHIP

If fear of man leads to distorted meditation and worship, then a holy fear of the Lord leads to genuine worship. For those of us coming out of abuse, it's important to understand what this proper fear looks like. Psalm 19:9 tells us that "The fear of the LORD is pure, enduring forever." The purity of this fear stands in contrast to the unholy fear of man that ensnares (Proverbs 29:25). In fact, it is "a fountain of life, turning a person from the snares of death (Proverbs 14:27). To fear God is to reverence Him, and to care more about honoring Him than anything or anyone else. It is rooted in a deep love and respect for God that compels us to serve and obey Him (John 14:15, 2 Corinthians 5:14). This means that correcting faulty beliefs about Him is crucial. We must know that He is loving and does not delight in punishing us. His love is "patient and kind. It does not envy, it does not boast, it is not proud. It does not dishonor others, it is not self-seeking, it is not easily angered, it keeps no record of wrongs. [It] does not delight in evil but rejoices with the truth. It always protects, always trusts, always hopes, always perseveres. [It] never fails (1 Corinthians 13:4-8). There is peace in surrendering control to One who loves us that well. When we do we will be like the man who built his house upon the rock in Matthew 7:24-25. No matter what life brings our way, we can persevere and overcome because He holds us, and His love overcomes destructive fear (1 John 4:18).

As we begin to understand God's amazing love for us, we will want to worship Him—that is, to elevate Him about all else. There is so much power in making Him bigger than our abusers, our fears, our circumstances, and anything else we have made all-consuming. "Therefore, since we are receiving a kingdom that cannot be shaken, let us be thankful, and so worship God acceptably with reverence and awe, for our "God is a consuming fire" (Hebrews 12:28-29). Let Him consume all the fears that have overwhelmed you. Psalm 100:4 instructs us to "Enter His gates with thanksgiving and His courts with praise." I believe this gives us a strategy for intentionally communing with God. We begin with thanksgiving. We may just start by thanking Him for the blessings in our lives, then move to thanking Him for who He is and what He's done. I believe gratitude prepares our hearts to enter His courts with praise. In my mind, "His courts" represent His presence, where there is fullness of joy (Psalm 16:11). Praise and worship may include singing, reading Scripture about His goodness, spending time in nature, and just imagining being held by Him. As we praise Him, He gives us strength for our weakness (2 Corinthians 12:9); sorrow is replaced by joy, and fear is replaced by faith. That is my prayer for you, friend. I pray that as you choose to cast ungodly fears at His feet and worship you will experience the beauty and joy of intimately knowing Him. There is nothing better in this life (Philippians 3:8).

LESSON 14: WORSHIP HIM | 203

PRACTICAL CONSIDERATIONS

- We become like what we worship. (Psalm 115:8)
- Idolatry yields misery. (Psalm 16:4)
- Idolatry is the result of misplaced fear that leads to a desire to control. We want things on our terms rather than yielding to Him.
- God offers healing for the wounds of His people, but we look to shallow substitutes to find the healing only He can provide. (Jeremiah 2:11-13)
- God created us for fellowship with Himself but laments that we "refuse to know" Him (Jeremiah 9:6). When we are living under the control of an abusive person, it warps our view of God so that we can't see clearly or know Him.
- This sort of fear leads to bondage, but the fear of the Lord leads to freedom. Fearing God is not related to punishment like the fear of an abuser is (1 John 4:18). It is simply honoring Him above all else and yielding ourselves to Him rather than grasping to control everything out of fear. [79]

> But the eyes of the Lord are on those who fear Him,
> on those whose hope is in His unfailing love…"
> ~ *Psalm 33:18.*

---

[79] Note: this does not mean we ignore safety concerns. Scripture is filled with examples of people fleeing for safety. We must be wise when it comes to dealing with abusers, and careful safety planning reflects wisdom.

LESSON 14 EXERCISES

1. Has fear unintentionally made something, or someone other than God, the lord of your life? If so, describe what happened.

2. Review the fear section in Chapter 12, "Managing Your Emotions," in *Called to Peace*. Can you relate to the experience of making your marriage or your spouse an idol? How will knowing God's great love help you put God on the throne? Write out your experiences and proclaim God's truth over yourself.

3. When we think we desperately need something from someone, we give them power in our lives. This week, look up the following verses and write out what Scripture tells us about what we truly need.
   - 2 Peter 1:3 (divine power—everything we need)

   - Luke 10:38-42 — Mary at Jesus' feet

   - Psalm 27 — My light and salvation—comes when we're forsaken (10)

   - Psalm 73:23-28 — He's always with us and guides and counsels us.

   - Matthew 4:4 — live on every word that comes from the mouth of God.

4. Fear can become an opportunity to proclaim His power. When we can say we were afraid, but still moved forward in faith, it shows the world that it is His power rather than our own. As hard as it may seem, rejecting fear of man is a choice. How will this choice look for you? What specific steps will you take?

5. Write out a confession to God for having idolatrous fear in your life and commit to serving Him alone.

6. List some practical ways you can make God the center of your life rather than a man or an idol.

LESSON 15

FINDING BEAUTY IN SUFFERING

Some people never recover from the trauma of living with coercive control, so you may be wondering if there really is a way to move from victim to victor. The question is, will you choose to believe God's assurances to the afflicted? "We are hard pressed on every side, but not crushed; perplexed, but not in despair; persecuted, but not abandoned; struck down, but not destroyed" (2 Corinthians 4:8-9). Coming out of abuse, I held tightly to passages like this. I also camped out in Psalms for a few years and found great comfort in them. I simply had to remind myself that God is for me. When the person you love most has been against you for so long, sometimes it's hard to believe anyone can be on your side. That is why it's so important to learn to counter negative thoughts with the truth about who He is.

We serve a God who specializes in redemption. This means that He can take the worst of your suffering and use it for good. The ultimate example of this is seen in Jesus. He willingly came into the world and suffered in order to reconcile us to God. He was despised, rejected, and abused beyond recognition, yet God had a good plan. I often read Isaiah 53, which describes Jesus's earthly suffering, to abuse victims because I want them to know that God truly understands their suffering. Hebrews 12:2 tells us that Jesus endured the shame and misery of the cross because of the "joy set before him." He knew the Father's plan was to use it to reconcile a lost world to Himself, and He knew it would allow Him to fully relate to those who suffer. Before I go any further, let me just say that I am not saying you should stay and suffer abuse! By all means, make every effort to get yourself and your children out of harm's way. If you want to move forward and heal, recognizing that God wants to redeem your pain will be immensely beneficial.

Consider the story of Joseph found in chapters 37-50 of Genesis. When his wrongful suffering was over, God used him to save a whole nation, as well as the same brothers who had betrayed him. Although he had the power to destroy them, Joseph chose mercy instead. Genesis 50:20 is one of my favorite Bible passages. This verse records Joseph's response to his brothers when they stood before him seeking forgiveness. While many people would savor the opportunity to get even, Joseph pointed to God's sovereign and good purposes. He told them, "As for you, you meant evil against me, but God meant it for good in order to bring about this present result, to preserve many people alive" (NASB). The truth is that bad things happen in this fallen world. Many of us end up as victims at some point, and it grieves God's heart. We suffer unjustly and it isn't fair, but God knows exactly how that feels (Hebrews 4:15). Our God is a redeemer, and nothing is wasted when we know Him. He can turn our mourning into dancing (Psalm 30:11) and use tribulation to mold us into the image of His son (Romans 8:29). But amid our troubles, we must choose to trust Him. Choose to focus your thoughts on truth that lines up with His Word. The process of biblical meditation summarized in Lesson 5 is a powerful way to internalize that truth. Refuse every deceptive thought (2 Corinthians10:5) and resolve to dwell on things that are good (Philippians 4:6-8). Remind yourself that He promises to work all things together for good (Romans 8:28), He always leads us in triumph (2 Corinthians 2:14), and He uses trials to build character in us (Romans 5:3-5).

Do you believe God could ever use your suffering for good? I can tell you, without a doubt, that if I had not suffered abuse, I would not be in this ministry. I can also tell you that my experiences drove me into my Savior's arms and deepened my relationship with Him beyond anything I would have ever imagined. When we see ourselves as victims, we can be too self-consumed to care for other people, but God wants us to use our pain to help others. "Praise be to the God and Father of our Lord Jesus Christ, the Father of compassion and the God of all comfort, who comforts us in all our troubles, so that we can comfort those in any trouble with the comfort we ourselves receive from God" (2 Cor. 1:3-4).

It's not easy, but God has given you all the resources you need to overcome. You have the very same Spirit who raised Christ from the dead dwelling in you (Romans 8:11)! You also have His Word that is alive and active to perform the spiritual surgery needed for change (Hebrews 4:12). You have a choice; you can allow our Lord to use your suffering for good, or you can let your past define you. My prayer is that you will choose God's way and make the transition from victim to victor. Beauty can be found in suffering when we allow it to drive us into His arms and into a deeper relationship with Him.

REALITIES OF SUFFERING

1. *Suffering is an inevitable part of life in the world.*
    - The righteous person may have many troubles, but the LORD delivers him from them all. – Psalms 34:19
    - I have told you these things, so that in Me you may have peace. In this world you will have trouble. But take heart! I have overcome the world. – John 16:33
2. *We have an enemy who seeks to destroy.*
    - Be alert and of sober mind. Your enemy the devil prowls around like a roaring lion looking for someone to devour. – 1 Peter 5:8
    - The thief comes only to steal and kill and destroy; I have come that they may have life and have it to the full. – John 10:10
3. *Jesus suffered and shares in our suffering.* He chose to suffer extreme abuse on our behalf!
    - I offered My back to those who beat Me and My cheeks to those who pulled out My beard. I did not hide My face from mockery and spitting. Because the sovereign Lord helps Me, I will not be disgraced, Therefore I have set My face like a stone, determined to do His will. And I know that I will not be put to shame." – Isaiah 50:6- 7
    - Because He Himself suffered when He was tempted, He is able to help those who are being tempted. – Hebrews 2:18. **Note:** the word tempted here can also refer to trials.
4. *Our Lord understands your suffering and promises to redeem it according to His good purposes for your life.* He didn't promise we would have it easy here on earth, but He did promise to use our suffering for good.

- The Spirit of the Sovereign Lord is on me, because the Lord has anointed me to proclaim good news to the poor. He has sent me to bind up the brokenhearted, to proclaim freedom for the captives and release from darkness for the prisoners, to proclaim the year of the Lord's favor and the day of vengeance of our God, to comfort all who mourn, and provide for those who grieve in Zion—to bestow on them a crown of beauty instead of ashes, the oil of joy instead of mourning, and a garment of praise instead of a spirit of despair. – Isaiah 61:1-3
- He will redeem my soul in peace from the battle which is against me, For they are many who are aggressive toward me. – Psalms 55:18 (NASB)
- And we know that in all things God works for the good of those who love Him, who have been called according to His purpose. For those God foreknew He also predestined to be conformed to the image of His Son, that He might be the firstborn among many brothers and sisters. – Romans 8:28-29

5. *We must make a choice about how we will respond to suffering and choose to believe His truth.*
    - Therefore, we do not lose heart. Though outwardly we are wasting away, yet inwardly we are being renewed day by day. For our light and momentary troubles are achieving for us an eternal glory that far outweighs them all. So we fix our eyes not on what is seen, but on what is unseen, since what is seen is temporary, but what is unseen is eternal. – 2 Corinthians 4:16-18
    - Not only so, but we also glory in our sufferings, because we know that suffering produces perseverance; perseverance, character; and character, hope. - And hope does not put us to shame, because God's love has been poured out into our hearts through the Holy Spirit, who has been given to us. – Romans 5:3-5

6. *Suffering can deepen our relationship with Him.* He fights our battles for us.
    - The Lord makes firm the steps of the one who delights in Him; though he may stumble, he will not fall, for the Lord upholds him with His hand. – Psalm 37:23-24
    - Yet I am always with You; You hold me by my right hand. You guide me with Your counsel, and afterward You will take me into glory. Whom have I in heaven but You? I desire You more than anything on earth. My health may fail, and my spirit may grow weak, but God remains the strength of my heart; He is mine forever… But as for me, how good it is to be near God! I have made the sovereign Lord my shelter, and I will tell everyone about the wonderful things You do. – Psalm 73:23-28
    - The Lord is close to the brokenhearted; He rescues those who are crushed in spirit… Calamity will surely destroy the wicked, and those who hate the righteous will be punished. But the Lord will redeem those who serve Him. No one who takes refuge in Him will be condemned. – Psalm 34:18, 21-22
    - So do not fear, for I am with you; do not be dismayed, for I am your God. I will strengthen you and help you; I will uphold you with My righteous right hand. "All who rage against you will surely be ashamed and disgraced; those who oppose you will be as nothing and perish. Though you search for your enemies, you will not find them. Those who wage war against you will be as nothing at all. For I am the LORD your God who takes hold of your right hand and says to you, Do not fear; I will help you. – Isaiah 41:10-13

7. *Recognize suffering is temporary and cultivate an eternal perspective.*
   - I consider that our present sufferings are not worth comparing with the glory that will be revealed in us. – Romans 8:18
   - If only for this life we have hope in Christ, we are of all people most to be pitied. But Christ has indeed been raised from the dead, the first fruits of those who have fallen asleep. – 1 Corinthians 15:19-20
8. *Entrust yourself to God.* Choose to believe and meditate on His goodness.
   - In you, Lord my God, I put my trust. I trust in You; do not let me be put to shame, nor let my enemies triumph over me. – Psalm 25:1-2
   - They will have no fear of bad news; their hearts are steadfast, trusting in the Lord. – Psalm 112:7
   - Why, my soul, are you downcast? Why so disturbed within me? Put your hope in God, for I will yet praise Him, my Savior and my God. – Psalm 43:5.
9. *Choose to make God bigger than your circumstances.* When we are suffering, we can end up magnifying our problems more than Him, and whatever we magnify gets the most power in our lives.
   a. I will glory in the Lord; let the afflicted hear and rejoice. Glorify the Lord with me; let us exalt His name together. I sought the Lord, and He answered me; He delivered me from all my fears. Those who look to Him are radiant; their faces are never covered with shame. – Psalm 34:2-5
   b. I will extol the Lord at all times; His praise will always be on my lips. I will glory in the Lord; let the afflicted hear and rejoice. – Psalm 34:1-2

QUOTES ABOUT SUFFERING

"We all know people who have been made much meaner and more irritable and more intolerable to live with by suffering: it is not right to say that all suffering perfects. It only perfects one type of person, the one who accepts the call of God in Christ Jesus." Oswald Chambers

"But pain insists upon being attended to. God whispers to us in our pleasures, speaks in our conscience, but shouts in our pains: it is His megaphone to rouse a deaf world." C.S. Lewis

"You may never know that Jesus is all you need, until Jesus is all you have." Corrie Ten Boom.

LESSON 15 EXERCISES

1. "While you are in the wilderness, what are you seeing in your own heart? How are you relating to God? Do you avoid Him? Ignore Him? Get angry at Him? Do you act as though He is very far away and too busy with everything else to attend to your suffering? Are you frustrated that God is powerful enough to end your suffering, but hasn't? In your depression, let God reveal your heart. You might find spiritual issues that contribute to, or even cause, your depression. "You are suffering, and suffering brings God into view."[80] Take time to journal your response to suffering, and where God is in the midst of it.

2. Does your response to suffering line up to God's truth? If not, write out a Bible verse from the study above that counters it.

---

[80] Welch, Ed…*Depression: A Stubborn Darkness* (Greensboro, NC, New Growth Press, 2008).

3. Read Isaiah 53:4-5 about Jesus's suffering. Does it help to know He experienced extreme suffering on your behalf?

4. I wrote the following journal post in 1996 after identifying how God was using suffering for good in my life.

   I do know one thing; I have learned so many valuable lessons this year that I am now actually grateful for all the tragedy. It has drawn me closer to the Lord and shone a light on some dark places in my heart. He was certainly not first in my life.

   Can you relate? Can you see how God may already be using your suffering for good? If so, write it below. If not, be honest with Him. Ask Him to help you see how He may be redeeming it.

Notes

AFTERWORD

Victim or Victor? The Choice is Yours!

WHERE DO WE GO FROM HERE?

There's no subtle way to say it. If you don't find healing after your abusive relationship, there's a good chance you could end up with some negative repercussions. You may find yourself moving on to another abusive relationship. You could end up suffering from severe depression or anxiety, or worst of all you might find yourself chronically angry, perhaps even abusive yourself. This assessment might seem harsh, but in my work with thousands of victims over the years, I've seen these outcomes countless times. I've seen so many women move from one abusive relationship to another because they were still operating out of trauma from previous relationships, and because they never became healthy enough to recognize what to look for in a new relationship. The hardest part of overcoming abuse is overcoming the warped thinking that comes with it. I often tell people that it took a lot longer to get the abuse out of me than it did for me to get out of the abuse—and getting out wasn't easy or quick! I had come to believe many lies, which were aggravated by the physical impacts of PTS. These lies were so deep-seated in me that took years to recognize and replace them with truth. Meditation on His Word was powerful, but even after attaining the major healing milestone of forgiving my ex-husband, I had a long way to go. Forgiveness did help alleviate the anger that almost destroyed me, but it did not stop the fear and anxiety that continued to rule me. Healing was a process that required honest self-appraisal, dependence on the Holy Spirit, and sheer determination not to allow lies to control me any longer.

CHOOSE HIS PATH TO HEALING

I urge you to look back over this workbook. Are there lessons in here that you still need to learn? Have you truly learned to apply God's truths to your life? How are you doing emotionally now compared to when you started this study? Are you overwhelmed with grief or anger? Are you able to wisely stand up to sinful mistreatment? Do you still find yourself overreacting to minor irritations or have you learned to respond gracefully and firmly while speaking truth?

Has abuse left you angry, fearful or distrusting of people in general? Do you have difficulty with relationships? Are you easily offended, or do you assume evil motives on the part of people who are truly trying to help you? If so, you are not alone. These are typical responses to trauma and betrayal. The abuse was not your fault, but regardless of what some say, finding healing after abuse is your responsibility—nobody can do it for you. Are you afraid to face the truth of what happened? Unless you are willing to face it you're likely to stay stuck in trauma and repeating destructive patterns. Many times, people start the work toward recovery but then try to skip over necessary steps like forgiveness, grief or self-examination. Are you willing to take an honest look at yourself? If you struggle with any of the bullet points below, I'd say you still have some healing work to do.

TEN SIGNS YOU HAVEN'T HEALED AFTER ABUSE

1. *You feel a desperate desire or need to be in another relationship*—or maybe even back in the destructive one you left. You may have no idea of what a healthy relationship looks like, but that doesn't stop you from trying again. Do you feel like you need to be in a relationship to be happy or fulfilled? Healthy relationships are never born out of need, and it's so important to find your fulfillment in God. No person on earth will ever be able to give you lasting satisfaction. To have a healthy relationship, you must be healthy. Seek Him first, and healing will come. (Lesson 2)
2. *You still see yourself as a victim.* While someone did victimize you—you were a victim—but allowing it to become your identity is very dangerous. You may find yourself unable to trust even those who have good intentions towards you, and assume their motives are evil even when they are not. (Note: this does not apply to those who may still be in an abusive situation). (Lesson 2)
3. *You find yourself easily triggered* by anything that reminds you of the abuse you experienced. A sound, smell, or even a word can thrust you into a state of panic or dissociation. (Lesson 5)
4. *You struggle with depression or anxiety.* While there are chemical and hormone imbalances that can contribute to these conditions, it's important to recognize the impacts of trauma on the brain. Recovery work with a trauma-informed counselor and Scriptural meditation on truths to counter warped thinking can help heal the brain so that it may be possible to overcome depression and anxiety. (Lessons 8 & 9)
5. *You can't move past the anger.* Anger, in and of itself, is not wrong. We are made in God's image, and there are things that anger Him. The problem comes when we become consumed with anger and are unable to let it go. Anger like this becomes destructive and compels us to want to control things rather than releasing control to God. It is self-focused versus righteous anger, which is God-focused. (Lessons 8 & 13)
6. *You are easily offended and overly defensive.* When we haven't healed, we tend to take things too personally. We often read into the motives of others and make faulty assumptions based on our past experience rather than reality. This can cause problems in most of our relationships.
7. *You are critical and controlling of others.* Part of healing after abuse involves learning to let go of the need to control things that are beyond our control, particularly other people. When we become hyper-aware of others' faults and feel it's our job to correct them, we are in danger of treating others the way our abusers treated us. (Lessons 7 & 14)
8. *You struggle to make decisions.* It is hard to move forward and feel confident about our choices when we've been controlled and criticized for years,. Most of us were told we couldn't do anything right, so the simple act of making a decision can become paralyzing. This is particularly true for survivors of domestic abuse. Survivors of childhood abuse may become highly reactive and prone to impulsive decisions.

9. *You can't move past grief and regret.* There's hardly anything more traumatic than being maliciously betrayed by someone we love. It's hard to get over the shock that their intentions were so evil, especially when we loved them so much. Many times, we struggle to get past the regret of failing to recognize the abuse sooner. Grief is a normal part of the healing process that we can't avoid, but it becomes a problem when it turns to self-pity. (Lesson 10)
10. *You feel hopeless and have lost your faith.* Living with abuse can make us feel like our abusers are even more powerful than God. It's especially difficult when they use Scripture as a weapon to convince us that God is on their side. Nearly every victim of abuse I've ever met found their faith was damaged in some way and most struggle with hopelessness at some point. (Lesson 3)

Many of the victims who have experienced these outcomes have told me they've forgiven their abusers, but deeper conversations have revealed that they didn't truly understand forgiveness. When I find someone who can't talk about the abuse without being overwhelmed with sadness, anger, and tears, my first thought is that they haven't truly forgiven. True forgiveness trusts God's justice instead of feeling a need for revenge. There's something about forgiveness that takes the sting out of our memories. It also prevents us from staying angry. However, I've met hundreds of victims who have not been able to overcome their rage. Not only were they mad at their exes, but many were upset with their churches, the legal system, or one of the many other entities or people that failed them. As mentioned in our lesson on anger, it's natural and right to be upset about injustice. The problem is that if we don't handle it properly, it can consume and destroy us.

On social media there are many advocates who are fueled by this sort of anger. Their messages can be very validating for those who have suffered injustice and abuse. They speak out against centuries of victim blaming, but their solutions fall short of offering the healing victims need. Unfortunately, their backlash against victim blaming has progressed to the point that challenging victims to examine their own broken responses to the abuse is considered victim blaming. While it is not helpful to focus on the sins of those who have endured condemnation and abuse, there comes a point in the recovery process in which we must become willing to honestly examine ourselves if we want to move forward and truly heal.[81] I constantly point survivors coming out of abuse to God's unconditional love, which is almost always obscured by abuse, and to the fact that He does not condemn us. Yet, we also know that His kindness leads us to repentance (Romans 2:4). At some point, we must be willing to allow the Holy Spirit to do His work in our lives by being open to His conviction. Those who teach otherwise do it under the guise of love but are not loving well at all. Instead, they create a huge barrier to healing.

It is natural to put up walls and try to protect ourselves (self-protection) when we've been hurt. The problem is that those walls very often turn into self-made prisons. We grasp for control to ensure nobody will ever hurt us that way again, and usually, the outcome is that we end up hurting ourselves and others. We become quick to judge and slow to listen. We even assume evil motives in people who are genuinely on our side. Many victims who fail to heal end up repeating the same abusive patterns that caused them harm. They may not become physically abusive, but they are masters at stirring up

---

[81] Counselors, pastors, and other people helpers should be aware that it is best to point survivors to God and His unconditional love for them, rather than focusing on their sin. When their relationship with Him is repaired, His kind Spirit will convict them of sin (Romans 2:4). However, if we focus on their sin, we risk pushing them further away from God by doing exactly what their abusers have done for years.

misery. They come across as self-righteous and critical of those who disagree with them. They twist your words to fit their own self-seeking agendas and don't have ears to hear. They only hear what they already believe based on their past experiences. When you try to reason with them, it only ends up hurting you. Filled with self-pity, they use guilt to control you. They are easily offended and assume evil motives on your part. Basically, their actions are the exact opposite of God's description of love in 1 Corinthians 13:4-7. Rather than giving their hurts to God and applying His truths for healing, these wounded abusers simply continue to give power to their abusers by carrying on their traditions.

When I work with victims who have ended up becoming abusive themselves, I try to direct them to God's promises toward them. They will usually give me a thousand reasons not to believe those promises. This attitude reminds me of the man Jesus healed at the pool in Bethesda in John 5. Even though he stationed himself where the angel stirred the healing waters, he told Jesus it was impossible because somebody always beat him to the water. He was full of bitterness and excuses. When Jesus healed him despite his negativity, he showed no joy, nor did he bother to thank Jesus. Instead, when the religious leaders rebuked him for carrying his pallet, he blamed Him. Jesus knew his heart and came to him later with a warning saying, "See, you are well again. Stop sinning or something worse may happen to you" (John 5:14). But he simply went out and reported Jesus to the leaders. He had been set free, but he chose to remain bitter.

That's the problem with so many victims; they fail to see and appreciate God's provision in their lives. Instead, they choose to make excuses for hanging on to their anger. They essentially cut themselves off from God's blessings and blame everyone around them, even God, for their difficult circumstances. I love to contrast the story of the man at the pool with the healing of the man born blind in John 9. When Jesus healed the blind man, his life was changed immediately. He became a Believer and was willing to profess his faith despite harsh opposition. As far as outward circumstances go, he probably fared worse than the man healed at the pool. Yet he was filled with joy over what Jesus had done for him. Like King David, who spent years running from abuse, he chose to praise God in the presence of his enemies rather than cling to unforgiveness and anger. Our God is a redeemer, and nothing is wasted when we know Him.

He can use our tribulations to mold us into the image of His Son (Romans 8:29). But during our troubles, we must choose to trust Him. We must choose to let go of the bitterness that poisons every relationship in our lives and keeps us in bondage (Hebrews 12:15). The problem is that many of us are not willing to make this choice. Instead, we hold tenaciously to our right to be miserable and angry and become perpetual victims. If you are reading this, I pray that this will not be your outcome, but that you will choose the path to freedom our God offers.

KNOW WHO YOU ARE

While many victims of abuse become angry or depressed, others find themselves moving into subsequent abusive relationships. Over the years, I've met hundreds of victims who have moved from one destructive relationship to another. Some have even been married multiple times. Often, this is an indirect result of the mind games abusers play. They get into our heads, we begin to believe their harsh assessments of us, and they condition us to accept mistreatment as normal. On top of that, we may carry shame from being divorced. It doesn't help that many times Christians treat divorce as the unpardonable sin. Yet, I don't believe that those who condemn the divorced reflect God's heart. Our

Lord went out of His way to reach a Samaritan woman who had been married five times and had a live-in lover (See John 4:1-42). I often wonder about this dear woman. What had she experienced? Had one or more of her husbands been abusive? We know back then, only men could initiate divorce, so at the very least, she had been rejected five times. Shame was likely a constant companion as she went to draw water in the heat of the day long after all the other women were gone. Perhaps it was to avoid their judgmental stares. Yet, as she arrived, a Jewish man showed her kindness. Can you imagine her surprise when He spoke to her? The very act went against everything cultural protocol demanded. Men were not supposed to speak to women without their husbands present, and Jews looked down on Samaritans. Generally, they would not associate with them at all. Besides all that, no self-respecting rabbi would ever be seen conversing with such a blatant sinner. But Jesus was different. He showed her that she mattered by offering her a relationship with God. He did not condemn her for her past; He simply offered her new life. She was so overwhelmed that she immediately went out and told the whole town about Him.

There's nothing in the text that tells us this woman changed her ways after that encounter, but I believe she did. The Messiah Himself told her she was valuable to God. She caught a glimpse of God's amazing love and received it. An encounter like that is life-changing and that is my prayer for you, dear friend. May you deeply know just how much you matter to God—regardless of what a person has told you. He treasures you! He does not, and never wanted you to be abused. You are worth so much more. When you can internalize that truth, you will be much less likely to tolerate mistreatment. I believe that knowing your identity in Him will help protect you from future abuse, and this is all tied into knowing God and His great love. Please take time to learn these truths so that you can heal and live a healthy life! This will involve correcting faulty interpretations of Scripture that have kept you in bondage. There is so much power in God's Word, and in you, because His Spirit dwells in you.[82] If you still feel overwhelmed by what has happened to you, I urge you to go back and repeat lessons that relate to struggles you are having. Jesus came to set you free, so don't settle for anything less than true freedom and deliverance. Looking back over my life, I am filled with gratitude for the way God stooped down and delivered me, but there's nothing special about me. He offers salvation and abundant life to whoever will come to Him in faith. He promises that you will find Him if you seek Him with all your heart (Jeremiah 29:13). Once you genuinely connect with Him and receive His healing truths, I believe you can, and will, find victory over your past.

> I waited patiently for the Lord; He turned to me and heard my cry. He lifted me out of the slimy pit, out of the mud and mire; He set my feet on a rock and gave me a firm place to stand. He put a new song in my mouth, a hymn of praise to our God. Many will see and fear the Lord and put their trust in Him.
>
> ~ *Psalm 40:1-3.*

---

[82] If you have received Jesus as your savior and surrendered your life to Him, the same power that raised Jesus from the dead dwells in you and empowers you. See Ephesians 1:13, Romans 8:11, and Acts 1:8.

Illustration by Shari Ellis (Used With Permission)

SUPPLEMENTAL LESSONS

IS IT SEXUAL ABUSE?

Working with survivors of abuse has shown me that many women are very confused about their sexual relationships with their husbands. It is extremely common for abusive men to have issues with pornography and sexual sin; it fits with their lack of respect and objectification of women. Statistics show that 40-45% of men who abuse their wives also sexually abuse them, but since many women do not recognize the signs of sexual coercion in their marriages, the numbers are likely higher. As with every other area of their lives, abusive men have a sense of entitlement that spills over and perverts what God intended to be a blessing. They enjoy exerting power over their wives. Maybe you have been forced to do things that were uncomfortable, or even painful, yet you do not see it as abusive because your husband has used Scripture to tell you that you have no right to refuse any of his demands. Basically, a husband like this is saying that Scripture supports his selfish desires, but that does not reflect the heart of God for His people. Many abusers misuse 1 Corinthians 7:1-5 regarding spouses having rights to each other's bodies to justify their harmful behavior.

However, in this passage, Paul makes the sexual relationship reciprocal between husbands and wives. The wife is meant to have equal rights when it comes to sex. Both partners should have the right to say "No." The gist of the whole passage is that spouses should agree and work together. There is nothing in the Bible that indicates one person should lord it over the other or treat that person like a sexual object. This reciprocity is intended to occur within a loving relationship where both people are seeking to honor God rather than selfishly use their partners.

Signs you are being sexually abused:[83]

- You're being forced to do something you don't want to do.
- You go along with his demands out of fear of repercussions.
- Your feelings about it are dismissed, and you're not allowed to say no.

The sexual relationship is intended by God to express intimacy within the marital relationship. It is part of the two becoming one flesh and a picture of Christ's union with the church. Ephesians 5:29 tells us that abusing that relationship is entirely contrary to God's design: "For no one ever hated his own flesh, but nourishes and cherishes it, just as the Lord does the church."

---

[83] Vernick, Leslie, "How Do I Know I'm Being Sexually abused in My Marriage?" (2018). Accessed July 21, 2024 at https://leslievernick.com/blog/know-im-sexually-abused-marriage/.

We have a right to be safe and to tell our partners that what they are doing is not OK. The following notes were taken from an online class with Darby Strickland. You can learn more at her website www.darbystrickland.com.

Common Responses to Sexual Abuse in Marriage:

- Denial: refusing to believe it was sexual abuse or minimizing it because he's your husband.
- Rationalization: involving self-blame or making excuses for him.
- Minimizing: denying the severity of the incident. Dissociation: having no feelings about it or refusing to talk about it.
- Focus on the good parts of the relationship; this makes it easier to rationalize that it's not that bad overall.
- Placating: agreeing to certain acts to avoid unpleasant consequences or injury.
- Normalizing: doing something routine (like housework) because doing something "normal" helps bring you back to normalcy.
- Self-soothing: activities that calm or help you escape, such as long baths or watching a movie.
- Self-numbing: using drugs or alcohol to numb the pain. This often results in another set of problems.

Effects of Marital Sex Abuse:

- Depression Anxiety PTSD
- Eating Disorders Distorted Body Image Sexual Distress
- Trust Issues
- Sleep Disturbances Shock
- Suicide

Common Misconceptions About Marital Rape:

- You can't rape your wife.
- It's not rape; it's an obligation.
- It's not rape if I stay with him or return to him.
- It's not rape if I sometimes enjoy sex with my husband.
- It's not rape if you haven't brought it up before, or if you still love him.

Impacts:

- Studies show that the effects of partner rape are more severe and last longer than stranger rape.
- The impact of partner rape is comparable to that of a hostage situation. Survivors of partner rape experience the highest degree of physical injury and are more likely to have been raped multiple times.

- Many victims of sexual abuse by a spouse or partner find themselves confused. They wonder if it was truly abuse if they agreed to it. One way to tell is by asking yourself the right questions; were you threatened in any way? Perhaps he used financial control or threatened to go elsewhere for sex if you didn't give in to his demands. Did he try to make you feel guilty for not giving in? The bottom line is that if you felt pressured to do something you didn't want to do, it most likely was abuse.

As with any abuse, healing is always possible with our God. The first step is always admitting the truth and calling it what it is—abuse! Then we must identify lies we have come to believe because of the abuse and confront them with God's truth. Remember that healing is a process, not a one-time event. It will happen over time as we surrender to His love and apply his truth to our lives.

LOVING YOUR ENEMY

The most harmful enemies are those we've been close to at one time. They have more power in our lives because we care for them. Scripture has much to say about how we should deal with those who have treated us like enemies even when we still love them and don't see them in the same way.

God, listen to my prayer and do not ignore my plea for help. Pay attention to me and answer me. I am restless and in turmoil with my complaint, because of the enemy's voice, because of the pressure of the wicked. For they bring down disaster on me and harass me in anger. My heart shudders within me; terrors of death sweep over me. Fear and trembling grip me; horror has overwhelmed me. I said, "If only I had wings like a dove! I would fly away and find rest. How far away I would flee; I would stay in the wilderness..." Now, it is not an enemy who insults me- otherwise I could bear it; it is not a foe who rises up against me- otherwise I could hide from him... But it is you, a man who is my peer, my companion and good friend! We used to have close fellowship; we walked with the crowd into the house of God... But I call to God, and the Lord will save me. I complain and groan morning, noon, and night, and He hears my voice. Though many are against me, He will redeem me from my battle unharmed. God, the One enthroned from long ago, will hear, and will humiliate them because they do not change and do not fear God. He acts violently against those at peace with him; he violates his covenant. His buttery words are smooth, but war is in his heart. His words are softer than oil, but they are drawn swords. Cast your burden on the Lord, and He will support you; He will never allow the righteous to be shaken.— Selected passages from Psalm 55

How to Respond

- **We are not to respond in kind.**

"Bless those who persecute you; bless and do not curse. Rejoice with those who rejoice; mourn with those who mourn. Live in harmony with one another. Do not be proud but be willing to associate with people of low position. Do not be conceited. Do not repay anyone evil for evil. Be careful to do what is right in the eyes of everyone. If it is possible, as far as it depends on you, live at peace with everyone. Do not take revenge, my dear friends, but leave room for God's wrath, for it is written: 'It is mine to avenge; I will repay,' says the Lord. On the contrary: 'If your enemy is hungry, feed him; if he is thirsty, give him something to drink. In doing this, you will heap burning coals on his head.' Do not be overcome by evil but overcome evil with good." — Romans 12:14-21

- **Understand the contagious and harmful nature of anger.**

"Don't associate with an angry man; make no hot-tempered man your companion. If you do, you may learn his ways and find yourself caught in a trap."— Proverbs 22:24-25

"In your anger do not sin: Do not let the sun go down while you are still angry, and do not give the devil a foothold." — Ephesians 4:26-27

- **We are to avoid foolish arguments.**

"Don't have anything to do with foolish and stupid arguments, because you know they produce quarrels. And the Lord's servant must not quarrel; instead, he must be kind to everyone, able to teach, not resentful."– 2 Timothy 2:23-24

"He who observes discipline is on the way to life; but he who ignores correction is making a mistake. He who covers up hate has lips that lie, and anyone who slanders is a fool. When words are many, sin is not lacking; so, he who controls his speech is wise." – Proverbs 10:17-19

"Do not answer a fool according to his folly, Or you will also be like him. Answer a fool as his folly deserves, That he not be wise in his own eyes." – Proverbs 26:4-5

- **Our reaction can hurt us.** We may find ourselves angry at God for what we've been through and find ourselves acting like our abusers. This often causes helpers to believe we are just as responsible for the issues in our marriages as our abusers. We need to follow Jesus's example of love—not allowing the selfish control of others. He was never selfish in his response but always pointed them to God's truth.

"A stone is heavy, and sand is weighty, but the resentment caused by a fool is heavier than both." – Proverbs 27:3

"Make every effort to live in peace with everyone and to be holy; without holiness no one will see the Lord. See to it that no one falls short of the grace of God and that no bitter root grows up to cause trouble and defile many." – Hebrews 12:14-15

- **Follow Jesus' Example.**

He often withdrew and spent time with the Father in frequent prayer and fellowship. (Luke 5:15-16)

He did not let people pull him into foolish arguments. (Matthew 21:23-27, 22:15-22)

He did not trust those who had not earned his trust. (John 2:24)

- **Remember that God's love allows people to face consequences.**

He offered freedom and relationship, but His people rejected it. His response was, "Your own sin will punish you." – (Jeremiah 2:19)

The bottom line is that we should never react to sin with sin or cover up our partners' sin. On the other hand, we are not to set ourselves up as their judges either (Matthew 7:1-5). We must continually entrust them to God and ask him for wisdom to respond calmly and kindly when provoked. This could mean we detach ourselves and treat them more as strangers (Lesson 11), and we set limits on sinful mistreatment (Lesson 12). Either way, when we stop reacting, we take control from our abusers and unleash God's power to work in the situation.

THE IMPORTANCE OF COMMUNITY IN THE HEALING PROCESS

One of the most effective tools of coercive control is isolation. Our abusers cut us off from people who might provide us with support, making it extremely difficult to get help. The interesting thing about this dynamic is that, often even when we escape the abuse, we continue this pattern of isolation. Depression or shame prevents us from tapping into the healing power of being in a community. One night in our local group, I asked participants to share some of the things that had been most helpful in their recovery process to date, and very quickly the idea of community came up. When I think back on my own story, I realize that without the help of dear friends, my kids and I might have never gotten out. Besides that, the Bible studies I did with a group of trusted Christian ladies played a powerful role in my healing process.

Sadly, many survivors of abuse have been judged by Christians rather than supported and have given up on church altogether. It's true that there are toxic Christians out there, but there are many loving and supportive ones as well. The key is to find people who are worthy of your trust. When your trust has been betrayed time and again, it feels risky to try again. However, we are called to trust God, and His intentions toward us are only good. As we grow stronger and more grounded in His Word, we will begin to recognize which of His people are safe. There are also resources to help you learn wise trust in relationships. I particularly like Georgia Shaffer's "Rebuild After Divorce" and other information on building healthy relationships. See Appendix C.

Jesus knew that some men were unworthy of His trust (see John 2:24). He also said true disciples are known by their fruit; there won't be a disconnect between their words and their actions. They will respect your boundaries and won't try to pressure you into doing something before you are ready. They will love and value you unconditionally and set no conditions for you to receive their support or affection. Take time and observe your new friends. Don't feel you need to disclose private information to everyone. It is easy for survivors of abuse to fall back into what feels familiar, so don't feel you need to share your story until long after trust has been established. It is a good idea to seek out women who have experienced abuse and have found healing or who are moving toward it. Support groups can be a great place to start your journey back into community. Called to Peace Ministries offers both local and online groups in the US and abroad. Visit www.calledtopeace.org to learn more.

Benefits of Genuine Community

- We receive support and encouragement.
- We have people speaking into our lives who can help correct faulty beliefs and point us to God's truth.
- It helps us fulfill the ministry God has for us. You have others who will hold you up in prayer. You have a place to grow as a disciple.
- Community with others can help prevent depression.

Scriptures About Community

- Two are better than one, because they have a good return for their labor: if either of them falls down, one can help the other up. But pity anyone who falls and has no one to help them up. – Ecclesiastes 4:9-10
- But in fact, God has placed the parts in the body, every one of them, just as He wanted them to be. If they were all one part, where would the body be? As it is, there are many parts, but one body. The eye cannot say to the hand, "I don't need you!" And the head cannot say to the feet, "I don't need you!" On the contrary, those parts of the body that seem to be weaker are indispensable, and the parts that we think are less honorable we treat with special honor. And the parts that are unpresentable are treated with special modesty, while our presentable parts need no special treatment. But God has put the body together, giving greater honor to the parts that lacked it, so that there should be no division in the body, but that its parts should have equal concern for each other. If one part suffers, every part suffers with it; if one part is honored, every part rejoices with it. Now you are the body of Christ, and each one of you is a part of it. – 1 Corinthians12:18-27
- Brothers and sisters, if someone is caught in a sin, you who live by the Spirit should restore that person gently. But watch yourselves, or you also may be tempted. Carry each other's burdens, and in this way, you will fulfill the law of Christ. – Galatians 6:1-2
- Instead, speaking the truth in love, we will grow to become in every respect the mature body of Him who is the head, that is, Christ. From Him the whole body, joined and held together by every supporting ligament, grows and builds itself up in love, as each part does its work. – Ephesians 4:15-16 (Also see verses 1-14)
- A friend loves at all times, and a brother is born for a time of adversity. – Proverbs 17:17
- For where two or three gather in my name, there am I with them. – Matthew 18:20
- And let us consider how we may spur one another on toward love and good deeds, not giving up meeting together, as some are in the habit of doing, but encouraging one another—and all the more as you see the Day approaching. – Hebrews 10:24-25

CHARACTERISTICS & TACTICS OF COERCIVELY CONTROLLING PEOPLE

- *An attitude of superiority.* They think they're always right - prideful. There is no mutuality in the relationship.
- *Sense of entitlement.* There's no give and take. It's their way or no way.
- *Impossible to please.* Your efforts are never enough – you find you are walking on eggshells.
- *Use of various control measures.* They may use the silent treatment, stonewalling, threats, intimidation, or even physical harm. They will attack or berate you when they don't get their way. It's not about anger, but control.
- *Gaslighting & Crazy-Making.* They convince you that your perception is wrong. They try to convince you that your perception of a disturbing incident is inaccurate. They cause you to feel confusion and even mistrust of your own vision, hearing, and the very sound mind that God has given you. They twist your words (Psalm 56:5).
- *Making Excuses.* They make excuses for their behavior rather than owning it.
- *Extremely selfish and self-focused.* This may include self-pity and playing the victim. They are also jealous and easily offended.
- *Very deceptive* — This includes hidden sins and hidden agendas.
- *Dual personality.* Dr. Jekyll/Mr. Hyde Syndrome (Psalm 55:21). Their personality in public can be charming and kind, but behind closed doors they are tyrants.
- *Intimidation.* They instill fear! It could be physical, like breaking things, punching walls, blocking exits, screaming, and threatening. It can also be subtle.
- *Emotional abuse.* This happens more often than physical abuse. It includes constant put-downs, name-calling, or inferences that you are less than. You feel you can't do anything right in their eyes. They want you to feel inadequate and to think you need them to survive. They are extremely disrespectful and dominating. Many victims have told me they would prefer physical beatings to emotional abuse.
- *Isolation.* They attempt to cut you off from support systems to keep you from hearing other opinions that differ with theirs or to prevent others from helping you. They want to be able to control your thinking. They spy on you and have to approve your contacts. They may move you away from friends and family or perhaps take your phone or computer to limit outside contact. This stems from a belief that they own you.

- *Minimizing, denying, or blaming.* They turn everything back on you. Everything that's a problem in the house is blamed on you. The kids may know what really happened, but take on your partner's thinking to stay safe. You're blamed for their abusive outbursts. Victims are blamed so much they begin to take the blame on themselves.
- *Using the children.* They threaten to take them if you leave or use them as leverage in an argument. Many times, abusers try to turn the children against their own mothers through extreme manipulation. Some even harm their own children to hurt their partners. They will attack whatever is most valued by you.
- *Use of male privilege.* This is a driving force behind most abuse. They believe they are entitled to have you submit and bow down. They don't believe you're equal. They believe that allowing you equality diminishes them somehow.
- *Economic abuse.* They control all the money or may give you control of the household bills but complain about the way you do it. They limit your financial resources, so you can't leave. They may give you a strict allowance for necessities that usually won't cover them all, but they can spend whatever they want (double standard). If you work, they may take your money. Many abusers don't allow their wives to work or make it impossible for them to work.

The bottom line is, if they don't get their way about something that's important to them, they will be sure to make you miserable for it. You feel more and more controlled and devalued by them over time. They refuse to accept responsibility for their own actions. Despite how angry, hurt, insecure, or unhappy your partner may appear to be, their abusive behavior is rooted far more in how they think than in how they feel. The answer to what has gone wrong lies primarily in their warped belief system of entitlement.

How to Respond

- *Admit the truth and stop helping to cover it up.* Perhaps you've even lied to yourself. Does it line up with His truth? Pray & Praise God. Make Him bigger than any person, and replace fear with faith. It's a choice. His Word and His Spirit will empower you as you choose to believe His truth over your feelings.
- *Examine your response to mistreatment.* While nothing you've done caused the abuse to heal and grow, it is important to be willing to look at and admit your own mistakes and sin. Have you given His glory to another? Caution: confessing to abusers gives them ammunition, so this is not an option. However, you must confess to God and commit to change.
- *Learn all you can to respond wisely without sinning.* Good resources include Leslie Vernick's *How to Act Right When Your Spouse Acts Wrong* and *The Emotionally Destructive Marriage*.
- *Avoid joint counseling.* Abuse is not a marital problem, so marriage counseling is not helpful. He must find help to deal with his control issues, and that help should be specifically geared to coercive control/domestic abuse. Seek individual counseling to help overcome the trauma you have experienced and to overcome the lies you have come to believe.
- *Respectfully take a stand against sin.* Do not react in kind, berate, or shame them. If you can't avoid them, don't let emotions control you. Guard your words.

- *Don't let unforgiveness consume you.* Understand forgiveness is not approving the behavior but committing that person to God. It's letting go and becoming free. It may not lead to reconciliation because forgiveness doesn't necessarily restore trust. Trust must be earned over time; forgiveness is freely given.
- *When possible, remove yourself from the situation* and do not allow yourself to be pulled into arguments or manipulation. Love from a distance if necessary. If you have to leave, don't give into fear, but stay safe.
- *Make a plan of escape.* Find resources to help—DV Shelters (www.ncadv.org), Called to Peace Ministries (www.calledtopeace.org). The earlier in a relationship you do this, the better. Statistics show emotionally abusive relationships often become violent after separation, so make a safety plan.
- *Fear God more than your abuser.* Whatever we fear will control us. Usually, the more we give in, the worse it gets, but the fear of God relieves destructive fears.

APPENDICES

APPENDIX A

FINDING PEACE AFTER ABUSE RECOVERY GROUPS: GROUND RULES

1. This group is for YOU. While we believe there is healing in sharing your story, we realize that some people are not ready or even able to share, so feel free to share or pass when it's your turn to talk.
2. Everything said in the groups is confidential and stays in the group.
3. Please limit your sharing to 2-3 minutes. While we want to hear your story, we need to allow everyone time to talk. Share bullet points and not details.
4. Do not attempt to rescue or fix other group members, nor give unsolicited advice. Share what is helpful to you using "I" statements, but please do not tell others what to do!
5. Be respectful when others are speaking. Give them your attention (no side conversations when someone is sharing), and do not interrupt.
6. Avoid comparing your experience of abuse with another's or minimizing their experience.
7. Recognize that some group members do not handle unsolicited hugs or touch well because of past trauma. If you want to comfort or hug someone you don't know well, ask them if it would be all right to give them a hug.
8. Avoid the use of profanity.
9. Avoid theological and political debates.
10. For online groups, remember the following:
    - Your camera must be on at all times with a view of your face.
    - Make sure you are located in a confidential zoom space or use headphones.
    - Do not record the meetings.
    - Be attentive on Zoom just like if you were in person.

OTHER IMPORTANT TIPS

We want everyone to have the freedom to share parts of their story but ask you to keep sharing what you experienced to general summaries. Remember that many in the group are suffering from PTS which could be triggered if you give too much detail. There is a time and place to share the details of what you've experienced (first with God and then a trusted counselor experienced with domestic abuse), but the point of this group is to focus on solutions. Help us try to keep the group moving in that direction.

NOTE FOR GROUP LEADERS

This workbook is designed to be a 16-week study, when including a week to go over the "Afterword" and discussing group participant progress. Some leaders choose to meet over an entire school year, taking breaks for the holidays and summertime. When I led groups, we covered the entire workbook twice a year between September and May. We did the supplemental lessons in the summertime. Some leaders choose to slow down the pace by spending extra weeks on longer lessons. You can also make the study shorter by eliminating a few lessons. The bottom line is that the way you schedule classes is flexible, and each class stands alone, so it is possible to allow new people to join at various times during the year.

For best results, urge your participants to repeat the classes at least once— many have found benefit from repeating multiple times. Healing takes time, so working and reworking lessons can be beneficial as participants struggle with different issues at different stages of the healing process.

If you are interested in becoming a Called to Peace Ministries affiliated support group leader, visit www.calledtopeace.org, click on "Connect" and "Lead a Support Group." Someone will get back to you with various options for training.

APPENDIX B

Power & Control Wheel

Used with permission from the
Domestic Abuse Intervention Program (DAIP) of Duluth, MN
www.duluth-model.org

APPENDIX C

Now that we've seen what an abusive relationship looks like, we thought we'd add this resource as a guideline for a healthy relationship. Also see 1 Corinthians 13:4-7 for a picture of true love.

THE CONTRASTING TRAITS OF HEALTHY VS. UNHEALTHY PEOPLE:

▶ Healthy

Take responsibility.
Learn & grow.
Overcome problems.
Bounce back.
Own their feelings.
Understand pain.

▶ UnHealthy

Blame others.
Stay the same.
Make excuses.
Stay stuck.
Act out their feelings.
Avoid pain.

Learn more at https://georgiashaffer.com

APPENDIX D

Developing A Safety Plan

Adapted from FocusMinistries1.org

If you are a victim of domestic violence, it is important to make a safety plan to help you figure out what to do if your partner becomes dangerous. If you are unsure about potential danger, you can chat with a domestic violence advocate 24/7 at thehotline.org. Below are some measures to consider in case you find yourself in danger.

- **Escape Route** — Determine how you will get out safely the next time you are attacked. (What doors, windows, elevators, stairwells, or fire escapes will you use?) Take your children with you.
- **Call 9-1-1** — If possible, call 9-1-1. If you cannot safely call from where you are, place the call as soon as you are out of the house and out of danger. Alert your neighbors to call 9-1-1 for you if they hear suspicious sounds coming from your apartment or house.
- **If Injured go directly to the nearest emergency room.** Tell the doctor who attacked you (please do not try to protect the abuser). Ask that your injuries be documented and photographed.
- **Plan Ahead** — Think ahead of about 4 places you can go if you cannot return home (friends, family, church). If you don't know where to go, the police or emergency room personnel will provide you with information about the nearest shelter. It is not safe to use a credit card to pay for food, travel, or lodging, since the abuser can find out where you are, and can cancel the card without your knowledge.
- **Organize Important Papers** — Keep money, car keys, important papers, and clothes in a safe place where you can get them quickly. A safe place does not mean in your home or car (he could easily find them). Ask friends or family to keep them for you. Important papers include:

1. Birth certificates (for you and your children)
2. Marriage certificate
3. Social Security cards
4. School and medical records
5. Bank and credit card statements
6. Medications
7. Passport
8. Deeds and titles (car and house, etc.)
9. Insurance papers
10. Address book
11. Cash
12. Videos, pictures and sentimental mementoes
13. Children's favorite books, toys, blankets
14. Keys to house, car, office
15. Unpaid bills
16. Journals or a diary
17. Tax returns and other financial documents
18. Documentation of criminal activity, etc.

Some of the above documents can be photocopied to avoid suspicion, while you will need the originals of others. Make sure you make an extra set of keys for the house, car, post office box, safe deposit box, etc. for storage in a safe place.

In addition to the tips above, there are apps available to help you create a personalized safety plan. MyPlan Safety is available for both Apple and Android devices.

APPENDIX E

CHECKLIST OF ABUSIVE BEHAVIORS

- Select all that apply to your relationship. Does Your Partner...?
  - Destroy your property, possessions or documents?
  - Make you feel like you're walking on eggshells?
  - Intimidate you with looks, gestures cursing, or a loud voice?
  - Make you afraid to voice your opinion?
  - Make all the decisions about money?
  - Make you feel crazy?
  - Use weapons to scare you?
  - Try to isolate you by controlling where you go, who you see & what you do?
  - Threaten to hurt or punish you if you don't do what he wants?
  - Often seem angry at someone or something?
  - Push, grab or shove you?
  - Check up on you excessively?
  - Minimize or deny his abusive behavior?
  - Act extremely jealous?
  - Use the children to control you? Try to turn the children against you?
  - Embarrass or humiliate you in front of others?
  - Threaten to leave you, hurt you, or to commit suicide?
  - Deprive you of sleep?
  - Pressure you for sex in ways that make you uncomfortable?
  - Often criticize you, your friends or your family?
  - Claim that he is a victim of something or someone?
  - Prevent you from leaving an area or restrain you?
  - Disregard your feelings?
  - Use Scripture to condemn you?
  - Lie to you regularly?
  - Degrade you, make you feel insignificant, powerless and/or worthless?
  - Ignore you or give you the silent treatment?
  - Blame you for how he treats you, or for anything bad that happens?
  - Tell you how to dress or act?

Experiencing just one of these behaviors on a regular basis could mean you are experiencing coercive control, also known as domestic abuse. You can contact a domestic violence advocate at thehotline.org (24/7) or calledtopeace.org to help determine abusive patterns.

APPENDIX F

SCRIPTURE DATABASE

ANGER

Jonah 4 - Jonah's anger at God's mercy. Ephesians 4:26 & 31 - Do not sin in your anger. Colossians 3:8 - Put anger aside.

Galatians 5:16–20 - A deed of the flesh will affect our inheritance in the kingdom.

James 1:19–21 - Anger does not achieve the righteous life God desires for us. Our anger is rarely righteous.

Luke 9:54–56 - The disciples ask Jesus to pour out wrath on those opposed to Him.

ANXIETY

Matthew 6:25–34

Philippians 4:6–9

I Peter 5:7

COMFORT

Isaiah 54:11 - The storm tossed, but God rebuilt.

2 Corinthians 1:3–4 - God comforts us so we can comfort others.

Hebrews 4:15 - He knows our affliction and is touched by them because he has experienced similar experiences.

Psalm 119:76

CONFESSION

Psalms 32 & 51

1 John 1:9

FEAR AND ANXIETY

2 Chronicles 20:15 - The battle is not yours, but the Lord's.

Psalms 56:3-4, 18 - When I am afraid I put my trust in You…what can mere man do to me?

Isaiah 51:12–14 - I am He who comforts you. Who are you that you should fear the oppressor bent on destruction?

Zephaniah 3:16–17 - The Lord is in your midst, He will quiet you with His love…will sing over you.

John 14:27 - Don't let your heart fear…you must choose to believe.

Psalms 34 - Seek the Lord and He will deliver you from all your fears.

Psalms 46 - He is a very present help in trouble.

Isaiah 41:10 - Don't be afraid. He will strengthen you

Romans 8:15 - We have not received a spirit of fear.

Psalms 27 - My heart will not fear (regardless of the circumstance).

Matthew 6:25–34 - Do not worry.

Philippians 4:6–9 - Do not be anxious.

I Peter 5:7 - Cast your anxieties on Him.

Psalms 27 & 46

FEAR OF MAN/CONFRONTATION

Proverbs 27:5–6 - Better an open rebuke than the wounds from a false friend

Matthew 10:28 - Don't fear those who can destroy the body.

Romans 14:23 - Whatever does not come from faith is sin.

Hebrews 13:5–6 - Find contentment in Him knowing that he'll never desert you

Galatians 1:10 - You can't aim to please/serve man and also be a servant of God. We serve whomever or whatever we fear.

BIBLICAL EXAMPLES OF HANDLING FEAR WELL

Saul - 1 Samuel 28:5–20 - Saul grasped for control

David - 1 Samuel 30:3–6 - David strengthened himself in the Lord (Psalms 27:3)

Hezekiah - 2 Kings 19:14–19 - Hezekiah brought his fears to God and chose faith

NOTE: Scripture is filled with passages about fear and contains 365 commands not to be afraid— one for each day of the year)! These verses are just a start. If you struggle with fear, you will find lots of good company in Scripture—from the likes of Saul who chose to handle it in his flesh and destroyed himself, to David who brought his fears straight to God and waited for his redemption. Each time fear rolls in, we have a choice to make. We can either give in to it or choose to believe God.

FORGIVENESS

Matthew 6:12–14

Matthew 18:21–35 - God has forgiven us of every murder- ous/adulterous thought (Mt. 5:21-28), we must extend the same grace to others.

Mark 11:24–26

Ephesians 4:32

Colossians 2:13 & 3:12–13

Matthew 5:23 - If you are presenting your offering and remember someone has something against you, God says to make amends first. This only works in normal relationships, though. With abusers, we often have to go to God instead and ask Him to rid us of unforgiveness.

GOD'S LOVE

Psalm 56:8–9 - God watches over you. God is on your side. Isaiah 53 - He willingly came and suffered because of His love for you.

Psalm 57:1–3

Isaiah 53 - this prophecy about Jesus shows what He did on our behalf

Isaiah 49:14–16 - People may forget, but God never forgets.

Zephaniah 3:16–17 - He rejoices over you with singing.

Isaiah 54:4–8 - The Lord, your maker, is your husband.

Psalm 130

Romans 8:15, 31–37 - We are His children, and nothing can separate us from His love.

GRIEF

I Thessalonians 4:13 - We can grieve with hope.

2 Corinthians 5:1–8

1 Corinthians 15:35–57

GUILT

1 John 1:9

Hebrews 10:19–23

Psalm 32:1–5 - Until we confess our sins, there is misery, but there is peace in the blessing of His forgiveness.

HOPE

Jeremiah 29:11–12

Romans 8:28–29

Psalm 25

Psalm 34:19

Psalm 42

Psalm 130

Isaiah 50:2

Romans 8:31–37 - We are more than conquerors.

Psalm 55:18 - God will redeem your soul, He will give you peace to help you recover from the battle against you.

Psalm 56:9 - God is for you!

Isaiah 54:11–17 - Our heritage as His children. 1 Corinthians 1:19–20

INADEQUACY

Philippians 4:11–13

2 Samuel 22: 28–30

Psalm 18:28–36

1 Timothy 4:11-16

OPPRESSION

Jeremiah 22:3

Isaiah 58:9-10

Psalms 12:5, 35:10, 82:3-4

OVERCOMING

Philippians 3:12–14 - Forget the past and look forward. Philippians 4:13 - We can do all things through Christ

2 Peter 1:3–4 - His divine power has given us everything we need pertaining to life.

2 Corinthians 12:7–10 - God has strength in our weakness.

PRIORITIES

Philippians 3:7–15

Matthew 6:19-21, 31-34

THOUGHT LIFE

2 Corinthians 10:3–5 - We must take every thought captive. Philippians 4:8–9

Isaiah 26:3–4

Psalm 16:7–11 - Praise the Lord who has counseled you.

TRIBULATION

2 Corinthians 4:17–18 - Our troubles are light, momentary afflictions working for eternal good in our lives.

Hebrews 12:2–4 - Look to Jesus—the author and finisher. Romans 5:2–3 - Rejoice in suffering, it produces perseverance. Romans 8:18 - Our sufferings are nothing in comparison to the glory waiting for us.

James 1:2

Philippians 3:7–10

Psalm 32:6–11 - God surrounds us with songs of deliverance. Psalm 119:67 & 71 - God uses the affliction to sanctify us.

Psalm 25 - Look to the Lord, for He alone can rescue us.

1 Corinthians 10:13 - God is faithful. He won't let us be tempted or tried beyond what we can bear. Other people have faced similar trials—and Jesus has faced even worse.

2 Corinthians 1:3–11

SATISFACTION IN HIM

Habakkuk 3:17–19 - Though bad things are happening, rejoice in Him.

Psalm 42 - You should long for Him as a parched animal longs for water—instead we seek cheap substitutes.

Psalm 17:8 & 15 - He treasures you. Be satisfied in Him. Jeremiah 2 & 3 - We often turn from God and seek other things/ways to find satisfaction, but it leads us into misery. God compares this kind of idolatry to unfaithfulness in marriage, yet He longs to heal and restore.

Jeremiah. 9:23–24 - Boast only in knowing Him. Psalm 16:11 - In His presence, there is fullness of joy. Psalm 34:8–9 - Taste and see that the Lord is good.

Hebrews 13:5 - He will never leave or forsake you. Be content.

SELF PITY

Jonah 4

1 Corinthians 15:19 - We have eternal hope beyond temporary circumstances.

Matthew 16:24

TEMPTATION

1 Corinthians 10:13

Hebrews 4:14–16 - Jesus was tempted in every way and is still without sin. He was able to say no to temptation. He is our priest and enables us to approach the throne of grace with confidence. Grace will aid us in times of trouble.

2 Corinthians 12:7–10

TRUTH

Jeremiah 17:9 - Truth is not in us, but in Him.

John 8:32 - The truth sets us free!

Psalm 51:6

Psalm 119:160 & John 17:17 - His word is truth. John 14:6 - Jesus (the Word made flesh) is the truth.

Philippians 4:8 - Think on things that are true. We must replace the lies we believe with His truth.

APPENDIX G

ADDITIONAL RESOURCES

Books

DYNAMICS OF DOMESTIC ABUSE/ COERCIVE CONTROL

- Chris Moles, *The Heart of Domestic Abuse: Gospel Solutions for Men Who Use Control and Violence in the Home.* Bemidji, MN: Focus Publishing, 2015.
- Darby A. Strickland, *Is It Abuse? A Biblical Guide to Identifying Domestic Abuse and Helping Victims.* Phillipsburg, NJ: P&R Publishing, 2020.
- Leslie Vernick, *The Emotionally Destructive Marriage: How to Find Your Voice and Reclaim Your Hope.* Colorado Springs: WaterBrook Press, 2013.

UNDERSTANDING TRAUMA

- Judith Herman, *Trauma and Recovery: The Aftermath of Violence—from Domestic Abuse to Political Terror.* New York: Basic Books, 1997.
- Edward S. Kubany, Mari A. McCaig, and Janet Laconsay, *Healing the Trauma of Domestic Violence: A Workbook for Women.* (Oakland, New Harbinger Publications, 2004).
- Diane Langberg, *Suffering and the Heart of God: How Trauma Destroys and Christ Restores.* Greensboro: New Growth Press, 2015.

OVERCOMING ABUSE & TRAUMA

- Christine Chappell, *Midnight Mercies: Walking with God Through Depression in Motherhood.* Phillipsburg, NJ: P&R Publishing, 2023.
- Brad Hambrick, *Making Sense of Forgiveness: Moving from Hurt toward Hope.* Greensboro, NC: New Growth Press, 2021.
- Diane Langberg, *On the Threshold of Hope: Opening the Door to Healing for Survivors of Sexual Abuse.* Carol Stream, IL: Tyndale Refresh, 2012, and On the Threshold of Hope Workbook. Maitland, FL: Xulon Press, 2014.
- Sydney Millage, *37 Ways to Be Taken Captive: Warning Signs and Prevention for Destructive Relationships.* Monee, IL: 2023.
- Georgia Shaffer, *A Gift of Mourning Glories: Restoring Your Life After Loss.* Friendswood, TX: Bold Vision Books, 2017, and *Taking Out Your Emotional Trash: Face Your Feelings and Build Healthy Relationships.* Irvine, CA, Harvest House Publishers, 2010.
- Esther Smith, *A Still and Quiet Mind: Twelve Strategies for Changing Unwanted Thoughts.* Phillipsburg, NJ: P&R Publishing, 2022.
- Curtis Solomon, *I Have PTSD: Reorienting after Trauma.* Greensboro, NC, New Growth Press, 2023.

- Lysa TerKeurst, *Forgiving What You Can't Forget: Discover How to Move On, Make Peace with Painful Memories, and Create a Life That's Beautiful Again.* Nashville: Thomas Nelson, 2020.
- Leslie Vernick, *The Emotionally Destructive Marriage: How to Find Your Voice and Reclaim Your Hope*: Colorado Springs, Waterbrook Press, 2013, and *How to Act Right When Your Spouse Acts Wrong*, Colorado Springs: Waterbrook Press, 2001.
- Edward T. Welch, *Shame Interrupted: How God Lifts the Pain of Worthlessness and Rejection.* Greensboro, NC: New Growth Press, 2012.

MINISTRY RESOURCES

- Dan and Shannon Boeck, *Domestic Abuse and the Dechurched: Are People Abandoning the Church, or Is the Church Abandoning Its People?* Middleton, DE: 2023.
- Chris Moles, Editor, *Caring for Families Caught in Domestic Abuse*, Greensboro, NC: New Growth Press, 2023.
- Jeremy Pierre and Greg Wilson, *When Home Hurts: A Guide for Responding Wisely to Domestic Abuse in Your Church.* Ross-shire, Scotland: Christian Focus Publishing, 2021.

Training Resources

- Advocacy Training:
  - Called to Peace Ministries, in conjunction with House of Peace Publications, offers a one-year advocacy training comprised of 12 courses on issues related to dynamics of domestic abuse and trauma, best practices for helping survivors, avoiding common pitfalls, and more. While these courses are designed for counselors, ministry leaders, and other people helpers, many survivors have reported that the courses were beneficial in their healing processes. Learn more at www.calledtopeace.org.

- Counseling Care for Domestic Abuse:
  - 9-video case series from The Institute for Biblical Counseling and Discipleship (IBCD). DVD. https://ibcd.org/product/counseling-care-for-domestic-abuse/

- PeaceWorks University:
  - An online membership site that exists to train and support helpers in a variety of ministry contexts to address domestic violence with the gospel of peace, available at www.chrismoles.org.

Organizations and Additional Resources

- **Called to Peace Ministries** — Offers support groups, advocacy training, and retreats for survivors, as well as resources, training and mentoring for churches. Learn more at https://www.calledtopeace.org.

- **ChrisMoles.org** — Provides resources on domestic abuse as well as resources for men who use control and violence in their relationships.

- **Counseling Care for Domestic Abuse** — 9-video case series from The Institute for Biblical Counseling and Discipleship (IBCD). DVD. https://ibcd.org/product/counseling-care-for-domestic-abuse/.resources.

- **Focus Ministries** — https://www.focusministries1.org. Faith-based domestic violence resources.

- **GeorgiaShaffer.com** — Rebuild after Divorce, coaching, healthy relationships, and more.

- **HerestheJoy.com** — This is Rebecca Davis' website. She has a series of books on Untwisting Scripture, as well as a blog covering a range of issues related to abuse.

- **LeslieVernick.com** — Biblically-based resources and virtual coaching for women in unhealthy and destructive marriages.

- **The Domestic Abuse Hotline:** 1-800-799-7233. Domestic Violence Support, National Domestic Violence Hotline (thehotline.org)

- **The PeaceWorks Podcast** — A weekly podcast featuring teaching from Chris Moles, interviews with experts, and stories from survivors. http://www.chrismoles.org/podcast.

Acknowledgments

I am especially thankful for the many Called to Peace Ministries' support group leaders and group participants who have provided feedback on the *Called to Peace* book and *Workbook* since support groups began in 2018. Your input has been invaluable, and I pray that incorporating your suggestions will multiply the benefits of the books exponentially.

Thanks to the faithful volunteers who invested the time to read these manuscripts and make suggestions— Katharine Crompton, Dan Boeck, John Felser, and Helenmary Brown. A special thanks to John for checking every Scripture reference in both books. That was no small task! Helenmary, thank you so much for your amazing editing skills. Thank you so much for the many hours you spent on this project, and I thank you for your heart for the cause. I can't thank you enough!

Thank you to my monthly "summit "group, Chris Moles, Darby Strickland, Greg Wilson, and Kirsten Christianson, for being a safe place to think through and discuss a multitude of issues related to domestic abuse and trauma within the church. I am so grateful for your friendship, wisdom, and even the constant running text thread that keeps me up to date on all issues related to abuse and the biblical counseling world. A special thanks to Darby and Kirsten for helping me better express my overall motivations for the book revisions.

As I ponder those who have contributed to these new editions, I must acknowledge how very grateful I am for Dr. Debra Wingfield. What an amazing answer to prayer you have been! When people were asking me to teach an advocacy class, I didn't have the capacity to launch another initiative, and honestly, my knowledge paled in comparison to yours. I'm so grateful for how you showed up with multiple courses on domestic abuse and advocacy and for your willingness to allow us to incorporate a biblical perspective along with the materials you present. Your advocacy classes have better equipped the entire staff of Called to Peace Ministries, hundreds of volunteers, and so many others. I believe the ripple effects of these classes will continue for generations to come.

I end this section filled with overwhelming gratitude for all that God has done at Called to Peace Ministries since the original publication of these books. It has been far beyond anything I would have ever imagined. He has given me a front-row seat to watching Him perform miracles daily. The work is hard, but He always shows up for those who trust Him. My prayer is that these new editions will better help those who have experienced the trauma of abuse to find the path to restored faith and freedom.

ABOUT THE AUTHOR

JOY FORREST is the Founder and Executive Director of Called to Peace Ministries. She is author of *Called to Peace: A Survivor's Guide to Finding Peace & Healing After Domestic Abuse* and the *Called to Peace Companion Workbook*. Joy holds an M.A. in Biblical Counseling from Southeastern Baptist Theological Seminary and has been active in counseling ministry since 2005. She has been an advocate for victims of abuse since 1997 and is a certified advocate with the NC Coalition Against Domestic Violence. Joy is a contributor to DivorceCare's recovery support group curriculum, the Institute for Biblical Counseling and Discipleship's Counseling *Care for Domestic Abuse* videos, and *Caring for Families Caught in Domestic Abuse* (Chris Moles, ed). In her spare time, she loves traveling and spending time with her family– especially her eleven grandchildren.

www.ingramcontent.com/pod-product-compliance
Lightning Source LLC
Chambersburg PA
CBHW081428070526
44586CB00020B/2519